LINEAGE ORGANIZATION IN SOUTHEASTERN CHINA

Sketch Map
of
Southeastern
China
N
Chekiang
Hunan
Kiangsi
Fukien
Foochow
Kwangsi
Kwangtung
Amoy
Formosa
Canton
Swatow
Hong Kong
Hainan
0
Miles
500
EW

LONDON SCHOOL OF ECONOMICS
MONOGRAPHS ON SOCIAL ANTHROPOLOGY
No. 18

Lineage Organization in Southeastern China

by

MAURICE FREEDMAN

Routledge
Taylor & Francis Group
LONDON AND NEW YORK

First published 1958 by THE ATHLONE PRESS

Published 2020 by Routledge
2 Park Square, Milton Park, Abingdon, Oxon OX14 4RN
605 Third Avenue, New York, NY 10017

First issued in paperback 2021

Routledge is an imprint of the Taylor & Francis Group, an informa business

Publisher's Note

The publisher has gone to great lengths to ensure the quality of this reprint but points out that some imperfections in the original copies may be apparent.

ISBN 13: 978-0-367-71697-4 (pbk)
ISBN13: 978-1-8452-0008-4 (hbk)

Preface

This essay is the work of a social anthropologist but it is not based upon field work. It is concerned with Chinese matters but it is not written by a sinologue. To explain why I have ventured to write a book about China I must go back to a subject which I have studied as a field anthropologist. In the years 1949 and 1950, under the auspices of the Colonial Social Science Research Council, I carried out a study of family and marriage among the Chinese living in the Colony of Singapore.[1] While this study was in progress and during the years which followed I pondered the significance of what I gathered both from my Singapore informants and from my reading of the works in European languages on the nature of Chinese society in the two provinces of Fukien and Kwangtung. To begin with I was interested in these provinces as the homeland of the Chinese in South-east Asia, but I came gradually to see in the material I was able to collect problems of a general sociological importance. If political and academic circumstances had been in my favour I should have gone to south-eastern China to study at first hand the questions which engaged my attention, but as matters have turned out I have seen no more of my field than glimpses of Kwangtung seized during a flying visit to Hong Kong and Macao in 1955.

I have set out in this essay my reflections on certain aspects of south-eastern Chinese society during the last hundred and fifty years. What I write cannot amount to a complete study, but it may help to interpret a kind of social complex which has much interested anthropologists in recent years. Unilineal kinship organization in a differentiated society and a centralized political system forms the main theme of the essay.

My attention was attracted to Fukien and Kwangtung because this region of China has specialized not only in large-scale unilineal organization but also in sending people overseas. Although I am concerned here with China itself, I hope that some of the matters I discuss will be of use to students of overseas Chinese society; for this is a field which, while of great interest in its own right, tends to grow in importance the longer China remains inaccessible.

It is possible that Chinese rural society will soon have changed beyond recognition. If China opens its doors to field investigation before this happens, we shall have the fruits of first-hand work to set against the

[1] The main published results of this investigation are embodied in 'Colonial Law and Chinese Society', *Journal of the Royal Anthropological Society*, vol. 80, 1950 (published 1952), and *Chinese Family and Marriage in Singapore*, H.M.S.O., London, 1957.

ruminations of armchair anthropology. Otherwise it is obvious that the conclusions of this essay must be tentative. They may, however, be improved upon and tested whether or not living China remains a closed book; for there are still literary sources for the study of Chinese society in the past which, as I understand the position, have not yet been fully exploited. The gazetteers and other works dealing with conditions in Fukien and Kwangtung might tell us much that we need to know. Some years ago Dr. Hu Hsien-chin whetted our appetites by bringing together literary evidence on lineage organization in China as a whole.[1] May we hope that the detailed social history of particular areas of China will in the future add to the body of comparative sociology? Anthropologists who respect, enjoy, and use the fruits of historical sociology would certainly not be slow to welcome reconstructions and analyses of China's past.

There is another way in which some of the speculations about south-eastern China can be tested. In the New Territories of Hong Kong both historical research and anthropological field work are possible. From my own brief experience of this area and from the discussions I have had with Miss Barbara Ward, who knows it well, I should say that anthropologists could answer certain important questions about south-eastern China from a study of the small part of it which is under British rule.

I have tried to remedy the sinological shortcomings of this essay in only one major respect. Two works in Chinese struck me as being especially likely to help me with material on south-eastern China and these, with financial aid from the Geographical and Anthropological Research Division, London School of Economics, which I gratefully acknowledge, I have had translated. They have proved extremely useful.[2] Apart from these two sources, all the published material I have used has been taken from works written in European languages. Some of this material is avowedly sociological, but a great part of it derives from a very heterogeneous collection of books and articles. In trying to find pieces to fit together to make a convincing picture of rural society in Fukien and Kwangtung, I have had to use whatever materials I could lay my hands on. When we know so little about a wide area over a long period of time, we must be dismayed by the jumps in space and time which an attempt at a systematic account entails. The provinces of Fukien and Kwangtung cover an area of some 150,000 square miles and have been inhabited by a population

[1] *The Common Descent Group in China and its Functions*, Viking Fund Publications in Anthropology Number 10, New York, 1948. How heavily I am indebted to Miss Hu's work will be apparent in this essay.

[2] They are: Lin Yueh-hwa, 'An Enquiry into the Chinese Lineage-Village from the Viewpoint of Anthropology', *She Hui Hsüeh Chieh*, No. 9, 1936; and Liu Hsing-t'ang, 'The Structure of Kinship Groups in Fukien', *Shih Huo*, vol. 4, no. 8, 1936. In connexion with the work done on these translations I wish to thank Mrs. S. van der Sprenkel and Mrs. Y. C. Liu of the School of Oriental and African Studies, London University.

which has probably varied around the figure of fifty millions during the last century. Within this range of time and distance the facts about rural life are very thinly spread.

The tenuousness of the data, however, while defeating any approach to a detailed social history of rural south-eastern China, does not prevent us, at least in principle, from building up a model of certain structures which were apparently common in the area and seemingly persistent over a considerable period of time. In the last section of this essay I discuss the validity and uses of the model of the south-eastern Chinese localized lineage which I try to construct. At the outset I must make it plain that, while I attempt to remain faithful to the facts I have been able to adduce, the picture I gradually build up inevitably departs from reality by subsuming many variations under generalized heads. But if my picture of the localized lineage in fact corresponds to no lineage which has ever existed in Fukien and Kwangtung, it is at least a summary of the characteristics of a great number of such lineages. From it we may draw certain conclusions and make certain predictions about real lineages.

In gathering the material for this essay and in thinking about the problems it raises, I have been helped in many ways by different people. The earliest version of what appears here was a series of lectures given at Professor Max Gluckman's invitation in 1952 in the Department of Social Anthropology, University of Manchester, and in the same year at the London School of Economics and Political Science. I wish to thank all the scholars who have given me the benefit of their criticism. In particular on the sinological side I gratefully acknowledge the help, advice, and encouragement which Mr. O. B. van der Sprenkel has given me, and I thank Mrs. H. M. Wright most warmly for reading and criticising the typescript of this book. If I have committed sinological blunders they are my own responsibility. I am in the debt of Professor Raymond Firth, who has watched over all stages of this study, and Dr. E. R. Leach, whose knowledge of Chinese matters and insight into Chinese questions were more than once placed at my disposal. The typescript was read by Professor Meyer Fortes, Miss Barbara Ward (Mrs. Stephen Morris), and Dr. J. B. Loudon; they offered me valuable criticism on many points; I am very grateful for their help. Miss Ward read the essay against the background of her general knowledge of the New Territories, and I am greatly encouraged by her opinion that in the main my argument is correct. My wife has helped me in many ways to prepare this essay for publication, and I should like to express my gratitude to her. I have also to thank the Geography Department of the London School of Economics and Political Science for preparing the map and diagrams which appear in this book. Finally, I wish to thank Professor Isaac Schapera for reading the proofs.

London School of Economics and Political Science, M.F.

October 1957.

The Monographs on Social Anthropology were established in 1940 and aim to publish results of modern anthropological research of primary interest to specialists.

The continuation of the series in letterpress has been made possible by a generous grant-in-aid from the Wenner-Gren Foundation for Anthropological Research. Any profits from the series will be returned to a rotating fund to assist further publication.

The Monographs are under the direction of an Editorial Board associated with the Department of Anthropology of the London School of Economics and Political Science.

Contents

I

Village and Lineage in Fukien and Kwangtung

Nearly everywhere in China the more or less compact village formed a basic unit of rural society. The clan (as the lineage is often called in the literature) was usually but one section of a village. In the provinces of Fukien and Kwangtung, however, the lineage and the village tended markedly to coincide, so that many villages consisted of single lineages. This coincidence of agnatic and local community was found in other parts of the country too, especially in the central provinces, but in the south-east it appears to have been most pronounced.[1]

With what this regional peculiarity is to be connected has never, so far as I am aware, been satisfactorily looked into. It is true that in Chinese terms the south-east is an area of fairly recent settlement by people of Chinese culture. This is why the inhabitants of Fukien and Kwangtung speak of themselves as Men of the T'ang rather than as Men of the Han dynasty.[2] Yet it is difficult to see exactly what factors may have led to the perpetuation of a wide scale lineage structure in this region when it has apparently tended to disintegrate or generally failed to emerge elsewhere. My wording here is deliberately cautious because I do not wish to associate myself with those who assume that at some time in the past all parts of China displayed the wide-ranging localized lineage which is now peculiar only to certain areas.[3] If I draw attention to this important problem here only to pass over it quickly, I do so because I lack the competence to handle the historical material which might throw light on so interesting a social difference.[4]

Wittfogel, in the context which I have just cited, refers to the 'clan familism' of south China as an 'enigmatic phenomenon'. Other writers on China have also been puzzled by the appearance of large-scale lineages in Fukien and Kwangtung and by their working. It is instructive to note

[1] Cf. Hu, op. cit,. pp. 11, 14.

[2] The Han dynasty spanned the beginning of the Christian era, while the T'ang reigned in the seventh, eighth and ninth centuries. On the use of the term 'Man of T'ang' see, e.g., J. Dyer Ball, *The Chinese at Home or the Man of Tong and his Land*, London, 1911, pp. xif.

[3] Cf. K. A. Wittfogel, *New Light on Chinese Society, An Investigation of China's Socio-Economic Structure*, New York, 1938, p. 9, and O. Lang, *Chinese Family and Society*, New Haven, 1946, p. 173.

[4] I refer to this question later. See below, p. 129.

that the south Chinese 'clan' fits Fei Hsiao-tung's scheme of Chinese society so badly that he is inclined to discount it. Having asserted that the 'clan' is a speciality of the gentry, he says: 'I shall leave the question open as to the nature of the so-called clan village. I rather suspect that such an organization among the peasants is a local organization, not a kinship organization.'[1] Lineages of the kind we see in south-eastern China are of course essentially political and local organizations. If we fail to realize this and think of lineages as inflated families, we must naturally wonder how they can persist in a complex and differentiated society. As I hope to show, if the south-eastern village-lineage is an enigma, the puzzle is in its history and not in its operation.

The coincidence of lineage and village or village-section is phrased in different ways. I cite some of the general statements which have been made. After pointing out that in the last six or seven centuries the centres of strongly developed *tsu* (lineages) have been in central and south-eastern China, Miss Hu Hsien-chin says that in this area 'many villages are inhabited completely or predominantly by people of a single surname'.[2] In a work dealing with Kwangtung in the 'twenties of this century Chen Han-seng states that at least four out of every five peasants 'live with their clans' and that usually one village is inhabited by one 'clan'. He goes on to say that 'Even if there is more than one clan, each clan occupies a distinct section of the village; there is hardly a mixed neighborhood'.[3] J. J. M. de Groot writes of the Fukien he knew at the end of the nineteenth century that the people of one village bore one 'clan name' only.[4] In more recent times Miss Olga Lang reports that in Fukien and Kwangtung some villages are inhabited almost exclusively by the members of one 'clan', but 'in most places, two, three, or four clans live side by side'.[5]

As for observations on particular cases we have D. H. Kulp's account of Phoenix Village in Kwangtung in the second decade of this century,

[1] 'Peasantry and Gentry: An Interpretation of Chinese Social Structure and its Changes', *American Journal of Sociology*, vol. 52, no. 1, 1946, p. 5.

[2] Op. cit., p. 14.

[3] *Agrarian Problems in Southernmost China*, Shanghai, 1936 (also published as *Landlord and Peasant in China*, New York, 1936), p. 37.

[4] *The Religious System of China*, 6 vols., Leyden, 1892–1910, vol. I, 1892, p. 191. De Groot also deals with this point in *Het Kongsiwezen van Borneo, Eene Verhandeling over den Grondslag en den Aard der Chineesche Politieke Vereenigingen in de Koloniën, Met eene Chineesche Geschiedenis van de Kongsi Lanfong*, The Hague, 1885, pp. 82f. He points out that people with strange surnames (e.g., who find better economic opportunities in their wives' villages than in their own) may be living in the community, but that the general rule holds that every village in China is like a single family writ large ('ieder dorp in China is als één gezin in het groot'). Although de Groot appears to generalize here about China, he is in fact discussing the homeland of overseas Chinese: Fukien and Kwangtung.

[5] Op. cit., pp. 173f.

which was one 'sib' except for a couple of teachers and a few shopkeepers;[1] Lin Yueh-hwa's village of I-hsü[2] and the Hwang village he describes in his sociological novel,[3] which were single lineage settlements in north Fukien; and G.-E. Simon's description of Oang-Mo-Khi, also in north Fukien, where there were said to be at least 10,000 people 'presque tous issus du même couple en descendance masculine'.[4]

'Sib', 'clan', and 'single surname' mean in such contexts that there were local communities consisting of male agnates with unmarried female agnates and the wives of the men. The rule of lineage exogamy followed, as we shall see, from the rule of surname exogamy. The relationship between agnatic group and village may be set out in a number of alternatives, of which the first was clearly very common.

One village might consist either of a single lineage or a lineage with a few 'strangers' whose presence was due to their special economic role.

One village might include two or more lineages, in which case these units were territorially distinct within the village.

A single descent-group might be spread over more than one village. T'ien Ju-k'ang cites an example of four villages in south Fukien arranged in this fashion.[5] One of my informants in Singapore came from one of a cluster of seven villages in north Fukien which were all branches of a single descent group, and presumably Simon's figure refers to an aggregation of this sort.

Quite apart from this last possibility, we must notice that a particular localized lineage was not likely to be the only one bearing its surname in the area. This followed from the Chinese system of surnaming which, while in theory consisting of some five hundred names in modern times, has had in practice a restricted range. I have come across no material to indicate the distribution of surnames in Fukien and Kwangtung, but it seems likely from what we know of overseas Chinese that there are considerably fewer than five hundred surnames current in their homeland.[6]

[1] *Country Life in South China, The Sociology of Familism, Volume I, Phenix Village, Kwangtung, China*, New York, 1925. (No other volume was ever published.)

[2] Op. cit.

[3] *The Golden Wing, A Sociological Study of Chinese Familism*, London, 1948. I-hsü and the Hwang Village may well be the same. See below, pp. 37f.

[4] *La Cité chinoise*, 3rd edition, Paris, 1886.

[5] *The Chinese of Sarawak: A Study of Social Structure*, London School of Economics, Monographs on Social Anthropology, London, [1953], p. 23.

[6] H. A. Giles, *A Chinese-English Dictionary*, 2 vols., 2nd ed., Shanghai, &c., 1912, pp. 1–8, lists 2,174 surnames, and this figure by no means covers all those surnames known to Chinese history. Li Chi, *The Formation of the Chinese People, An Anthropological Inquiry*, Cambridge [Mass.], 1928, p. 127, counts 3,736 surnames recorded up to A.D. 1644 in Section XIV of the Chinese Encyclopaedia completed during the reign of the K'ang-hsi Emperor, and cites a Ming source giving a total of 4,657 surnames. In modern times the so-called *Hundred Family Names*, a work included in some editions of the Chinese almanac and often printed

Moreover, it is certain that the surnames which were to be found in Fukien and Kwangtung, as no doubt elsewhere in China, were very unevenly represented. Surnames such as Ch'ên, Lin, and Hwang were very common and must have embraced a large number of localized lineages in various places.[1]

All people bearing one surname were by that fact agnates, for they were considered to be descendants of a common ancestor in the male line. Bearing a common surname, people might not marry. Although in some parts of China marriage between people of the same surname was permitted by local custom, the official view in China was that such a marriage constituted a breach of exogamy.[2] In Fukien and Kwangtung the official rule appears to have been closely reflected in customary practice.[3] It has been reported, however, of one district of Fukien that people of the same surname but of different *souches* might marry,[4] and Kulp, after asserting that 'sib' exogamy was based on surname exogamy, says that the difficulties created by the wide casting of the exogamous net were sometimes

[1] For the distribution of surnames in Singapore see my *Chinese Family and Marriage*, p. 69.

[2] The legal code of the last imperial dynasty has: 'Whenever any persons having the same family-name intermarry, the parties and the contractor of the marriage shall each receive 60 blows, and the marriage being null and void, the man and woman shall be separated, and the marriage-presents forfeited to government.' See Sir George Thomas Staunton, *Ta Tsing Leu Lee; Being the Fundamental Laws, and a Selection from the Supplementary Statutes of the Penal Code of China; . . .*, London, 1810, p. 114. See also G. Boulais, *Manuel du Code chinois*, Variétés Sinologiques, no. 55, Shanghai, 1924, p. 277f., and P. Hoang, *Le mariage chinois au point de vue légal*, Variétés Sinologiques, no. 14, Shanghai, 1898, p. 43. The punishment for marriage with an agnate was in fact graded. If people of the same known descent but not related within the agnatic mourning grades (i.e. having a common agnatic ancestor not closer than great-great-great-grandfather) married, they were to receive 100 blows. Marriage within the agnatic mourning grades was to be punished by (*a*) exile, (*b*) death by strangling, and (*c*) death by beheading, according to the closeness of the relationship. Hoang, op. cit., pp. 46f.

[3] Cf. de Groot, *Het Kongsiwezen*. p. 105.

[4] F. Théry, 'Les Coutumes chinoises relatives au mariage,' *Bulletin de l'Université l'Aurore*, Shanghai, Série III, tome 9, no. 36, 1948, p. 390.

---

by itself as a booklet, gives nearly 500 surnames. Apparently it is rare nowadays for anyone to bear a surname not found in this little work. Cf. Hu, op. cit., p. 47. A Westernized version of th *Hundred Family Names* is to be found in a Malayan publication, Tan Pow Teck, *The Pek Kah Seng*, Kuala Lumpur, 1924. Tan lists 453 single-character and 60 double-character surnames. As for Chinese surnames actually to be found among Fukienese and Kwangtungese abroad, we may note that only 48 were to be found in the Singapore telephone directory in 1949. I have myself counted approximately 70 Chinese surnames in Singapore in all and we may certainly assume that a round 100 will cover the number of surnames to be found in this large section of overseas Chinese. For material on surnames in a different type of Chinese area see S. D. Gamble, *Ting Hsien, A North China Rural Community*, New York, 1954, pp. 53f.

resolved by the device of making slight changes to the surname, in order to allow two people of the same surname to marry, provided that they were 'five generations removed'.[1] It is possible that in this passage Kulp is drawing on his general knowledge of China and is not speaking specifically of Phoenix Village, but in any case his data and those given by Théry go against the general flow of the evidence. In Fukien and Kwangtung men rarely married women of their surname.

The fact of having a common surname at the least set up between any two lineages a bar on marriage. But, however remote the genealogical connexions they traced between them, the possession of a common surname might in certain circumstances lead to formal co-operation such that localized lineages were grouped into wider agnatic units.[2] However, lineages might be grouped not only by similarity of surname but also on the basis of certain traditional alliances between surnames. In these alliances, which appear to have differed from area to area in the surnames they linked, the bond of no-marriage was extended beyond the limits of any exogamic rule dictated by general custom.[3] A bar on marriage, on the other hand, could evidence not only solidarity but its diametrical opposite. When lineages of different surnames quarrelled they sometimes broke off connubium, swearing an oath before the ancestors that brides would no longer pass between them. We thus find a situation in which any localized lineage at a given point in time might be grouped in alliance with certain lineages and in hostility against others. Alliance might be based upon agnation, linked surnames, or connubium; hostility might exist both between lineages which were agnatically connected, and between those which, of different surnames, were tied by bonds of marriage and matrilateral descent.

The localized lineages were of considerable size. Phoenix Village in northern Kwangtung appears to have been fairly small. About the year 1920 its population was 650.[4] However, Kulp says that the villages in the area were small, not one of them having ever maintained a population

[1] Kulp, op. cit., p. 167. On the restriction of the rule of exogamy to people who can trace close common agnatic descent cf. Fei Hsiao-tung, *Peasant Life in China; A Field Study of Country Life in the Yangtze Valley*, London, 1939, pp. 84, 86. Officialdom did in fact recognize that peasants of like surname might marry, and was apparently prepared to tolerate such marriages provided the partners were not of the same *tsung*, i.e., not members of the same known line of descent. See Hoang, op. cit., p. 43.

[2] Cf. Hu, op. cit., p. 42.

[3] Cf. ibid., pp. 50f. and T'ien, op. cit., p. 30. It is sometimes said that alliances between surnames must be based on the titles which appear against each surname in the *Hundred Family Names*. There are only some 125 of these titles and several surnames may be shown to have the same title. These titles are thought to refer to the ultimate place of origin of each surname. To judge by the behaviour of overseas Chinese, however, the alliances between surnames in south-eastern China were largely independent of the titles.

[4] Kulp, op. cit., p. 32. In addition, 55 members of the village were abroad.

of more than 2,000.[1] Of the Hwang village in Lin's *The Golden Wing* we know only that in the 'thirties it had 'several hundred' inhabitants,[2] while the size of I-hsü is not indicated. It is possible to infer the size of four villages from some of J. L. Buck's statistics. One Kwangtung village had a population of some 1,800 and three Fukien villages had populations of about 2,000, 1,400 and 1,100.[3] Of course, we do not know how these last villages were agnatically constructed. Miss Lang says of 26 'clans' investigated in Fukien and Kwangtung in connexion with her study that they ranged in size from 4 to 546 'families', most of them falling within the range of 40 to 70 'families'.[4] One account of Fukien, after pointing out that there were no isolated farmhouses, says that villages varied in size from hamlets to settlements of several thousand inhabitants.[5] The part of mainland Kwangtung which came into British hands in 1899 held settlements ranging from 10 to 5,000 souls, the average size of a settlement being about 240.[6] Except where mountainous country intervened, the villages of south-eastern China were very close together and within short walking distance of one another.

The large size of localized lineages obviously depended to a considerable extent on the time they had existed. Not only was Phoenix village comparatively small but it was also comparatively recent, having been founded at the end of the sixteenth century. Kulp says that some nine generations had elapsed between the beginning of Phoenix Village and the time at which he wrote.[7] The Hwang lineage of *The Golden Wing* was also shallow in time depth, Dunglin, the protagonist of Lin's story, belonging to the eighth generation.[8] Against these two examples the weight of the evidence suggests that the south-eastern Chinese lineage commonly extended to

[1] Ibid., p. 11.

[2] Op. cit., p. 1.

[3] *Land Utilization in China: Statistics*, Nanking, 1937, pp. 300, 469, 471. These are the only villages in Fukien and Kwangtung for which Buck gives the total population of farm families. I have multiplied the numbers of farm families by the average size for farm families in each village.

[4] Op. cit., p. 174.

[5] F. Hurlbut, *The Fukienese, A Study in Human Geography*, n.p. (U.S.A.), 1939, p. 53.

[6] *Papers Laid Before the Legislative Council of Hong Kong 1899*, Hong Kong, 1900, 'Extracts from Papers Relating to the Extension of the Colony of Hong Kong, no. 9/99, Appendix 3, p. 19, and Appendix 5, pp. 21ff. See also *Papers Laid Before the Legislative Council of Hong Kong 1900*, Hong Kong, 1901, 'Report on the New Territory During the First Year of British Administration', no. 15/1900, p. 252. (These *Papers*, together with *Report on the New Territory at Hong Kong*, Cmd. 403, London, H.M.S.O., 1900, form a very useful source for data on rural Kwangtung. I am very grateful to Mr. Paul K. C. Tsui, M.B.E., of Hong Kong for drawing my attention to them.)

[7] Op. cit., pp. xxiii, 68. But the lineage actually traced its origin to a founder who set it up in Chaochow in Sung times.

[8] Op. cit., p. 60.

about twenty-five generations in recent time. This figure roughly expresses the average generation depth in lineages about which I heard from their members in Singapore. T'ien in Sarawak found that one group bearing his surname traced twenty generations and another nineteen, while a group of a different surname ran to twenty-one generations.[1] The generations in the Chinese lineage could multiply indefinitely, for no fixed time scale was imposed upon it. Each new generation was given a written character which its male members incorporated in their personal names,[2] the system being capable in principle of indefinite extension. If we assume, as Chinese themselves do, that lineage depth is a statement of historical time, and if we allow about thirty years to each generation, then we arrive at the conclusion that south-eastern lineages were commonly extablished some seven hundred years ago.[3] In fact we know that the truly Chinese population of the region goes back much further; by T'ang times the south-east was a real part of the Empire.[4] It is therefore a problem to decide why the lineage system as we know it in modern times should not extend back conceptually to the full depth of Chinese settlement in the area.[5] This problem, because of the historical questions involved,

[1] Op. cit., pp. 26n., 29n.

[2] Chinese formal names nearly always consist of three characters, of which the first is the surname, the last the purely personal element, and the middle commonly the generation name.

[3] Yuan I-chin, 'Life Tables of a Southern Chinese Family from 1365 to 1849', *Human Biology*, vol. III, no. 2, May 1931 (Baltimore), accepts a Kwangtung genealogy as reasonable material for demographic analysis. In this genealogy the fourth generation appears in 1365 and nineteen more generations are counted by 1914. Each generation occupies roughly thirty years, therefore. Note that most of the 'Puntis' (i.e. the Cantonese-speaking and long-established population, as distinct from the Hakka-speaking) in the New Territories of Hong Kong at the end of the last century were said easily to 'trace their descent from ancestors who were settled' in the area in the Southern Sung dynasty (A.D. 12th and 13th centuries). See *Papers Laid Before the Legislative Council of Hong Kong 1899*, 'Extracts from Papers Relating to the Extension of the Colony of Hong Kong', no. 9/99, p. 6.

[4] Cf. H. Bielenstein, 'The Census of China during the Period 2–742 A.D.', *Bulletin no. 19 of the Museum of Far Eastern Antiquities*, Stockholm, 1947.

[5] Hu, op. cit., p. 45, points out that in China generally few genealogies of localized lineages go back beyond the Sung dynasty. It is of course true that, although a considerable Chinese settlement of the south-east took place in T'ang times, a great influx of Chinese into this region occurred in the Sung dynasty, when the Court moved to the south. See H. J. Wiens, *China's March Toward the Tropics*, Hamden, Conn., 1954, pp. 144, 180, 182. The rising scale of Chinese—as distinct from barbarian—occupation of the two provinces may be seen from the following data taken from Li Chi, op. cit., p. 235:

Number of Districts with more than 10,000 *Chinese People*

	A.D. 464	A.D. 740	A.D. 1102	A.D. 1280–1367
Fukien	2	9	40	58
Kwangtung	8	24	?	42

The tracing of lineage origins to founders arriving in Sung times may, therefore, be either a reflection of some historical reality or a conventional idiom of descent. Of course, the Chinese population grew not only by immigration and natural

lies outside the scope of this essay, but we shall later need to examine the bearing of written genealogies on the development and structure of the lineages for which they constituted the charters.

The south-eastern Chinese village was not merely highly nucleated; it was often so formed as to constitute a kind of embattled settlement, a physical fact which takes on a sociological allure when it is set against the background of the bureaucratic peace theoretically ruling in the Empire. John Scarth writing about the Chaochow district in the middle of the last century says that: 'All the neighbouring country was in a state of chronic anarchy; the villages, towns, and hamlets were all walled, and each seemed prepared to fight with its neighbour. There were villages, certainly not a quarter of a mile distant from each other, both surrounded with distinct walls about sixteen to twenty feet high. . . .'[1] Another Western visitor to the same area a little later refers to the campaign of pacification carried out by the Governor of Kwangtung and Kwangsi, who successfully suppressed 'the village clans which for many years previously had set all authority at defiance. These villages were like a garrisoned fortress, inhabited by one large family or clan, and at feud with all other surrounding villages and clans'.[2] When British administrators took over a slice of Kwangtung province to form the New Territories of Hong Kong at the end of the nineteenth century, they found that there were 'several walled villages in the territory, which are invariably inhabited by the members of one clan only. They are rectangular or square in shape, and are enclosed within brick walls about 16 feet in height, flanked by square towers, and surrounded by a moat some 40 feet in width. They have one entrance protected by iron gates.'[3] The significance of this warlike architecture we shall see more clearly when we have looked into the relations both between villages and between the state and its village population.

[1] *Twelve Years in China*, Edinburgh, 1860, pp. 66f.

[2] J. Thomson, *The Straits of Malacca Indo-China and China*, London, 1875, p. 258.

[3] *Papers Laid Before the Legislative Council of Hong Kong, 1899*, 'Extracts from Papers Relating to the Extension of the Colony of Hong Kong', no. 9/99, p. 6.

---

increase but also by the assimilation of barbarians who at some time or other occupied every part of south China. (See Wiens, op. cit., p. 268.) In modern times the absorption of barbarians into the Chinese population has been so complete that, as far as Fukien and Kwangtung are concerned, one may in a general study ignore the remnants of barbarian population still displaying non-Chinese social characteristics.

2

The Economic Basis of Village Life

Before we turn to the analysis of social groupings within the villages of Fukien and Kwangtung we must examine the general economic framework within which social life was conducted. This framework, which was a complex of agricultural and commercial institutions, allowed wealth to accumulate in differing degrees in different small areas of village society, and provided certain opportunities for individuals and families to raise (or depress) their standard of living and to increase (or decrease) their command of socially desirable goods and services. The uneven distribution of resources and the possibilities of mobility were an important aspect of the heterogeneity of rural life, for they provided the basis for a large measure of political and ritual differentiation.

China as a whole has been an overwhelmingly agrarian state; those who lived in its villages were nearly all in some way connected with land and its working. In Fukien and Kwangtung irrigated rice fields were the commonest agricultural land and rice was, at least ideally, the staple food. In the 'thirties of this century some three-quarters of the total area of the two provinces under food crops were devoted to rice, while the crude agricultural statistics available show how largely rice bulked in the volume of production. In the years 1931–7 the annual averages of the production of the most important food crops in Fukien and Kwangtung were ten and a half million metric tons of rice, three million metric tons of sweet potatoes, and one million metric tons of wheat and barley.[1] In J. L. Buck's classification of Chinese agricultural zones Kwangtung and the southern part of Fukien fall within the double-cropping rice area, while northern Fukien lies in the rice–tea area.[2] Intensively worked, the region was able to provide some sort of a living for a dense population.

Rice was not, however, uniformly important in the regional economy. Some rural areas round Canton and Swatow, two of the main Kwangtung emigration ports, have been deficient in rice, while Amoy and Foochow in Fukien, in addition to the two Kwangtung ports, have been the main inlets for the rice imported from abroad.[3] Some areas produced a marketable

[1] See T. H. Shen, *Agricultural Resources of China*, Ithaca, New York, 1951, pp. 374f. and 376f. Minor crops included peas, broad beans, rapeseed, kaoliang (sorghum), millet, maize, soya beans, peanuts, and sesame.

[2] *Land Utilization in China*, Nanking, 1937, p. 27.

[3] See Shen, op. cit., p. 202.

surplus of rice. Sugar and tea were important cash crops in the region, while the production of silk has also been a source of peasant income. Fluctuations in the fortunes of tea and sugar greatly disturbed the rural economy.[1] It appears, for example, that the replacement of Chinese tea on the Western markets by Indian and Celyon tea towards the end of the last century was a spur to emigration.[2] Demographically and economically the region was by no means stable.

It happens that the most complete account we have of a village in the region shows us how far a particular settlement could diverge from the 'normal' wet-rice farming pattern. Phoenix Village in north Kwangtung had, in the second decade of this century, forty-four 'gardeners' but only thirteen 'farmers'. Oranges were the principal crop of the district and these, together with other horticultural produce, were clearly more important than rice.[3]

Whatever the main crop of a particular village, it put much of its produce on the market, partly in direct sale and partly in rent, and relied for many consumer goods on the wider economy.[4] Fukien and Kwangtung were, of course, heavily affected by foreign trade, and the impact of this trade on their handicraft industries further tied the peasantry to the greater economic world. Yet, despite the economic changes of modern times, the village maintained its corps of specialized workers who, together with the business men and the local gentry, ensured that the village scene was not entirely peopled by farmers.[5]

[1] For an account of the effect of the decline of these crops on the peasantry in north-eastern Fukien, see *Agrarian China*, Institute of Pacific Relations, London, 1939, pp. 251–5.

[2] Cf. Chen Han-seng, 'The Present Prospect of Chinese Emigration,' in I. Bowman, ed., *Limits of Land Settlement*, New York, 1937, p. 138; and see C. T. Gardner, 'Amoy Emigration to the Straits,' *The China Review*, vol. XXII, no. 4, 1897, pp. 623f. Gardner, who was H.B.M. Emigration Officer at Amoy, speaks of the abandonment of large tracts of country formerly planted with tea and the dependence of 'a vast proportion of the population' on remittances from their relatives overseas. He also suggests that yearly fluctuations in the ordinary harvests played their part in determining the flow of emigration. 'Thus many villages now talk of a twenty, thirty, or forty crop, or a nobody crop—meaning the crop is such that twenty, thirty or forty of their clan will have to emigrate, or the crop is so good that all the clan can, if they like, stay at home.'

[3] Kulp, op. cit., pp. 84f. and 90.

[4] R. H. Tawney, speaking of China in general, but with evidence from Fukien and Kwangtung before him, suggested that 'more than a quarter of the goods consumed by agricultural families are purchased'. See his *Land and Labour in China*, London, 1932, p. 54.

[5] In Phoenix Village, apart from the 44 gardeners and 13 farmers, there were 39 clerks and salesmen, 11 merchants, 10 fruit dealers, 9 boatmen, 9 servants, 6 cooks, 4 varnishers, 3 officials, 3 beancurd makers, 2 tailors, 2 teachers, 2 dyers, 2 professional gamblers, 1 carpenter, 1 silversmith, 1 pottery painter, 1 Christian preacher, 1 doctor, 1 priest, 1 tax-collector, and 1 fortune-teller. The total population of the village was 650. See Kulp, op. cit., pp. 89f.

We may catch a glimpse of the importance of economic activities other than farming from material collected by J. L. Buck in twelve counties (*hsien*) of Fukien and Kwangtung. In the samples the percentage of net income from other than farm sources ranged from 1 to 43, the subsidiary occupations listed being: farm labourer on other farms, skilled labourer, unskilled labourer, home industry worker, merchant, scholar, soldier. official, professional occupation.[1]

The general pattern of land tenure in Fukien and Kwangtung followed that of the greater part of China; small—sometimes minute—holdings of land were vested in the heads of small households. In one important respect, however, the two south-eastern provinces showed a significant difference from the greater part of the rest of the country: corporate holdings of land played an important part in the economy.[2] The chief corporations holding land were lineages and villages (that is, both agnatic and territorial groups), but in some few cases the corporate holders were groups of other kinds. A survey conducted in the 'twenties of this century along the East River in Kwangtung produced the following data on the importance of 'common' lands, which, although they included some 'village' and 'school' lands, were mainly 'ancestral'.

District	*No. of villages investigated*	*Per cent. common land*	*Per cent. private land*	*Per cent. other land*
A	2	57	38	5
B	1	60	35	5
C	4	50	50	–
D	2	15	85	–
E	2	50	50	–
F	2	39	61	–
G	2	15	85	–
H	2	35	65	–
I	1	30	70	–
J	3	11	89	–
K	1	15	85	–
L	3	55	42	3
M	3	20	78	2
N	4	57	43	–
O	3	21	79	–
P	1	5	95	–
Q	1	45	55	–
R	2	45	55	–
S	2	30	70	–
T	1	10	90	–

(Adapted from 'Kwangtung Agricultural Statistics', *Chinese Economic Journal*, vol. II, no. 4, April 1928, Table IV, p. 331.)

The high incidence of corporately owned land in parts of Kwangtung is confirmed by Chen Han-seng's investigations. 'Indeed, we can safely

[1] *Land Utilization in China: Statistics*, p. 310.

[2] Cf. Chen Han-seng, *The Present Agrarian Problem in China*, China Institute of Pacific Relations, Shanghai, 1933, pp. 12f.

say that one-third of the cultivated land of the entire province is clan land. . . .'[1] 'Clan land is the one single dominating form of land owned in common which accounts for the continuing influence of collective landlordism in Kwangtung.'[2] Chen distinguishes various forms of corporate holdings. Land owned by 'public bodies and charity organizations' was not very considerable. 'Education' and temple lands were relatively small, and while at one time the land held by associations of merchants for religious and 'social' purposes was considerable, it had by the modern period declined in importance.[3]

In Phoenix Village corporately owned lands fell into three categories: land owned by the village; land owned by the 'sib' (the lineage); and land owned by various segments of the 'sib'. The first category of land accounted for about sixty *mow* (about ten acres), and the second for some twenty *mow*. (The total area of cultivated land is not stated.) Village land was exploited in the interests of the village as a whole: for underwriting the expenses of lawsuits in which the village was engaged; for making loans to poor people and to students; for making awards to scholars and chaste widows; and for repairing public buildings, graves, bridges, and streets. The use of the lineage land circulated among its segments, the segment entrusted with the land being charged with the provision of the expenses for festivals and ceremonies. Land owned by lineage segments circulated among component members, the current holder providing the means for ancestor worship.[4]

Similar facts emerge from Lin Yueh-hwa's work on north Fukien. Of the Hwang Village described in *The Golden Wing* Lin says that the 'ancestral plot', held in the name of the founding ancestor of the lineage, was cultivated in turn by the various 'families' of the lineage ('by the different families among the different lineages of the clan'). The 'family' which in any one year held the ancestral land enjoyed the right to its fruits but must furnish the lineage sacrifices and provide a feast for the lineage in that year.[5] More data on lineage lands are given by Miss Hu in

[1] *Agrarian Problems in Southernmost China*, p. 35. The same proportion is given by Tawney, *Land and Labour in China*, p. 32n., as the area of Kwangtung occupied by public land (ancestral, village, and school); he is citing T. C. Chang, *The Farmer's Movement in China*, 1928. It is interesting to note that at the present time one-third of the land in the Hong Kong New Territories is said to be 'held on trusts for ancestral worship'. See *Chinese Law and Custom in Hong Kong, Report of a Committee Appointed by the Governor in October, 1948*, The Government Printer, Hong Kong, 1953, p. 62.

[2] Chen, op. cit., p. 27. Note that in the 24 Kwangtung 'clans' investigated in connexion with Olga Lang's study in 1937 clan land varied from 10 to 90 per cent. In most cases the clan claimed between 50 and 70 per cent of the area cultivated by its members. In Fukien clan lands were less extensive. See Lang, op. cit., p. 174.

[3] Chen, op. cit., pp. 24ff.

[4] See Kulp, op. cit., pp. 86f., 101ff., 123f. Kulp's account of these various types of land is not clear and I have had to try to systematize his statements.

[5] Op. cit., p. 60.

her general survey of the 'common descent group' in China. She distinguishes between school land, land devoted to ritual purposes, and land set aside for welfare functions.[1]

Perhaps the most interesting account of lineage lands comes from Liu Hsing-t'ang's article, 'The Structure of Kinship Groups in Fukien', in which evidence is cited for various parts of the province during the Ch'ing dynasty.[2] Liu's data bring out very clearly the important points that there was much variation in the incidence of common lands and that the variation was associated with differences in status between different localized lineages. Poor lineages held no common lands. The author of one of Liu's main sources[3] wrote, for example: 'Once I was travelling on official business. I saw men and women walking one behind the other on the road carrying wine and meat. When questioned, they said: "We do not have a sacrifice-field from the profit of which we may offer sacrifices to our ancestors; so that each of us prepares a small offering, and we have just been sacrificing to our ancestors with our kinsmen".' Setting up common land and maintaining it intact over the generations required that the lineage be and remain prosperous.

Liu says that common landed property fell into two categories: 'book-lamp-fields' and 'sacrifice-fields'. '"Book-lamp-fields" are the fields specially set aside, the benefits of which are used to encourage the students in the lineage.' The 'sacrifice-fields' were rotated among members of the group to which the fields belonged, the people working them at any one time providing the ancestral sacrifices out of the benefits. The smaller the group the more frequently a member came to his turn. Ch'ên Shêng-shao wrote: 'The people of Chien-yang all take turns to administer the benefits from the "sacrifice-fields", in small lineages once in five or six years, in large lineages once in fifty or sixty years.' If a group expanded its numbers considerably in time the turn of each member grew less frequent. Of Chao-an *A Record of Customs* says: 'This kind of land is called *chêng-ch'ang-t'ien*. Afterwards as the descendants increase it comes to one's turn after a few years, sometimes more than ten years, sometimes even several tens of years.'

Some lineage land in south-eastern China was rotated among units of the owning group and some rented to tenants. The land cultivated by a particular household, then, might be either its 'own property' or the property of an individual or collective landlord. When the collective landlord was a lineage or a lineage-segment and the land was rented out to tenants, members of the group owning the land had better claims to

[1] Op. cit., pp. 65–80. For a statement on the functions and methods of exploitation of ancestral land in the New Territories of Hong Kong at the end of the last century, see *Report on the New Territory at Hong Kong*, p. 18.

[2] As I am working with a translation of this article (see footnote, p. vi above) I give no page references for my citations and quotations.

[3] Ch'ên Shêng-shao, *A Record of Customs*. I have not succeeded in dating this work.

tenancy of it than non-members. Miss Lang says of the 'clan' lands in Fukien and Kwangtung that they were rented to both 'clan' members and outsiders, but members had the first claim.[1]

The category of 'own property' now needs to be looked into. It is common in writings on land tenure in China to find statistics of peasants who own the land they cultivate, of peasants who rent their land, and of peasants who do both at the same time. The rights which people had over the land they owned outright were very wide. They could grow what they liked on it; they could mortgage it; they could sell it. Sale, on the other hand, might be restricted by two different sets of rights which inhered in persons other than the individual owner. First, it appears that where lineages formed large local groups, as they commonly did in south-eastern China, land was either alienable only within the lineage or alienable to outsiders only after options to lineage members had not been taken up.[2] Second, a man held his land in trust for his sons and any sale required their concurrence.[3]

[1] Op. cit., p. 176. In the Hong Kong New Territories ancestral land was 'nearly always leased to members of the clan, who cultivate it and pay a yearly rent. Sometimes the different branches of a clan cultivate the land in rotation, the branch in occupation of the land being held responsible for the payment of the expenses incurred on account of the objects for which the land was originally transmitted.' *Report on the New Territory at Hong Kong*, p. 18.

[2] Cf. *Agrarian China*, pp. 23f., where it is said that 'other families' of the 'clan' have first option to buy land for sale, but that this priority right had disappeared quickly since 1927 in south China. Cf. *Report on the New Territory at Hong Kong*, p. 18: 'If any owner wishes to sell his land, he is supposed to offer such land in the first instance to his nearest relatives, and is not at liberty to sell to anyone outside of his clan, unless the nearest relatives are unwilling to purchase. In large clans transactions in land take place, as a rule, between different members of the clan without the property ever being disposed of to outsiders.' Note the form of words used in land deeds quoted in *Papers Laid Before the Legislative Council of Hong Kong 1900*, 'Report on the New Territory During the First Year of British Administration', pp. 272, 276: 'The vendor, in the first instance, invited his nearest kin to purchase it, but as none of them had the necessary funds wherewith to purchase the property, he called the middle-man. . . .' '. . . the Vendor . . . in the first instance, invited his nearest kin to take it over, but as they had not the money, the Vendor asked the middle-man. . . .' Of course, these phrases reflect a legal usage common throughout China, but where, as in Fukien and Kwangtung, large communities were composed of agnates, it seems likely that the acquiescence of kinsmen was less a mere matter of form than elsewhere in the country.

[3] On this point cf. H. McAleavy, 'Certain Aspects of Chinese Customary Law in the Light of Japanese Scholarship', *Bulletin of the School of Oriental and African Studies*, vol. XVII, no. 3, 1955, p. 544. *Vis-à-vis* collateral descendants the head of a land-owning household was certainly obliged to obtain consent for the sale of land, but it has been argued that a man's direct descendants did not enjoy the same right. However, the weight of the evidence seems opposed to this last view. McAleavy points out that 'the result of the Japanese enquiries in North China during the war reveal that in many places people would at any rate not buy land from a father unless his sons joined in the conveyance'. Cf. also F. L. K. Hsu, *Americans and Chinese, Two Ways of Life*, New York, 1953, p. 290. For an account

These two restrictions applied not only to land owned outright but also to land held in some forms of tenancy. In Fukien and at least some parts of Kwangtung, as in other areas of China, a distinction was made between rights in the sub-soil and rights in the surface. The holder of the sub-soil rights collected rent from the holder of the surface rights but he could not arbitrarily terminate the latter's tenancy. With respect to the rights in the surface the tenant exercised the privileges of an 'owner'. He could dispose of his rights in the same manner as an outright owner disposed of his. The surface-holder might in turn take a tenant, but the latter did not enjoy the privilege of security of tenure inhering in surface rights. Tax to the state was paid, at least in theory, by outright owners and, in the case of surface tenancy, by the owner of the sub-soil rights.

These niceties emerge in the analyses made by anthropologists and some other observers,[1] but they are not taken account of in ordinary agricultural statistics. However, the crude figures available on 'ownership' and 'tenancy' can be put to some use. They show us two features of village life which are of importance for this enquiry. First, there was wide variation in land-holding. Second, the connexion between land-holding and domestic organization was such that the sizes of holdings and the sizes of households tended to vary together.

While China was not a country of large estates worked by tenants or labourers, it has often been pointed out that there was considerable concentration of land-ownership. Data for Kwangtung given in *Agrarian China*[2] and relating to 1933 show landlords making up 2 per cent of the 'families' and owning 53 per cent of the land; rich peasants making up 4 per cent of the 'families' and owning 13 per cent of the land; middle peasants making up 20 per cent[3] of the 'families' and owning 15 per cent of the land; and poor peasants making up 74 per cent of the 'families' and owning 19 per cent of the land. Chen Han-seng, using the same data on Kwangtung, gives the average holding per 'family' for each of the four categories of owners as: landlords, 203·3 *mow* (that is, roughly 34 acres); rich peasants, 24·8 *mow*; middle peasants, 6·0 *mow*; and poor peasants, 2·0 *mow* (roughly one-third acre). The general average is 7·8 *mow* per

[1] Cf. Lin Yueh-hwa, *The Golden Wing*, pp. 13f.; Fei Hsiao-tung, *Peasant Life in China*, pp. 177f.; *Agrarian China*, p. 25. The last source states that the permanent tenancy system is very common in Kwangsi, Fukien, eastern Chekiang, and southern Kiangsu. For sinological comment on the system of sub-soil and surface rights, see P. Hoang, *Notions techniques sur la propriété en Chine avec un choix d'actes et de documents officiels*, Variétés sinologiques, no. 11, Shanghai, 1897, pp. 30f.

[2] p. 4.

[3] The source has 12 per cent, but this must be an error.

of the rights exercised by sons and other agnates in the sale of land in another area of China where villages were often composed of single lineages, see R. F. Johnston, *Lion and Dragon in Northern China*, London, 1910, pp. 143f.

family.[1] Again in Kwangtung, a report made in the late nineteen-twenties gave the total agricultural population as 12·5 millions, of whom 1 million were farmers cultivating their own land, 8·75 millions were tenant farmers and part-owners, while 2·75 millions were farmers 'of other kinds'.[2] In a survey of twelve counties along the East River 34·5 per cent of the farmers were found to be owners, 29·3 per cent part-owners, and 36·2 per cent tenants.[3] In five counties in the central part of the province owners accounted for 5 per cent, part-owners and tenants for 85 per cent, and 'others' for 10 per cent.[4] Buck's data for sample farms in Fukien and Kwangtung show generally the same kinds of divisions, although farmers who owned all the land they cultivated appear to have been fewer in Fukien than in Kwangtung.[5]

The farms worked by most people in Fukien and Kwangtung were very small. Private holdings of land in Kwangtung in the 'twenties of this century seldom exceeded 15 *mow* (two and a half acres) and were often less than 10 *mow*.[6] In 1946 the average area of land worked per farm household was 0·79 hectare in Kwangtung and 0·86 hectare in Fukien.[7] Moreover, small as many holdings were, they were often dispersed in several parcels. Buck's data for sample farms in twelve counties in Fukien and Kwangtung show a range in the average number of parcels per farm of 2·0 to 9·3 and a range in the average size of parcel of 0·05 hectare to 0·75 hectare.[8] Various parcels of land represented inherited, bought, and rented land. Within the lifetime of any farmer the size and composition of his farm might change. In a survey of 161 farms in three villages in a northern Fukien county Buck found that the average size of the farm area when the operator began had been 0·73 hectare (of which 0·54 hectare was inherited) and that, because of buying and renting, the average size at the time was 1·01 hectares.[9]

From Buck's material we can also see how the sizes of farms and the sizes of the households running them generally correlated. The following

[1] *The Present Agrarian Problem in China*, p. 7.

[2] 'Kwangtung Agricultural Statistics', p. 328.

[3] Ibid., Table I, p. 329.

[4] Ibid., Table II, p. 329. See also Table III in which seven counties surveyed showed tenants and part-owners to account for 70 per cent.

[5] *Land Utilization in China: Statistics*, p. 58. Tawney, however, cites official figures which give tenants and part-owners as 65 and 66 per cent of Fukien and Kwangtung agricultural households respectively.—*Land and Labour in China*, p. 64. Another modern source (Leonard T. K. Wu, 'Merchant Capital and Usury Capital in Rural China', *Far Eastern Survey*, vol. V, no. 7, 25 March, 1936, p. 66) says that only 9 per cent of Fukien farmers were owners.

[6] 'Kwangtung Agricultural Statistics', p. 332.

[7] Shen, op. cit., p. 142. (1 hectare equals 2·471 acres and roughly 15 *mow*.)

[8] Buck, op. cit., p. 47.

[9] J. L. Buck, *Chinese Farm Economy*, Chicago, 1930, p. 35.

table is an adaptation of one appearing in *Land Utilization in China: Statistics.*[1]

Size of Farm and Size of Household (number of members) in Sample Farms in Twelve Fukien and Kwangtung Counties

County	Very small farms	Small farms	Medium farms	Medium large farms	Large farms	Very large farms	Very very large farms	All farms
Fukien								
A	—	5·3	4·9	5·9	5·8	6·2	7·5	5·7
B	—	4·4	4·8	5·4	6·4	7·1	—	5·5
C	—	2·8	4·4	5·3	6·0	5·3	—	5·0
D	—	3·4	4·8	5·7	8·3	6·0	—	5·2
E	2·3	5·6	5·3	6·0	8·9	—	—	6·0
Kwangtung								
A	—	5·4	6·3	8·2	10·9	—	—	6·7
B	—	5·4	5·5	5·5	5·4	6·1	—	5·5
C	4·0	5·2	7·1	9·4	11·5	—	—	7·2
D	—	3·3	4·6	5·6	6·1	7·3	—	4·9
E	—	3·8	4·8	8·0	8·0	15·5	—	6·4
F	—	4·6	7·0	8·2	11·4	12·5	—	7·6
G	—	3·6	4·6	6·6	8·3	9·3	—	5·5

This crude correlation as it stands masks an important problem. It is evident, as we shall see, that in peasant China holdings of land tended to split as the senior generation in a household died off and married sons took over full control. However, division did not invariably take place in this fashion, and it is therefore theoretically possible that even if the ratio of land to individual were uniform the correlation would appear because the few undivided households would have both a greater aggregate of land and a greater number of members. In fact, however, it is unlikely that this is the main explanation for the regularity in the connexion between size of farm and size of household. Recent evidence from another part of China shows that this correlation appears when it is clear that the larger the household, the higher is the ratio of land to individual member.[2]

Within a particular localized lineage there might be landlords, merchants, craftsmen, and peasants. The extent of mobility between these categories we shall need to consider later. We must bear in mind now,

[1] p. 300.

[2] See Gamble, op. cit., pp. 25, 66. At p. 66 Gamble says that there was an apparent tendency in Ting Hsien for the average size of the family to increase some 35 per cent when there was a 100 per cent increase in the size of the farm. In other words, the ratio of increase in family size to increase in farm size shows that the larger families have higher *per capita* holdings of land than smaller families. N.B. Table 17, p. 84, where, in a sample of 400 farm families, *mow* per individual range from 1·8 in families averaging 3·8 individuals and holding farms between 1 and 10 *mow*, to 9·1 in families averaging 13·5 individuals and holding farms of more than 100 *mow*.

however, that they did not constitute fixed orders of society between which no movement could take place, and that a cash economy, a relatively free market in land, and the flow of wealth in and out of the village community allowed people to hope for greater riches, even if they did not attain them. Moreover, the financial operations within the village rested on the assumption that each household was an independent economic unit and that the economic relations between households were regulated in fact or might in principle be regulated by the free play of the market. The high price of credit might be paid by neighbour to neighbour and kinsman to kinsman. The structure of the economic relations among kith and kin was certainly often at variance with the ideals of co-operative ties between relatives and neighbours.[1]

[1] Note, for example, the following passage concerning credit in the eighteenth century colloquial version of K'ang-hsi's Sacred Edict. '(Take for instance) the case of a poor villager. I ought to assist him, and if I give him a loan, must not take more than 36 per cent interest: (or in) a debt of many years' standing that cannot be repaid, the thing to do is to let him off on generous terms, and not exact compound interest, or exceed the current rate: (nor) presuming on my being well-to-do fleece another man who happens to be poor.' This occurs in the chapter 'Pacify the Local Communities in order to put an end to Litigation'. See F. W. Baller, *The Sacred Edict, With a Translation of the Colloquial Rendering Notes and Vocabulary*, Shanghai, 1892, pp. 32f.

3

Family and Household

The households between which economic relations were controlled by the market for labour and credit are not, however, altogether easy to define. It is sometimes wrongly assumed that the definition of what constitutes a household in any society is a simple matter. In societies in which there is a tight residential clustering and a regular sharing of activities between domestic units, any individual may in fact be a member at once of both more inclusive and less inclusive households. The material on Fukien and Kwangtung shows us that for the most part we can isolate only one household for each individual: the unit within which he normally ate and which constituted for him the primary property-owning group; yet, as we shall see, there were sometimes households of this kind which were also members of wider domestic units.

It has become almost customary during the last decade to begin discussions of the Chinese family system with a round denunciation of the older view that the 'large' or 'joint' family is the typical family of China. The point has by now been well enough made for writers on Chinese society to pass quickly over it. The statistics of household size should by themselves be a sufficient indication that complexity of family structure is not likely to characterize the domestic institutions of peasant China. A joint family of elderly parents, two married sons with their wives, and four children in the next generation requires nearly double the number of individuals to be found in the average peasant household. We have seen already that the average sizes for farm households in twelve Fukien and Kwangtung counties ranged from 4·9 to 7·6 individuals.[1]

The peasant household was nearly always a family unit; only well-to-do households could afford to incorporate non-kinsmen as servants and labourers. On marriage a woman was brought into her father-in-law's household, but the process of extension through marriage was quickly aborted by the tendency for the household and its property to be divided between brothers when the generation senior to them had disappeared. Division of the household might sometimes take place even during the lifetime of the 'father' of the family, although this step was contrary to

[1] See table, p. 17 above. Cf. F. L. K. Hsu, 'The Myth of Chinese Family Size', *American Journal of Sociology*, vol. XLVIII, May 1943.

official views of ideal kinship behaviour;[1] but the most common arrangement was for sons to wait for their father's death before dividing the home. In some cases the division was delayed until their widowed mother had also died. It follows that the number of married couples in a peasant household was likely to be small.

When extension took place, however, it was almost invariably in the male line. Only in exceptional circumstances did a man move into his father-in-law's house on marriage. We know from the general literature that the rule of patrilocal residence was closely adhered to and it is no surprise to encounter in Buck's data on 161 northern Fukien households a complete implementation of the rule. These data also illustrate the minor role given to extension in the kinship structures lying at the base of households. Buck gives, by generation, the percentages of all 161 households (with a total population of 808) which held particular kinds of kinsmen and affines in relation to the heads of the households. Thus:

Generation of the head of the household (living or dead): male heads, 99·4 per cent of the households; wives, 93·8 per cent; brothers, 18 per cent; married sisters, none; unmarried sisters, 1·9 per cent; cousins of all kinds, none.

First ascending generation: fathers, 1·9 per cent; wives' fathers, none; mothers, 27·3 per cent; wives' mothers, none; uncles and aunts, none.

Second ascending generation: none.

First descending generation: married sons, 26·2 per cent; unmarried sons, 75·8 per cent; married daughters, none; unmarried daughters, 36·0 per cent; daughters-in-law, 26·7 per cent; sons-in-law, none; brothers' sons, 3·1 per cent; sisters' sons, none; brothers' daughters, 1·2 per cent.

Second descending generation: sons' sons, 12·4 per cent; sons' daughters, 5·6 per cent; sons' sons' wives, 0·6 per cent.

Third descending generation: none.[2]

In his study of Phoenix Village in northern Kwangtung, Kulp provides a little material on household composition and structure. He distinguishes between 'natural-families' and 'economic-families'. By the former term he means an elementary family, and by the latter something which might sometimes coincide with what we usually call a household. Kulp

[1] Ch'ing statute law said: 'Sons or grandsons who form to themselves a separate establishment from their parents or grand-parents, and also make a division of the family property, shall, provided such parents and grand-parents personally prosecute, be punished, on conviction, with 100 blows.' See Staunton, op. cit., p. 92. Cf. Boulais, op. cit., p. 197.

[2] Buck, *Chinese Farm Economy*, p. 318. The imbalance in proportions between households showing brothers' sons and brothers' daughters, between those showing sons' sons and sons' daughters, and between those showing own unmarried sons and own unmarried daughters is in part at least a reflection of the sex ratio of the whole population. The 161 households held 467 males and 341 females.—Ibid., p. 338. The excess of males over females is frequently reported from China. Chen Ta, *Population in Modern China*, Chicago, 1946, p. 18, says that the preponderance of males is smaller than is usually thought: his samples give 111·2 males to 100 females. It is interesting to note, however, that his data on one Fukien county reveal a ratio of 128·4 males per 100 females (ibid., p. 81), a figure only a little smaller than that in Buck's Fukien sample.

writes: 'Members of the economic-family may all live under one roof, under several roofs joining [sic] one another, in houses somewhat apart as in Chaochow, Swatow or the South Seas. So long as there is no distinction between the income and outgo of funds and so long as the whole group is administered by a certain head or *chia-chang*, the persons living under these arrangements belong to an economic-family.'[1] It is clear, then, that the term 'economic-family' covers not only a family in a house but also a non-residential extended family operating as an economic unit. Kulp goes on to say that 'ordinarily' an 'economic-family' covers four generations, but that the range of size in Phoenix Village was from one individual to more than twenty. There were five one-person 'economic-families'. 'Many economic-families consist of widows with one or more small children. However, these are not modal cases but exceptions.'[2]

Miss Lang offers data on forty peasant families in Fukien in which she classifies families into conjugal (elementary), stem (elementary families with the addition of the husband's parents), and joint. Her analysis is as follows:[3]

	Conjugal	*Stem*	*Joint*
Poor peasants	10	8	3
Middle peasants	3	5	1
Well-to-do peasants	1	–	3
Merchants and landowners	1	1	4

The preponderance of simple kinship structures in the household was a reflection of the tendency for households to split in each generation. As sons came to maturity and married they began to assert their independence as heads of potential domestic units. As long as at least one of their parents was alive, married brothers were more likely to remain together, but with the passing of the senior generation the division of the household became, at least in peasant circumstances, almost inevitable. The process of division was sometimes seen by the Chinese themselves as the result of conflict between women. All married women in the house were, by the rules of agnatic exogamy and patrilocality, necessarily some sort of stranger. Yet, because the Chinese system of marriage identified the interests of a married woman strongly with those of her new family and severed her formal economic ties with her natal family, it forced her into the struggle which essentially turned upon the rivalry between her husband and his brothers. Her participation in this struggle might come to be looked upon as a primary cause of it.[4] The moralist of the colloquial

[1] Op. cit., p. 148.

[2] Ibid., pp. 148f.

[3] Op. cit., p. 350.

[4] Cf. the statement of a Chinese demographer that 'in the absence of a parent, family disputes and disorganizations occur between brothers, because of the inability of their wives to agree'. See Chi-ming Chiao, 'A Study of the Chinese Population', *The Milbank Memorial Fund Quarterly Bulletin*, vol. XI, no. 4, October 1933, p. 333.

version of the Sacred Edict speaks of the difficulties in fraternal relations and laments that 'All the squabbles that arise among brethren in the present day are on account of property. Some squabble about money, some about land, some about houses, some about food: all sorts of things.'[1] But he also accuses the wives and the undue attention paid to them. 'With men of the present day, the chief object of affection is the wife!'[2] 'But forsooth, you love to listen to what your wives have to say, and perceiving that there is some reason in their talk, you listen until before you are aware of it you believe them. The wife of the elder brother says to him, "How lazy, how prodigal, your young brother is! You laboriously make money to keep him, and he still finds fault: are we his son and daughter-in-law, that we ought to yield him the respect due to a parent?" The wife of the younger brother will also say to him, "Even if your elder brother knows how to make money, you have made money too; you do just as much as he does in the home: if you hire a labourer by the year, even he has not such hard toil. But *his* children forsooth, they *are* children, buying this, that and the other to eat—can it be that our children are not fit to live?" '[3] This eighteenth-century picture of domestic strife in the joint family household is a paradigm for the system we are discussing.

Although the process of division may be seen against the background of conflicts between conjugal couples in the ordinary round of domestic and agricultural life, it was more fundamentally grounded on the property rights which, vested in each son, tended to pull the component elementary families in a joint establishment apart. The head of a household held its property in trust; his control of it did not obliterate the individual rights of the men under his hand.[4] The junior men might be powerless to exercise their independent rights during the head's lifetime, but these rights were latent and were apt to find expression in bickering over the allocation of domestic duties and privileges. The strength of the insistence in Confucian ethics on the solidarity of brothers was matched by the pressure forcing them apart.

Household division was not simply the division of a domestic unit; it was a formal separation of both hearth and land. Chinese rules of inheritance generally ascribed to the oldest son an extra portion associated

[1] Baller, op. cit., p. 11.

[2] Ibid., p. 9.

[3] Ibid., p. 12. Cf. the Chinese proverb: 'If sister[s]-in-law live in harmony, the family will not be divided; if brothers live in harmony everything will go well'. See W. Scarborough, revised by C. W. Allan, *A Collection of Chinese Proverbs*, Shanghai 1926, p. 216.

[4] It was for this reason that the head of a household could not dispose of its major property without the concurrence of his juniors. See above, p. 14. Cf. H. F. Schurmann, 'Traditional Property Concepts in China', *The Far Eastern Quarterly*, vol. XV, no. 4, August 1956, p. 511: '. . . family property was not the private property of the elders of the family, but joint property subject to management by the elders.'

with his responsibilities for maintaining the ancestral shrine which passed to him alone among his brothers, but, this extra share aside, all brothers had equal claims on an estate. When they asserted their individual rights the division of a household became necessary.

Once separately established the households of two or more brothers ceased legally to form part of a co-operative economic unit. The members of one household had no automatic economic claims on those of another. Financial transactions between them might legitimately be regulated by the same contractual terms as governed similar dealings between strangers. Yet, at the same time, newly separated households were at least potentially members of one ancestor-worshipping unit in relation to recent forebears, and some forms of *ad hoc* economic co-operation might be instituted between them. In other words, while the formal division of house and land, which was a ritually established rupture at one point in time, created legally independent households, the relations between these households might diminish gradually in time rather than undergo a sharp transformation from involvement to indifference.[1]

We may consider these general points against the facts of two concrete cases. Both cases, although separated in time, are drawn from material on the same general area in northern Fukien. The first is dealt with in the fifth part, 'La famille de Ouang-Ming-Tse', of G.-E. Simon's *La cité chinoise*.[2] When in 1865[3] Simon met the man he calls Ouang-Ming-Tse, who was in his sixties, he was living with his oldest son Po-Y, about forty years old, and his widowed mother, in her nineties. All his daughters were married and lived in other villages. He had also a younger son, married and with six children, 'dont les intérêts sont séparés des nôtres, mais qui demeure tout près de notre maison'.[4] Po-Y had three sons and three daughters, the oldest of whom was a boy aged eighteen. Ouang said that his father had been the fourth child in a family of fourteen children, his elders being two brothers and a sister. The second of these older brothers studied to be a mandarin and became a 'gouverneur de district'. At that time—some eighty to ninety years before Simon's encounter—Ouang's paternal grandfather was poor, cultivating in all some fifteen *mow* of land, of which only half belonged to him. As the number of children grew, a decision was taken to teach the sons trades so that they might go to town and add to the family's resources. Ouang's father was the first of the sons to be apprenticed, choosing the trade of a

[1] Note the proverb: 'Three years after a family has been divided, its members are mere neighbours'. Scarborough, op. cit., p. 61.

[2] Op. cit. I am indebted to Miss Barbara Ward for drawing my attention to the significance of Simon's material. There is an English translation of this work: *China: Its Social, Political and Religious Life*, London, 1887. All references here are to the third French edition.

[3] Ibid., p. 356.

[4] Ibid., p. 247.

carpenter. Three of his brothers followed his example. With the money they brought in from their labours in town the farm was enlarged, and they returned to work on it except for one brother who remained in Foochow to become a big merchant.

When Ouang's paternal grandfather died, to be followed shortly by his wife, the family still kept together under one roof. There were many younger siblings to be looked after. Two of the sisters were already married; 'on ne les voyait guère qu'à l'époque du nouvel an où elles venaient, avec leurs enfants, passer trois ou quatre jours au milieu de nous'.[1] The brother who was a mandarin held office in another province and was well enough off to forgo part of his inheritance rights and leave them in the 'communauté'. Four of the brothers who remained in the family house were married and between them they had nine children. The household at that time consisted of twenty-four souls, besides four servants engaged on a yearly basis, three of whom were men working in the fields and one a woman employed in the house. 'Tant que dura la communauté, nous vécûmes dans une grande aisance avec les quatre-vingt méous de terre que nous possédions.' [2]

But when the sisters had been married off and one brother had settled in Foochow, things changed. The brother in Foochow wanted his share of the property to invest in business, and the mandarin also withdrew his share. The seven brothers began by dividing the patrimony into eight equal shares, two of these shares in addition to the house being allocated to the oldest brother. The merchant's and mandarin's shares were bought by the other five brothers jointly for a sum of money to be paid in three years with interest. At the same time the five brothers rented some fields from neighbours with the intention of buying them later on. The whole estate was divided into five parcels, one for each of the five brothers. New houses were built for the five new households. At the end of three years the land was all paid for and the division complete. 'On continua cependant à faire en commun les principaux travaux des cultures et des récoltes; on continua à se prêter aide et assistance en toute occasion; mais on vécut chacun chez soi, et les produits des champs appartinrent à ceux auxquels ces champs avaient été attribués et qui les cultivaient à leur guise.'[3] The mandarin and the merchant later replaced the patrimonial fields they had sold to their brothers with other land they bought in the area. Although after division the five households consisted of forty people, there were only seven men to work on the fields. Ouang himself, aged about fifteen or sixteen, was destined for an official career and spent his time in study. Three yearly workers were employed. The five households jointly owned and used two water buffaloes.

[1] Ibid., p. 261.

[2] Loc. cit.

[3] Ibid., p. 263.

The process of division in Ouang's father's generation is, then, fairly clear. The data on the subsequent division within his father's household are more sketchy. Ouang said that he had twice failed in the public examinations, but, thanks to his father's brother's influence, he had got a small job in a prefectural office, intending to make a third attempt in the examinations. Time passed and his academic ambitions remained unfulfilled. 'Me trainer comme bien d'autres dans une position infime et besogneuse, à la suite de mon oncle dans tous les postes où il était envoyé, me répugnait profondément. . . .'[1] Finally he decided to stick to a farmer's life. He was then forty years old. His father's death encouraged him to come to this decision. His brothers helped him to marry off his three eldest daughters, whose marriage had up to then been delayed by his straitened circumstances. Until two years before Simon's interview with him, Ouang and his brothers had harmoniously worked their land in common although they had separate houses. About that time Ouang married off his second son, and the new daughter-in-law created trouble because she thought her husband was not being fairly treated. Division became necessary; the younger son was given his share of the common property and went off to live apart.

Family division, as we may see from this example, might be precipitated by domestic conflict, but it did not necessarily lead to the creation of new units which were not included in some wider one. The establishment of new households, and therefore of new independent economic units, did not preclude the possibility that these households might continue to co-operate economically in some way. The religious aspect of continued co-operation emerges from Ouang's answer to Simon's question about the effect of family division on the cult of the ancestors. Ouang said that a new household had the right to carry on independent worship, but usually it did not do so until one of the founders (the father or the mother) of the new household was dead. Until then, and beyond this time if people wished, everyone assembled at the house of the oldest son who, with his extra share of the inheritance, paid for the expenses of the festival.[2] In time, of course, the economic and religious ties must break; presumably a subsequent division of households which created a new group of co-operating households disrupted the earlier group. There is clearly no expectation in Ouang's answer to the question on ancestor-worship that the cadet households would continue for very long to foregather at the shrine maintained in the senior household.

The 'family' of Ouang was clearly not one of simple peasants. Ouang's father's brother was an official; he himself entertained ambitions in the same direction. Commercial activities, centred upon the capital of the province, contributed to the expansion of the farm holdings. Of Ouang's

[1] Ibid., p. 281.

[2] Ibid., pp. 265f.

four daughters, one married a merchant and another a teacher.[1] Presumably this 'family' was affected by a national ideology which recommended many generations under one roof; yet in their case it is still clear that the tendencies inherent in an agrarian system which allocated equal rights to all brothers prevented the maintenance of large establishments over a long period of time.

I take my second illustration from Lin Yueh-hwa's *The Golden Wing*, which deals with the affairs of two northern Fukien 'families' seen from a point in time some seventy years after Simon's enquiries. I examine the process of household division among the people associated with the hero of the book, Hwang Dunglin. He was the younger of two brothers. Still unmarried, although of an age to take a wife, he lived in one household with his widowed mother, his brother Dungmin, and the latter's wife and three small children. His two sisters were already married. The land which had belonged to his paternal grandfather had been divided between the household of which Dungmin was the head and two other households whose heads descended from the grandfather's two other sons. Dungmin's household was poor.[2]

Dunglin's rise to fortune, which resulted from his business partnership with the husband of one of his sisters, led him finally to marry at the age of twenty-four.[3] Although he had now established himself in business while his older brother remained at home to cultivate the land, the whole property of the household was held as a unit. Since no division had formally taken place, the capital and income resources of the shop which Dunglin operated were part and parcel of the fraternal property.[4] However, the brothers soon decided to divide their property, and Dunglin, now with two small children, set up a separate hearth.[5] But Dungmin died within a year of the division and the old lady, his mother, demanded that the bereaved family be rejoined to Dunglin's.[6] In the reunited household tension grew up between Dunglin's older nephew, who managed the farming side of the household's pursuits, and his own sons. This nephew began to insist on the household being divided so that he might obtain a large share and be able to set up by himself. '[He] was of course the first-born of Dungmin, who was in turn the eldest son. In that division of a family the first-born had a legal right to an extra portion of the joint property. . . . Furthermore, the education of [two of Dunglin's sons] was proving a great drain on the family income and this frightened [the older nephew], who complained of it to his uncle from time to time. Beyond all this, [the older nephew] had grown more and more attached

[1] Ibid., p. 284.

[2] Lin, op. cit., pp. 1–3.

[3] Ibid., p. 11.

[4] Ibid., p. 13.

[5] Ibid., pp. 14f.

[6] Ibid., p. 15.

to his wife . . . and their three children. He wished now to live in a smaller and more peaceful household.'[1]

After some very hard and embittered bargaining over the partition of land, cash savings, and business shares, the family was finally divided. A deed was drawn up which began by describing family division as 'an event as natural as the continuous flow of water from a source or the spreading of branches in a tree'.[2] From that time on Dunglin's household, although occupying the same set of buildings as that of his two nephews, was a distinct economic unit. Property and hearth had been divided. The process of division, however, did not stop at this point, for the older nephew, having managed to set up a household distinct from Dunglin's, now wished to separate from his brother. After much bickering this second division was achieved, once again two new households continuing to live in the same buildings but in separate quarters.[3] Although Dunglin's mother was still alive, there were now three households where recently there had been one. Dunglin had wished to keep the 'family' intact in accordance with what local opinion held to be praiseworthy standards. 'But the internal conflict between the brothers, between the cousins and between the wives of the younger generation had made family life difficult on the scale he envisioned.'[4] The terms of the separation between the two brothers led to continued conflict between them, even though they were now neighbours and not members of one household.[5] In this conflict Dunglin managed to exert only a small measure of authority, but as long as he lived there was no total break in the relations between the several households.[6]

In this example the contrary pull between two principles is well brought out. On the one hand, men like Dunglin who had personal prestige to maintain in their community wished to keep their households undivided. On the other hand, the continuous assertion of fraternal property rights, reflected in the conflict between agnates and their wives, made the maintenance of an undivided household very difficult. The division of households was in fact 'as natural as the continuous flow of water from a source or the spreading of branches in a tree' because the rights of brothers to more or less equal shares of property and the image of these rights in the restiveness of the wives *vis-à-vis* their mother-in-law and their husbands' sisters entailed a constant pressure against unity.

Why do the data on China in general indicate that households of higher social status tended to hold together longer than households lower down in the social scale? Hsu has written that the fragmentation of holdings in

[1] Ibid., p. 123.

[2] Ibid., p. 125.

[3] Ibid., pp. 126–8.

[4] Ibid., p. 128.

[5] Ibid., pp. 160–4.

[6] Ibid., p. 164.

the Chinese agrarian system reduced them below the level of size for their most economic working, and that what really determined the fine division of land among the poor peasantry was the assertion in this stratum of the claims of the husband–wife tie against those of the tie between father and son. Higher up in the social scale people conformed more closely to the ideals of their society; in these ideals the father–son relationship was stressed and the conjugal relationship discounted.[1] Among the poor, that is to say, the solidarity between husband and wife might manifest itself without hindrance; among the better-off, who strove to approximate in their behaviour to ideal norms, the accent was shifted to the solidarity between father and son, such that, whatever the intensity of the personal bond between spouses, it must yield before the claims of the unity of the large unbroken household.

Arguments of this kind, however, appear to involve a certain circularity. The gentry maintained large households because they tried to behave as members of their social class. The humble peasant, relieved of the necessity to strive after gentry ideals, conformed to a pattern considered suitable for the humble peasantry. But why should two distinct models of behaviour have polarized Chinese practice in this fashion? There were many social ideals in China to which only the gentry sought to conform closely. In mourning customs, ancestor worship, wedding ceremonial, and the conduct of widows, we are likely to find the ideal norms of Chinese society reflected in practice only among the higher strata. Perhaps we cannot in general reduce to other factors this unequal distribution of conformity, but in the case of household size we are able to point to several reasons, apart from the differential efficacy of norms, why the richer rural households appear to have maintained larger establishments than their poorer neighbours.

The first of these reasons is very simple. Richer households had more children than poorer households. Plural marriage occurred almost exclusively among the better-off. Poverty postponed marriage, and sometimes prevented it altogether, while the poor were encouraged by their circumstances to rid themselves of 'unwanted' children, especially girls. Some of these children found their way by adoption or sale into the households of the rich.[2] It is also possible that, the later age of marriage apart, the

[1] 'The Myth of Chinese Family Size', pp. 556–9. See also Hsu's essay, 'The Family in China', in R. N. Anshen, ed., *The Family, Its Functions and Destiny*, New York, 1949, pp. 77f.

[2] Female infanticide in China has no doubt been exaggerated, but it seems to have occurred. Curiously enough, southern Fukien appears to have been particularly noteworthy for this practice. See E. T. C. Werner, *Descriptive Sociology . . . Chinese. Compiled and Abstracted Upon the Plan Organized by Herbert Spencer. . .*, edited by H. R. Tedder, London, 1910, p. 38. The legal rules governing the adoption of boys to fill vacancies in direct lines of descent required that they be sought from the closest collateral agnatic lines from which sons could be spared; but in fact some boys were brought in from other lineages, although they may have been related to the adopting fathers by non-agnatic ties. Cf. *Chinese Family and Marriage in Singapore*, p. 62.

reproductive span of the poor was limited by higher mortality, although I am not aware of detailed evidence which bears on this point.[1] The households of the rich were likely to expand their numbers in two other ways. Domestic servants, and sometimes hired farm labourers, lived in their masters' houses and came under their control. The poor lost sons who went off to seek their livelihood elsewhere, and some of these were taken into prosperous households, where there was a shortage of male heirs, as adopted sons-in-law whose children would assume their mothers' surnames.

A further reason why households seem to have been larger among the better-off is suggested by the examples I have taken from Simon and Lin Yueh-hwa. Analysed carefully the units which result from family division are seen to be distinct households; casually regarded, especially in the case of Dunglin's house, what is from the inside several households may appear from the outside to be one household.[2] In Simon's example, even though the several households were spatially separate, there was still enough common economic activity between them to make them appear to be one unit to some outside observer. We may well suspect that the units which Kulp calls 'economic-families' occupying more than one dwelling[3] were in fact groups of distinct households bound together for certain purposes and maintaining a common interest in a particular source of wealth. In *Under The Ancestors' Shadow* Hsu draws a distinction between a situation he found in West Town, Yunnan, where what appeared to be undivided households occupying single houses were in fact internally segmented into several households still linked together by common residence and ritual, and what he says is the situation elsewhere in China, where once a household is divided it is divided completely.[4] I suspect that Hsu's distinction in this matter between West Town and the remainder of China is too strongly drawn. Household division elsewhere in China may be quite clear-cut as a legal fact, but the two examples I have cited show that enough religious and secular co-operation might sometimes have continued after division between erstwhile components of the same household to lead to a situation similar to that found in West Town.[5]

[1] Fei, 'Peasantry and Gentry', p. 10, makes the surprising assertion that 'among the leisure class the birth rate is low because of their degenerated physical conditions. . . .' In fact, the rich were likely to be more fertile than the poor. Cf. F. L. K. Hsu, *Under The Ancestors' Shadow, Chinese Culture and Personality*, London, 1949, p. 214n.

[2] Cf. Wittfogel, *New Light on Chinese Society*, p. 38: 'Often a larger family splits into smaller units but continues to share the same compound. We had to draw attention to this situation again and again before all our assistants became alert to the possible pseudo-largeness of what appears superficially as one family.'

[3] See above, p. 21.

[4] p. 114.

[5] In Lin Yueh-hwa's article on a northern Fukien lineage, on which I shall be drawing later, the Chinese term *hu*, which is usually translated as 'household', appears as precisely the label for the combination of separate households within one set of buildings which we have seen illustrated in *The Golden Wing*.

The significance of this fact for our present purposes is that co-operation between closely related households of a kind to make them seem to resemble one household was more likely to occur among the better-off. Because of heavy capital investment in buildings and in agricultural equipment the richer households probably tended to live closer together and co-operate more fully than poorer households related in a similar fashion.

Another reason why larger households should have appeared among the rich lies in the focus of economic and political power provided by an influential household. Among poor peasants there was little to be lost by breaking away. Among the rich and the influential, it is reasonable to assume, possible alienation from a source of power would weigh with a man in his decision to press for a division of the household. It is possible that business property was a more effective centripetal force than agricultural property, while the important social connexions of gentry households formed a fund from which people might be reluctant to remove themselves even to the small extent implied in their setting up separate households.

Finally we might return to Hsu's explanation and consider it from a different point of view. If it was true that the bond between husband and wife was stronger among the poor than among the rich, then this fact may have been an aspect of a difference in the total configuration of social ties between rich and poor, such that the necessity for a man of high status to remain enmeshed in a wide network of relations outside his conjugal family led him to invest a minimum of emotional and social interest in his wife and her domestic problems. The social horizon of the humble peasant was considerably more restricted; the whole pattern of his conjugal relations may have been shaped by the narrowness of his extra-familial ties. From this angle the greater contribution to ordinary domestic affairs made by the wife of a poor man and the smaller distinction made among the poor between the man's world and woman's world might be seen as part of a system in which the poor household was more isolated than the rich.[1]

In this essay, so far as kinship is concerned, I am dealing mainly with agnatic organization, and I am not intending, therefore, to make a thorough analysis of the family. The discussion on family and household has been necessary in order to show the nature of the most elementary units which composed the structure of the localized lineage. From the unit of agnates living in one household and the unit of agnates living in closely related households the hierarchy of agnatic groups mounted through various segments to the lineage as a whole. Before I turn to this hierarchy, however, I wish to consider the place of women in the social units standing at the base of the pyramid of patrilineal groups. In what sense were women members of the families and households into which they had married?

[1] Cf. Max Gluckman, *Custom and Conflict in Africa*, Oxford, 1955, pp. 58ff., 77ff.

There is a Chinese proverb which says: 'A boy is born facing in; a girl is born facing out'.[1] In other words, from the moment she comes into life a girl is a potential loss to her family. Among Singapore Chinese coming from southern Fukien daughters are spoken of as 'goods on which one loses'. These statements reflect the rule that a woman left her family on marriage and contributed children to the group into which she married. Her domestic services, her fertility, and her chief ritual attachments were transferred by marriage from one family to another. The conveyance of rights in a woman from one group to another was validated by the passage of bride-price.

Although there appears to have been some regional variation in the nature of the control over women exercised by those who had given bride-price for them, it is clear that the legal rights vested in the families from which women married were very few. Once married a woman visited her original family as a kind of guest and, at least in theory, only with the permission of her husband's people. After the completion of the marriage exchanges no property flowed by right between the married woman's old family and her new family. The married woman found a permanent place in her new home, a place which, so to speak, was strengthened first by her bearing children and second by her death; for when she died she might lie by her husband's side both in the grave and on the ancestral altar.

A test of the married woman's absorption into her husband's group was her fate on widowhood. According to the ideals of gentry behaviour she did not remarry, but when, as seems to have been often the case among ordinary people, she chose to get or was given another husband, the rights over her in second marriage lay largely with her first husband's people. These people could not legally claim to continue their control over her by passing her to a brother of her late husband, because the law of the land incorporated a strict rule against widow inheritance[2]; although the inheritance of brothers' widows was certainly known, the law notwithstanding, in many parts of the country, especially among the poor.[3]

[1] See C. H. Plopper, *Chinese Religion Seen Through the Proverb*, Shanghai, 1926, p. 99.

[2] It did so in the setting of a general prohibition on marriage with the widows of agnates. See Staunton, op. cit., p. 115. This fact is itself an important reflection of the extent to which, from the official point of view at least, married women were absorbed into and identified with their husbands' groups. Note the wording, loc. cit., in the Ch'ing code: 'Whoever marries a female relation beyond the fourth degree, or the widow of a male relation equally remote, shall be punished with 100 blows. Whoever marries the widow of a relation in the fourth degree, or of a sister's son, shall be punished with 60 blows, and one year's banishment.—Whoever marries the widow of any nearer relation, shall be punished according to the law against incestuous connexions with such persons.' Cf. Boulais, op. cit., p. 278 and Hoang, op. cit., pp. 55ff.

[3] See a note on the 'levirate' in China in *The China Review*, vol. X, 1881–1882, p. 71; Théry, op. cit., p. 391; and M. H. van der Valk, *Conservatism in Modern Chinese Family Law*, Studia et Documenta Ad Iura Antiqui Orientis Pertinentia, Volume IV, Leiden, 1956, pp. 29f.

Théry, drawing on the compilation of customs published by the Chinese government in 1930 in connexion with legal reform, says that in some places the widow's original family were completely excluded from the right to dispose of her or were given second place; and in this connexion he notes the dictum reported from one county in Hupeh: a woman does not have two families. Two counties in Fukien followed this rule. However, there were also places where the widow's original family arranged her second marriage and received the gifts, one Fukien county appearing to ascribe the right of the remarriage of widows to their original families. Yet again, in several places the consent of the widow's own people was required even though the late husband's people had the right to marry her off.[1] Kwangtung was, unfortunately, not covered in the survey of customs. The evidence from Fukien, as we have seen, is not all of one piece, but generally it seems to indicate that the passage of bride-price gave those who paid it very wide and continuous control over women.[2]

The assimilation of the married woman into her husband's group was certainly never complete, despite the control exercised over her by this group. She retained her own surname through life and was ritually a part of her original family at least to the extent of mourning for her parents. In this respect she demonstrated her marginality; having, unlike men, two sets of parents to mourn, her own and her husband's, she was a link between two agnatic groups. We shall later see a reflexion of this tie in the relations between men and their maternal kin.

All units from the family to the lineage as a whole were agnatic in framework but had women attached to them. But there was an important difference in this respect between the family and higher kinship units. In the family the activities and functions of women were as prominent as those of men. Once we look beyond domestic units the formal roles of women disappear and their informal roles seem comparatively unimportant. Only when she was dead was a woman admissible, in the shape of an ancestral tablet, into the ancestral hall. In the government of the lineage she had no voice other than her husband's or her son's. When we discuss the household and the family, therefore, we cannot fail to take account of the importance of women. When we turn our attention to wider kinship units we may conveniently think of these groups as being composed primarily of men.

[1] Théry, op. cit., pp. 375ff.

[2] Van der Valk, op. cit., also draws on the 1930 compilation of customs. He speaks (p. 61) of the 'outright buying' of wives in some districts, especially in Fukien, and reports of Nan-an in Fukien that the husband, having 'paid' for his wife, was entitled by custom to 'sell' her to another person, her own family having no right to interfere. The Ch'ing code gave a widow's parents-in-law complete control of her remarriage. If, however, there were no competent survivors in the widow's husband's family, her own family could exercise the right to marry her. See Boulais, op. cit., p. 273.

4

The Hierarchy of Agnatic Units

Kulp isolated for Phoenix Village four types of 'family': natural, economic, religious, and conventional. The first, as we have seen, was the elementary family and the second a household or wider group with a strong economic unity. The religious family was 'the practical unit of ancestral worship', varying with the particular ancestor worshipped at a given time.[1] The conventional family was the 'sib' as a whole. The 'sib' was divided into two moieties which constituted the religious families of the highest order. The religious family 'includes all those persons who ordinarily come together for ancestor worship, whether of the moieties just beneath the sib in rank and size, or just above or identical with the economic-groups'.[2] It is evident that a particular elementary family might be a member of a series of Chinese box-like 'religious families' rising in a hierarchy. The picture of lineage segmentation is not, however, altogether clear. 'The ancestral-group is made up of a number of sex- and economic-groups. In fact there are cases where the sex- and economic- and ancestral-groups are identical. The ancestral-groups vary in size. They may stand midway between the sib and the economic-group, or between the sib and smaller ancestral groups.'[3] Both economic and religious families had their heads, *chia-chang*, but the functions of the two kinds of *chia-chang* were different. The administration of the resources owned by the economic family lay in the hands of its *chia-chang*, who came under the supervision of the *chia-chang* of the religious families or the leaders of the village. 'While the religious-family functions primarily for the stability of the community, the economic-family provides its maintenance.'[4]

Kulp's account is blurred for us because he was not interested in what we nowadays call lineage structure. Oddly enough, we may be almost as puzzled by the treatment of a Chinese lineage at the hands of an anthropologist aiming at great precision in structural analysis. In 1935 the late Professor Radcliffe-Brown visited China where, according to Lin Yueh-hwa, his lectures inspired the latter to present a treatment of his material

[1] Kulp., op. cit., pp. 145f.

[2] Ibid., p. 146.

[3] Ibid., p. 145.

[4] Ibid., p. 149.

on a northern Fukien village in terms of functional anthropology.[1] This village was I-hsü, inhabited by people of the surname Hwang.

'Now,' in Lin's words, 'let us take a glance at the situation as regards the lineage at I-hsü. The lineage is composed of fifteen sub-lineages. Since each sub-lineage has a head, the lineage has fifteen heads of sub-lineages. These sub-lineage heads are not elected or appointed but come to their position simply as a matter of natural succession as time goes on. That is to say, among the male members of each sub-lineage, whoever ranks highest in generation and in the same generation whoever is the oldest automatically becomes the head of the sub-lineage. . . . Among the sub-lineage heads there must be one man whose generation and age are superior to those of all the rest, and he is the head of the lineage. . . . However, there is one difficulty in giving priority to generation. Sometimes in the highest generation the old people have died off and there are no middle-aged members, so that only the young are left, and in such cases they may even have a boy in his 'teens or a child of seven or eight as head of the lineage. In order to remedy this defect there is a special device in I-hsü, which is to choose a village head to assist the head of the lineage. The choice of village head rests on age alone—generation is not a criterion; that is, the village head is the oldest male member of the lineage. He could be the head of the lineage as well, or the head of one of the sub-lineages, but it could happen also that he was neither lineage nor sub-lineage head but simply an ordinary male member of the lineage. In this way the village head must be an old man of wide experience, shrewd and firm in the management of business, in whom the lineage members have complete confidence. The head of the lineage of I-hsü was an old man of eighty-six with grey hair and beard, and he was also the village head because he was the oldest man in the village. . . .

'The difference between a lineage village and other kinds of village lies not only in the existence of the lineage ancestral hall and the worship of ancestors but, which is really much more important, in the natural interlocking structure which binds the family and the lineage, that is consanguineal relationship.

'The family is the smallest and most fundamental unit of the lineage, each family having its family head. Several families make up a compound, each with a compound head. Several compounds make up a branch, each with a branch head. Several branches make up a sub-lineage, each with a head. Several sub-lineages make up a lineage, which has a lineage head. This kind of structure builds up from the bottom in a very regular manner. The family is the basic economic unit, comprising all relatives in the

[1] 'An Enquiry into the Chinese Lineage-Village from the Viewpoint of Anthropology'. As this article is available only in Chinese I propose to quote translated extracts from it at considerable length. It is an extremely important source and deserves to be widely known. I give no page references for my quotations from the article. Cf. p. vi above.

paternal line who share a stove and prepare food together. The oldest man in the highest generation is the head of the family. Families are counted by kitchens [literally, stoves] while compounds are counted according to dwellings. The same dwelling may comprise several families, from among which the oldest of the family heads is made the head of the compound. For instance, if there are three brothers in a compound, each of whom has set up his own family, the oldest brother becomes the head of the compound as a matter of course. Branches are reckoned by lines of descent. For example, agnatic cousins belong to a common line of descent from the same paternal grandfather although they may live in different compounds. Above the branch there are further branches, for example the line of descent springing from the same patrilineal great-grandfather, or from the same patrilineal great-great-grandfather, or from any of the agnatic ancestors up to the point of sub-lineage division; therefore within one sub-lineage there will be many major and minor lines of descent. Each sub-lineage has a head and these heads, together with the head of the lineage, form the ancestral hall association. These then are the intermediate stages between the family and the lineage.

'The links between the family and the lineage are approximately according to the pattern we have just described. Naturally the real picture may not conform with this in every respect. As for the number of families, there are one-family compounds, and in such cases the family head is also the head of the compound. There may be cases in which there are two families in one compound belonging to different branches and both heads of family are compound heads. The function of the head of the compound is to attend meetings in the ancestral hall and to be the chief worshipper at times of ancestral worship in the compound. Hence the influence of the compound head is not economic but rather political, diplomatic, and religious. Orders from the ancestral hall can be transmitted direct to each compound, through which they are transmitted in turn to each family. Therefore lineage members often call this unit "family compound", thus indicating the close relationship between the family and the compound. As the head of each branch stands midway between the lineage and the sub-lineages, on the one hand, and the family and the compound, on the other hand, his position has neither the intimacy that comes of close kinship nor the importance of standing for the entire lineage. When members of the branch are still within the limits of the five mourning grades, on the occasion of wedding or mourning ceremonies communications are still sent out in the name of the head of the branch. However, the heads of larger branches can be in charge only of the worship and the sacrifices of their respective branches. From the functional point of view we can say approximately that the family is an economic unit, the compound a political and social unit, and the branch a religious and worshipping unit, while the heads of the lineage and the various sub-lineages, that is, the ancestral hall association, constitute a combined economic, political, social, religious, educational, and military (&c.) unit.'

Lin then proceeds to point out that, in principle, each of the units he has outlined has an ancestral hall. 'All halls from the sub-lineage and branch halls downwards, although they have special functions to fulfil, still have the original religious function as the most obvious one. Of course, it cannot be said that other functions are non-existent. For instance, a case of dispute between brothers should be settled first by the head of the family. If the decision is not accepted by either party, the case can be brought before the head of the compound. If again there is no settlement, the matter should be taken up to the head of the branch, or even to the head of the lineage and the ancestral hall association which can settle all kinds of disputes. If this fails to settle the dispute then it goes to the magistrate's court. However, lineage members all consider it dishonourable to bring an action into the official courts.'

No numerical information is given on the various units distinguished. Lin mentions a formula, 'Five persons constitute a family, five families a compound, five compounds a branch, five branches a sub-lineage, and five sub-lineages a lineage,' only to dismiss it as a falsely mechanical way of discussing lineage structure. On the structure and functions of the family he writes: 'We have referred to the family as an economic unit comprising relatives in the paternal line, of various generations and various orders of seniority within each generation. It is a communal group, sharing the same cooking stove, eating together, and it is often called a joint family in the literature of sociology. Each family often has so many *mow* of land which formally belong to the head of the family. Sometimes the head of the family retires because of his age, while still exercising control over the administration of the family's property. Once a male member of the family reaches the age of sixteen he has to go out and till the land, and all the produce of the land is kept in the family barn. The individual has no private savings and all his expenses on food, clothing, shelter, and travelling have to be paid for by the head of the family. . . . The family is not confined in function to the economic field. It is merely that, because common ownership of property and the sharing of a common life bind the family together, the economic factor is the fundamental condition of family solidarity.'

These are the essential data in Lin's account which bear on the question of how the lineage is segmented. I have translated some of his technical terms unconventionally from the sinological point of view in order to fit them more easily into anthropological discourse. *Tsung-tsu* I render as lineage, although when we turn to *The Golden Wing* we see that Lin himself translates the term as 'clan'. *Fang*, literally 'house', is the common Chinese term for a primary division of a lineage; I translate it as sub-lineage. I retain the literal meaning of *chih*, a branch. *Hu* is usually rendered as 'household', but it will clearly not bear this meaning in Lin's analysis of I-hsü because it designates a unit which, although occupying one set of dwellings, is or may be subdivided into distinct kitchen and property-owning groups. I have, therefore, translated *hu* as 'compound', taking a leaf from the Africanist's book. (We may note that Wittfogel, in a passage I have quoted earlier,[1] comes close to using the term 'compound' in the same way.) *Chia* is always translated as 'family' and I have followed this uasge. If we look at the diagram at the end of Lin's article, which is supposed to illustrate the interlocking groups and functions in the lineage, we see that he sets out the structural hierarchy in the following manner: individual, matrimonial group, elementary family, joint family, compound, small branch, large branch, sub-lineage, lineage.

The formal analysis on which Lin insists in a large part of his article leads him to present a picture of a lineage which is built up in a more or less orderly fashion from segments of increasing genealogical span. The structure mounts from residential units through branches and sub-lineages to the lineage as a whole. However, just as in the case of Kulp's account (which Lin correctly says to be inadequate in some respects), so in the treatment of the Hwang lineage of I-hsü, the status of the branch (Kulp's religious family) is unclear. Branches may nest within branches; this is certain; but how many types of this unit there are and what causes them to be distributed in a different manner in different areas of the lineage are left unstated. Nevertheless, we may gather from Lin's account that, unless a branch coincides with a group of agnates still within the five mourning grades, its functional status is not strong. We can take the Hwang lineage of I-hsü to confirm the impression given by other material that the structurally important units in the Chinese localized lineage were the lineage as a whole and its sub-lineages, at one end of the system, and the family and the compound, at the other end. The intermediate units, the branches of varying span, might express themselves in the context of ancestor-worship, but they seem to have done little else.

The shortcomings of Lin's outline of I-hsü[2] lie mainly in its treatment of the lineage as though it were a relatively isolated segment of Chinese society and in its bias towards one type of organizing principle: kinship. I propose now to show, on the basis of another work from Lin's pen, how these shortcomings can be seen to be important in distorting the picture of the village-lineage system. In the article I have just dealt with Lin follows what he takes to be a Radcliffe-Brownian method of analysis. The article was written in 1936. Some years later Lin returned to a sociological treatment of a northern Fukien lineage and in so doing offered a rather different account. *The Golden Wing*, published in England in 1948, makes no reference to the article in Chinese. It sets out to trace the fortunes of two 'families' in northern Fukien, one of which, the more central to the story, belongs to the Hwang Village. It seems to me that this Hwang

[1] See p. 29n. above.

[2] Lin says that his earlier account of I-hsü, unpublished, ran to 150,000 words. His article, which contains about 10,000 characters, is necessarily condensed.

Village and I-hsü must be the same place; but even if they are not, then they must have been close neighbours, for they were studied at the same time. Either, therefore, the two villages are one or they are two representatives of a regional type. To show, as I shall attempt to do, that the two accounts differ in interesting respects is to comment on the effect of changing theoretical preoccupations on an anthropologist's analysis. The influence of Radcliffe-Brown has evaporated from *The Golden Wing*. Since writing his article Lin had spent some time in the United States and had there absorbed other ideas. The theme of the article was structural and functional analysis; the aim of the book is to treat the ups and downs of individual and group fortunes as examples of the working of the principle of equilibrium, a concept which is naïve in its conception however dramatically it may be applied. Of course, *The Golden Wing*, as a kind of novel written in the pointed simplicity of Chinese style, has great charm and, incidentally to the story of the rise and fall of family fortunes, gives a great deal of fascinating information on life in China. But it is precisely in this information that we find suggestions that the analysis of I-hsü is inadequate.

I have already noted that the population of the Hwang village of *The Golden Wing* numbered 'several hundred'.[1] Apart from the innkeeper's family, all the inhabitants of the village belonged to one 'clan' which traced its descent from a common founding ancestor. Dunglin, the protagonist of the story, was of the eighth generation in the lineage.[2] When the founding ancestor had arrived from southern Fukien in the area now inhabited by the Hwang, he had found all the land already taken up, but by dint of hard work he had established himself, and his descendants came finally to enjoy almost sole occupation of the area. There was apparently a cluster of houses in the village centre, but some of the houses seem to have been scattered about in the agricultural land. Wet-rice farming was the base of the economy. If there is any general significance in the case of the land held by the people of Dunglin's family, the occupation of the area by the Hwang lineage did not mean that they owned all their land outright; they rented the surface rights in perpetuity from town landlords for about 40 per cent of the crop.

The lineage as a whole owned a rice mill, an ancestral hall, ancestral land which was exploited to finance lineage ancestor worship, and a tomb of the first ancestor where annual rites were carried out.[3] The lineage also owned a set of musical instruments for use on special occasions.[4] At one important wedding all the constituent families of the lineage were represented.[5] The only other evidence of common action in the lineage is

[1] See p. 6 above.

[2] Op. cit., p. 60.

[3] Ibid., pp. 60f.

[4] Ibid., p. 68.

[5] Ibid., p. 115.

the case in which money was collected all round to 'ransom' some of the village elders from the military,[1] and a case in which money was raised within the lineage to finance a member's education abroad.[2]

The segmentation of the lineage is obscure. Lin uses the word 'clan' for the descent group in its entirety and employs the word 'lineage' to label an unspecified division of the 'clan'. We do not know how many such divisions there were, how they came about, and at what levels they operated. 'Elders' are spoken of incidentally, but who they were and what they did are not clear. Of the lineage head we are told that he was the highest in generation and most senior in age. None of this contradicts what Lin writes of I-hsü; indeed, these data confirm some of the points he makes in his article; but when we turn to what can be gathered about the working of the lineage we receive a different impression from that created by the account of I-hsü.

In this latter account we are told only incidentally of the existence of a world outside the village with which it had social relations. What is striking in *The Golden Wing* is that, the import and export of brides quite apart, villagers were the whole time in close touch with people from other lineages. The boys of different villages played together. Outsiders came into the Hwang Village to work. Some of the landlords at least were not members of the lineage. Friendship on a non-kinship basis ramified in all directions. Moreover, the importance of matrilateral and affinal kinship is made manifest. Indeed the main theme of the book rests on the economic partnership between Dunglin and his older sister's husband. In all the stories of banditry, trade, political manoeuvring, and marriage arrangements we find friends, affines, and non-agnatic kinsmen playing a major role.

The events set out in *The Golden Wing* do not portray a regular arrangement of lineage parts, with quarrels rising in an orderly fashion through a hierarchy of segments. It is true that much of the action of the book is set in towns, to which the characters go in pursuit of their business, but even in the purely rural milieu we find the national legal system coming into play at the instigation of villagers. When Dunglin had trouble with his late brother's son over the division of the family property, outside mediators were brought in, and for years the matter was not satisfactorily settled. The apparatus of a segmented lineage does not appear in this example.

The most interesting dispute described was that between Dunglin and the descendants of his father's father's mother's brother, a member of the Ou lineage. This man had given his sister's sons permission to plant saplings on his own land. The trees now being fully grown, Dunglin wanted to cut them down to use in the building of a new house. His claim to the trees was physically resisted by the descendants of the loving

[1] Ibid., p. 154.

[2] Ibid., p. 121.

maternal uncle, and several lawsuits followed. In this serious dispute between members of two neighbouring lineages, with its fines, jailings, and violence, no people were directly involved other than those who made specific claim to the trees or the land on which they stood. The hostile party in the Ou lineage consisted of the descendants of the kindly maternal uncle. At the outset of the case Dunglin on his side was supported by men who were descended with him from the man to whom the right to plant the saplings had been given; but even they withdrew their claims, only Dunglin and his father's brother remaining to contest the trees. No principle of lineage solidarity seems to have come into play. The groups of men from the two lineages involved in the quarrel appear to have been defined in relation to the property rights in question.[1]

Naturally, one might argue that the facts which I have adduced from *The Golden Wing* are by their nature of a different order from the generalized statements made in the article on I-hsü. It is clear, however, that in his book Lin is trying to illustrate general matters through particular events, and I think it is fair to see in these events a partial contradiction of his earlier analysis.

In her general survey of the Chinese lineage Miss Hu Hsien-chin deals with the process of segmentation only at the higher levels. Her evidence shows that it was common for a lineage to be divided into a number of sub-lineages (*fang*), which traced their origin to different sons of the founder.[2] Miss Hu herself treats lower units of lineage structure in terms of the *chia*, which is the primary property-owning unit, and the circle of mourning relatives. The latter is a category of relatives defined with respect to a given individual so as to include, so far as agnates are concerned, the descendants of his agnatic great-great-grandfather. What Miss Hu refers to as the circle of mourning relatives is elsewhere in the literature called the *wu fu*, the five grades of mourning. We have seen that this category affects the nature of the ties between members of lower segments of the lineage in I-hsü. We must examine it in some detail.

[1] Ibid., pp. 26–32.

[2] Op. cit., pp. 18f.

5

Mourning Grades

Miss Hu speaks of the circle of mourning relatives as a unit 'larger than the family but smaller than the *tsu* [lineage]'.[1] She points out that, although it owns no property and is relatively impermanent and relatively informal in organization, its members have recognized obligations to one another.[2] They are supposed to attend one another's family celebrations and funerals, and 'also act as negotiators and arbitrators in disputes arising between the individual *chia*. At the division of property particularly, the elders in the circle of mourning relatives make decisions and witness the transaction.'[3]

The *wu fu* was in principle a category drawn up in regard to a given ego; it could not, therefore, be a discrete segment of a lineage. But, while the term was used to define the range of agnatic kinsmen to whom a given individual was supposed to hold himself closely related and with whom he should co-operate in a number of ways, in another sense it marked out different classes of relatives, both agnatic and otherwise, for the specification of types and durations of mourning due to them; whence the literal meaning of the expression. This ambiguity appears to have given rise to some confusion. It is interesting, for example, to find two Chinese anthropologists debating the meaning of *wu fu*.[4] We shall be concerned later with the non-agnatic categories covered by the term when it is taken in its literal sense of mourning grades.[5]

An individual defined his agnatic *wu fu* as: his direct line of ascent to father's father's father's father; his direct line of descent to son's son's son's son; his brothers and their agnatic descendants to the third descending generation; his father's brothers and their agnatic descendants to the level of second descending generation from ego; his father's father's brothers and their agnatic descendants to the level of the first descending generation from ego; his father's father's father's brothers and their

[1] *The Common Descent Group in China*, p. 17.

[2] Ibid., p. 9.

[3] Ibid., p. 17.

[4] See F. L. K. Hsu, 'The Problem of Incest Tabu in a North China Village', *American Anthropologist*, vol. 42, no. 1, Jan.–March 1940, p. 123, note 6, where he and Fei Hsiao-tung are shown to give different senses to the term. Literally, *wu fu* means "the five mourning grades."

[5] See below, pp. 101ff.

agnatic descendants to the level of ego's own generation; and all the sisters of the men included.[1]

It is this patrilineal category, including agnatic third cousins and rising and falling four generations in the direct line of descent, which is, as it were, the hard core of Chinese agnation. Where marriage was permitted by custom between people of the same surname the exogamous boundary was drawn at the *wu fu*.[2] We may judge how fundamental a characteristic of the Chinese kinship system this limitation is by the manner in which not only the Kuomintang civil law but also the more recent Communist marriage law have entrenched the irreducible exogamous area in their provisions for modernizing the family law of China.[3]

Within the agnatic *wu fu* a person dealt with his closest patrilineal kinsmen. They might not form a discrete segment of his community,

[1] Hsu, op. cit., p. 124, gives a diagram of the agnatic *wu fu* plus their wives in the traditional Chinese form. See also Fêng Han-yi (Fêng Han-chi), *The Chinese Kinship System*, Cambridge, Mass., 1948 (reprinted from *Harvard Journal of Asiatic Studies*, vol. II, no. 2, July 1937), p. 23.

[2] Cf. above, p. 4, and Hsu, op. cit., p. 123. In the community described by Fei in *Peasant Life in China* we find a situation where genealogical shallowness is reflected in the identification of *tsu* (lineage) and *wu fu*. The theoretical difficulty that *wu fu* must be defined afresh for each individual is not encountered in practice. Fei writes (p. 84): 'According to the accepted principle, all the patrilineal descendants and their wives that can be traced to a common ancestor within five kinship grades consider themselves as belonging to a kinship group called Tsu. . . . But in practice this strict genealogical accounting is not important. Firstly, there is no written document of genealogy and memory of descent is not very exact. . . . Secondly, if the principle were strictly observed, theoretically there would be a division of Tsu for each generation. But Tsu are seldom divided for this purpose. . . . The Tsu will not be sub-divided if there is no increase of members.'

[3] Cf. my 'Colonial Law and Chinese Society', pp. 107f. Article 983 of the 1931 Civil Code laid it down that a person might not marry, among others, a collateral relative by blood who was of the same generation and 'within the eighth degree of relationship but this provision does not apply to "piao cousins".' (*Piao* are cousins of a different surname.) See Ching-Lin Hsia et al. trans., *The Civil Code of the Republic of China*, Shanghai, 1931. Since degrees of relationship were computed in the Code by the Roman law system, the prohibition in this clause extended up to and included agnatic third cousins, who are, of course, at the limit of the *wu fu*. Article 5 of the Marriage Law of the People's Republic of China includes a statement that the prohibition of marriage between collateral blood relatives within the fifth degree of relationship shall be regulated by custom. See 'Colonial Law and Chinese Society', p. 123; other translations of the Communist code are to be found in *The Marriage Law of the People's Republic of China*, Foreign Languages Press, Peking, 1950, and *Chinese Law and Custom in Hong Kong*, Appendix 13, pp. 226ff. Van der Valk, op. cit., p. 26, paraphrases a Communist commentary on the new law by Ch'en Shao-yü: in modern economic conditions the old prohibitions on marriage between close collaterals can hardly hold, but 'in parts of the country with backward economy, where persons of common descent were living closely together it would be left to custom to decide whether marriages collateral of relatives [sic] within the fifth degree would be allowed, of which the marriages of *piao* cousins were only one kind.' This is an interesting example of the extension of custom into Communist reform.

but when the members of a segment were related within the *wu fu* they were particularly intimate. We may turn again to legal statements to see the special importance ascribed to the *wu fu*. The codified Ch'ing law expressed in a number of ways the assumption that close agnates were a category of particular significance. Among the ten offences singled out as being of 'treasonable' nature[1], four are concerned with action against or with kinsmen. '*Parricide*, is the denomination under which the murder of a father or mother, of an uncle, aunt, grandfather, or grandmother, is comprehended, and is a crime of the deepest dye; . . . *Impiety*, is discoverable in every instance of disrespect or negligence towards those to whom we owe our being, and by whom we have been educated and protected. . . . *Discord*, in families, is the breach of the legal or natural ties which are founded on our connexions by blood or marriage; under this head may be classed the crimes of killing, wounding, or maltreating any of those relations or connexions to whom, when deceased, the ceremony of mourning is legally due. . . . *Incest*, is the cohabitation, or promiscuous intercourse, of persons related in any of the degrees within which marriage is prohibited.'[2] 'Parricide' and 'impiety' concern only immediately related kinsmen; 'discord' and 'incest' on the other hand, are closely connected with the *wu fu*, as we may see from the wording quoted for 'discord' and, in the case of 'incest', from the explanation that, while the Code prohibited sexual relations between all agnates,[3] it regarded only the intercourse between close kinsmen, in particular between agnates within the mourning grades, as very serious.[4] The Code also expresses the desirability of harmony within the narrow range of kin by providing that relatives might legitimately conceal the offences of one another (except in cases of high treason and rebellion), either escaping punishment altogether or suffering a reduced punishment according to the closeness of the relationship;[5] and by making it an offence generally for close kinsmen to lay even just accusations against one another.[6] Of course, these codified rules do not represent for us the actual rules by which behaviour was necessarily regulated, but they reveal an official system of ideas in which close agnatic kinship was thought to set up special rights and duties standing apart from, and sometimes in opposition to, the rights and duties between man and man and between man and the state.

[1] Staunton, op. cit., p. 5: 'treasonable' offences are 'distinguished from others by their enormity, are always punished with the utmost rigour of the law . . . being likewise, in each case, a direct violation of the ties by which society is maintained'. Cf. Boulais, op. cit., p. 28.

[2] Staunton, op cit., pp. 3f. Boulais, op. cit., pp. 29f. Boulais, p. 30, instead of 'incest' has: '*Trouble intérieur* (comme d'avoir commerce charnel avec ceux de ses parents pour lesquels on doit porter au moins le petit deuil; . . . .).'

[3] Staunton, p. 406. Boulais, p. 686.

[4] Staunton, pp. 371f. Boulais, pp. 644f.

[5] Staunton, pp. 34f. Boulais, p. 92.

[6] Staunton, pp. 371f. Boulais, pp. 644f.

The obligations of mourning borne by a man towards his agnatic *wu fu* not only set this category of patrilineal kinsmen aside from other agnates but also discriminated among them in such a fashion as to show which were more important than others. We have seen that the imperial law determined the nature of certain duties and privileges in accordance with the types of mourning required of individuals in relation to others, and it was necessary for the state to lay down what the structure of mourning obligations was to be. The Ch'ing Code set out five main degrees or grades of mourning and allocated different kinsmen to these grades. The diagram below represents the mourning duties of a man towards his agnates within the *wu fu*. The numeral against each person shows the grade of mourning due to him or her. The five grades were defined in terms of duration and apparel as follows:

Grade 1: 27 months; coarse hempen garments (unhemmed), hempen headdress, grass sandals, and (in the case of mourning for parents) mourning staff.

Grade 2: (*a*) 1 year; somewhat finer hempen garments (hemmed), hempen headdress, shoes of grass, straw, or hemp, and mourning staff.
(*b*) 1 year; dress as for (*a*) but without staff.
(*c*) 5 months; dress as for (*b*).
(*d*) 3 months; dress as for (*b*) and (*c*).

Grade 3: 9 months; dress of coarse cloth.
Grade 4: 5 months; dress of fine cloth.
Grade 5: 3 months; dress of silky hemp.[1]

In the diagram the figure 1 in brackets against paternal grandparents and the lineal ascendants above them indicates that ego was to mourn for them in the first grade if he was the most senior direct descendant alive. The grade 2*a* does not appear on the diagram; it covered mourning for father's wife other than own mother, own remarried mother and own divorced mother. The grades ascribed to female agnates apply to them only if they are unmarried.

The official pattern of mourning in this fashion portrayed the diminishing intensity of relationships between agnates according to proximity. The grades declined towards patrilineal great-great-grandfather, towards patrilineal great-great-grandson, and towards third agnatic cousin. Yet, although this system expressed a legal grading of responsibilities couched in the idiom of mourning, we know that people in the villages, at least, did not follow the official rules in all their elaboration. Indeed, the official rules embodied one principle, mourning for juniors, which was rejected in the popular system. Lin Yueh-hwa brings this out very clearly in *The Golden Wing* when he comments on the fact that a man did not wear mourning for his wife. Although this failure was contrary to what Lin

[1] See de Groot, *The Religious System of China*, vol. II, pp. 547ff., Boulais, op. cit., pp. 17ff., and Hoang, *Le mariage chinois*, pp. 1ff. of 'Annotations aux tableaux du deuil d'après les lois chinoises'. I have not reproduced here all the details about costume. It was not to be worn in all its elaboration throughout the mourning period, and in practice full mourning apparel was used only during rites.

calls the ancient ritual, 'the present practice seems to be to enforce mourning only as a duty of younger to older, juniors to seniors, or inferior to superior. . . .'[1] Our knowledge of the behaviour of overseas Chinese

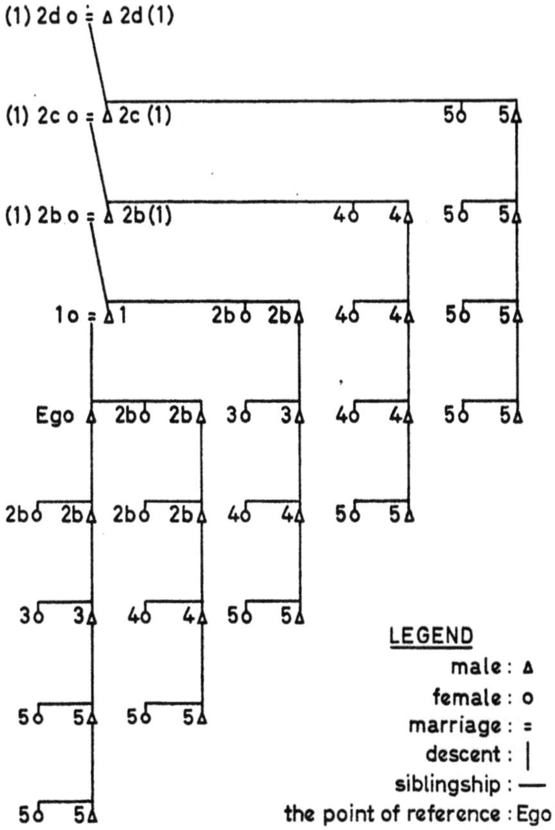

from Fukien and Kwangtung[2] and of people in other provinces of China[3] shows that the popular system of mourning was not on all fours with the ideological system propounded by the Confucian state. Apart from ignoring the duties of seniors to juniors, popular mourning simplified the grades; and in doing so probably reflected an agnatic system which was narrower in ritual range than that envisaged by the official system. I shall show in a later context that mourning for agnates in other households, except when these households were grouped with one's own to form an extended family, was likely to be on a contractual rather than a fixed basis.[4] The ritual mobilization of close agnates in mourning, therefore, defined a smaller core of patrilineal kinsmen than was required by the legal system.

[1] Op. cit., p. 106.
[2] See my *Chinese Family and Marriage in Singapore*, pp. 209ff.
[3] Cf. Fei, *Peasant Life*, p. 78; and Hsu, *Under the Ancestors' Shadow*, pp. 158f.
[4] See below, pp. 93ff.

6

The Segmentary System

The evidence which I have so far brought forward indicates that, while the lineage in south-eastern China may have segmented in relation to many different points in its historically long career, the segments of particular structural importance were the sub-lineage, the family in one household, and an aggregate of such families which were closely connected in agnation. I call this last unit an extended family. If all its component household-families occupied one set of buildings, it corresponded to the unit in I-hsü for which I have proposed the name 'compound'. Ideally, there was a close connexion between the extended family and the *wu fu* such that individual families whose adult males were no further removed than agnatic third cousins constituted the most effective extended family. But it is clear that the actual boundaries drawn for this lower-level segment of the lineage varied not only between but also within lineages. The extended family was a unit which might be based on domestic ancestor worship, a common interest in certain types of property, and a political and legal identity such that its head, *chia-chang*, might give orders to those under him and act as a mediator between disputants who were members of the group. Beyond this very general formulation we cannot profitably go, because it is evident that the range and effectiveness of the functions of the extended family were determined differently in different circumstances.

The passage of time added to the number of generations in the sub-lineage, but, because its focal point was constant, it remained structurally stable. The household-family and the extended family, on the other hand, shifted their focal points along the continuum of the generations. Unlike the unilineal descent groups explored by anthropologists in non-literate societies, the Chinese lineage did not operate on a stationary time-scale. Not only biologically but also socially it added new generations to its system. The way in which genealogies were kept in the Chinese lineage shows that there was no attempt to maintain a constant distance between founder and present generation.[1] Families, therefore, had constantly to redefine themselves in relation to different recent ancestors.

Yet, despite the fact that the various types of branches which interposed themselves between sub-lineages and their extended families appear to have been structurally of minor importance, we may certainly not dismiss

[1] See below, p. 70.

them from our attention without further ado. These intermediate segments, as we may call them, may have had little connexion with the maintenance of order, but they could emerge to form a descending series of less and less inclusive ancestor-worshipping units. It was in theory possible for a lineage which had members in the twenty-fifth generation[1] to display a hierarchy of intermediate segments emerging at a dozen or more levels.

These segments could not result from the *domestic* mode of ancestor worship. In this mode ancestral tablets descended by primogeniture until they were no more than about four generations from the man who maintained them. When they reached this stage of remoteness they were destroyed or buried. Tablets kept in this fashion in domestic shrines could serve as ritual foci for the component units of an extended family; but since they came in time to be removed from the domestic shrines no segment higher than an extended family could find a focus in them. However, when a tablet, having receded about four generations from its chief worshipper, was taken out of the domestic shrine it could be replaced by another kind of tablet to be set up in an ancestral hall. When ancestor worship shifted from the domestic plane to that of the ancestral hall a different kind of social grouping could result. Ancestor-worshipping segments might emerge in relation to a series of halls.

If an ancestral hall and property for its maintenance had been set up for forebears in every one or two generations, permanent foci would have existed for a large number of segments. It was apparently open to any man of means to tie a portion of the property he left either to the maintenance of an ancestral hall already in existence or to the establishment of a new one in respect of himself or some recently dead forebear. New segments coming into being were physically reflected in the ramification of halls. De Groot tells us, for example, that when a 'clan temple' became overcrowded with tablets, or for some other reason no further tablets could be added, some members of the 'family' formed a new 'temple' of their own, transferring from the old 'temple' to the new the tablets of those of their ancestors who were recently dead. In this manner they set up a 'temple' which was a branch of the older one.[2] Chen Han-seng writes of a village in Kwangtung, which had seven hundred inhabitants, all of one 'clan', that it maintained forty or more ancestral 'temples'.[3] This is a figure which we may take to represent a fairly high degree of segmentation.

[1] Cf. pp. 6f. above.

[2] J. J. M. de Groot, *Les fêtes annuellement célébrées à Emoui (Amoy), Etude concernant la religion populaire des Chinois*, trans. C. G. Chavannes, Annales du Musée Guimet, vols. 11 and 12, Paris, 1886, vol. 11, pp. 552f. See also de Groot, *Het Kongsiwezen*, p. 99, where the newly established branch is called *kleine clan* in relation to the *groote clan* from which it has sprung.

[3] *Agrarian Problems*, p. 41. Cf. also a statement about 17th century Kwangtung that a lineage of one thousand people had several tens of ancestral halls. See Hu, op. cit., p. 186.

The emergence of intermediate segments, then, depended not simply upon ancestor worship as such but upon the endowment of special places of worship. Domestic ancestor worship extinguished ancestors, so to speak, once they had moved up to a position some four generations from the worshippers. This form of worship also invested one line of descent with ritual superiority by making the tablets and sometimes an extra share of inheritance follow a primogenitory path; and this primogenitory structure of the domestic cult was in contrast to the principle seen at work in higher segments by which benefits and responsibilities were circulated among components of a segment on the basis of equality. Once an ancestral hall had been set up, the various member units of the segment which it expressed commonly took turns in enjoying the fruits of the property attached to the hall and in providing the expenses of the rites.[1]

Ritually expressed segmentation of this order depended directly upon economic resources. Without a hall and land or other property to support it, a segment could not come into being and perpetuate itself. Let us note Lin Yueh-hwa's statement on ancestral halls in his article on I-hsü. 'Just as the family and the lineage rank differently, so the ancestral halls are of different sizes.' Lineages, sub-lineages, branches, and compounds have their halls. 'The hall of each family is, if large, called a family hall and, if small, a family shrine. . . . This is not to say that all sub-lineages, branches, compounds, and families have such halls; for the establishment of a hall is related to economic conditions; therefore only the rich have halls for the sub-lineages, branches, compounds, and families, while the poor may even have only an ancestral shrine for the lineage.' I have shown in the discussion on land tenure that the corporate ownership of ancestral property was highly variable in Fukien and Kwangtung, despite the generally important role ascribed to it.

[1] Something of the same sort seems to operate, at least in theory, in the Annamite system of ancestor worship. The *huong-hoa*, 'incense and fire', is an institution by which property is set aside by an individual to pass by primogeniture for the upkeep of the ancestral cult. But after the fifth generation an ancestor is no longer worshipped as an individual, and the *huong-hoa* property established for him is converted into ritual property for his descendants as a group. See Le Van Dinh, *Le culte des morts en droit annamite (Essai historique et critique sur le Huong-Hoa)*, Paris, 1934, especially pp. 157–9. Customary practice incorporated into the modern Civil Code produces the rule that, after the fifth generation, the *huong-hoa* becomes family property: 'La gestion en est confiée, selon la décision de l'assemblée de la parenté, soit au membre le plus âgé, soit à tour de rôle . . . au représentant de chacune des branches, à charge de subvenir aux dépenses nécessitées par les principales célébrations rituelles'. Ibid., pp. 158f. See also Boüinais and A. Paulus, *Le culte des morts dans le Céleste Empire et l'Annam*, Paris, 1893, p. 111. The appearance of ancestral halls among Chinese overseas poses special problems in analysis. The most interesting information from South-east Asia appears in J. L. Vleming, *Het Chineesche Zakenleven in Nederlandsch-Indië*, Weltevreden, 1926, chap. 13, 'Familiefondsen'. See also my *Chinese Family and Marriage in Singapore*, pp. 90f., 212–18, 221.

It follows from this argument that, if one sub-lineage was richer than other sub-lineages, the degree of segmentation within it was likely to be greater. In a rich sub-lineage a man was a member, perhaps, of several branches, one within the other. In a poor sub-lineage a man might be a member of no unit between the family in the household and the sub-lineage. 'In fact there are cases,' Kulp writes, 'where the sex- and economic- and ancestral-groups are identical.'[1] Differences in wealth within a lineage produced unequal segmentation. In a system which knew great variations in riches and social status the horizontal divisions produced by these variations must to some extent have been translated into the vertical divisions between segments. A small segment, homogeneous in status and resources, might grow in numbers to include both powerful and weak, high and low, rich and poor; when it segmented it showed up this differentiation by tending to segregate the privileged from the underprivileged.

In such a system segments could not always stand balanced against other segments of like order within a more comprehensive segment. Let us suppose two sub-lineages A and B. A is symmetrically segmented into A1 and A2, but in B a segment B1 has emerged which is not balanced against any B2. This has come about because the members now forming B1 wished to mark out their separate identity from their other agnates in B and, having the resources, established their own ancestral hall to bring their new segment into existence. The members of a potential B2, however, lacking status and wealth (a deficiency which promoted the establishment of B1), do not express their existence in a formal segment; they are, like their agnates in B1, members of B, but, although they are differentiated from the members of B1 by the very existence of that segment, they are not poised against them as a formally constituted unit. A similar one-sided segmentation might occur at a later stage in B1 to produce a B1a which is not matched by any B1b. Thus, within sub-lineage B, of three men, one may be a member of ancestral units B1a, B1, and B; one a member of units B1 and B; and one a member of B alone. If any version of this simplified model was realized, then there could have been no orderly arrangement of segments in a hierarchy.

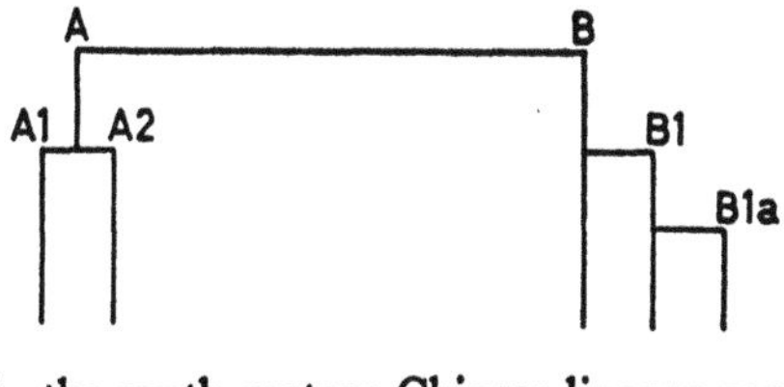

Segmentation in the south-eastern Chinese lineage appears to have been confined to units which remained geographically distinct either as villages, which was more common, or as groups of neighbouring villages. When

[1] Kulp, op. cit., p. 145.

individuals or families moved away, to other villages, to the towns, or to overseas settlements, either they remained members of the system as it existed at home or they ceased to be members of a series of segments. That is to say, they did not set up branches which continued in some sense to be part of the system at home. Past connexions which were traced between lineages through fission might be made the basis for some sort of clan grouping, but there was no regular framework for the expansion of a segmentary system beyond the limits of a local group. The lineage persisted in so far as it was a localized community.[1]

[1] Except in the case of segments which formed separate but neighbouring villages, it is not clear how far segments were geographically distinct.

7

Social Differentiation within the Lineage

The economic data which I have already adduced suggest that there were likely to be considerable differences in social status within the lineage. Some households held more land than others; some owned their land, while others rented it. There were important differences in occupation between the members of one community. Social differentiation turned more fundamentally, however, on the unequal way in which people enjoyed privileges stemming from the national political system. In order to study this inequality we must examine how men came to hold office in the bureaucracy and how they acquired the education necessary for social advancement.

There is mention of titled scholars in both Phoenix Village and I-hsü, even though these communities were described in republican times. Kulp writes that the titled scholars formed a second type of village leader, the 'elders' forming the first type. The scholars were greatly respected because of the bureaucratic significance of their learning. 'The examinations have always been open to anyone. The successful candidate is the boast and pride of the village. Scholastic tradition has from early times been strong in the sib of Phenix Village.'[1] Furthermore, the graduates of the new, Western-type, school system were equally accorded high status.[2]

In Lin's article on I-hsü we find: 'Formerly under the Ch'ing dynasty when official examinations were held, whenever any member of the lineage graduated as a *chü-jen* the hall was opened for worshipping and feasting, to do honour to the lineage ancestors for their continuing goodness. Even to this day the private school is attached to the ancestral hall; there the private teacher gives instruction and younger lineage members study. . . .' Lin says that members of the lineage who held official rank or title were invited to join the ancestral hall association by the lineage or sub-lineage leaders; 'that is, those who held government office and scholars who had obtained degrees of *chin-shih*, *chü-jen*, or *hsiu-ts'ai* under the Ch'ing dynasty. Even to this day there are still some old-style scholars and elders left in this lineage. Recently a new class has gradually arisen to take the place of the old scholars and officials, viz., the

[1] Op. cit., pp. 110f.

[2] Ibid., pp. 111f.

graduates of modern-style schools and those who have been successful in industry and commerce.'[1]

In Kulp's statements we have the heart of a common view of the imperial examination system and its bearing upon status in the village community: the bureaucracy recruited itself by competitive examinations which, because they were open to all, offered a *carrière ouverte aux talents* to ordinary countrymen; office-holding was the occupation which commanded the greatest respect in Chinese society; scholars with imperial degrees enjoyed very high status and exercised much influence in their village communities. In popular Chinese thought—and in the reflection of this thought in the writings of many Western observers—the examination system created a society with a high degree of social mobility.[2] I have myself heard the traditional peasant view of the opportunities offered by the examination system from the mouths of overseas Chinese. Whatever the objective chances of social mobility provided by the system, there is no doubt that it was often thought of as an efficient mechanism of social promotion. The industrious peasant lad conning his books and winning his way into the ranks of officialdom by sheer hard work and intelligence may have rarely existed in reality, but he lives as an important figure in popular imagination. The ideal of Chinese society could not envisage so readily the leap symbolized by the American formula of from log cabin to White House, but it offered the prospect of the magistrate's bench to the inhabitant of the mud hut.

Since I am not a sinologist I should not presume to dogmatize about the extent of social mobility in China, but, in order to establish my picture of the localized lineage, I must attempt to summarize what appears to be known on this topic at the present time. I shall consider the question of promotion to the ranks of officialdom and the relation between officialdom and the stratum of Chinese society often referred to as the gentry.

[1] In *The Golden Wing* Lin does not mention any old-style scholars in the village. He uses the term 'gentry' when speaking of a group of influential men in Kutien city who combine to secure somebody's release from gaol. These gentry were a retired prefect now a commander of militia, a district counsellor, the chairman of the Kutien Merchants' Association, and a man who was the richest merchant in the district. Op. cit., p. 172.

[2] The Chinese examination system long fascinated Westerners. As Miss Mason has pointed out, the system was of especial interest to the West in the middle of the nineteenth century when means of testing applicants for the civil service were being debated. See M. G. Mason, *Western Concepts of China and the Chinese, 1840–1876*, New York, 1939, p. 169. I cannot resist quoting from the report of the U.S. Civil Service Commission, 1873–4, which declared that 'with no intention of recommending either the religion or the imperialism of China, we could not see why the fact that the most enlightened and enduring government of the Eastern world had required an examination as to the merits of candidates for office, should any more deprive the American people of that advantage, than the facts that Confucius had taught political morality, and the people of China had read books, used the compass, gunpowder, and the multiplication table, during centuries when this continent was a wilderness, should deprive our people of these conveniences.' Ibid., pp. 171f.

Wittfogel has written: 'Some "fresh blood" may have been absorbed from the lower strata of society by means of the examination system; but on the whole the ruling officialdom reproduced itself socially more or less from its own ranks.'[1] This is doubtless a widely acceptable view,[2] although its exact significance must depend upon the meaning given to the phrases 'the lower strata of society' and 'from its own ranks'. For the most part the bureaucracy is seen as a specialized section of the gentry, and it is the gentry which is looked upon as the more or less closed area of society.

In the writings of Fei Hsiao-tung the gentry is identified with the land-owning ruling class of China. 'The class that is here called gentry is also sometimes referred to as *shih ta fu*, "scholar-official". Actually, the gentry class, although closely linked with the group of scholar-officials, should be distinguished from it. To be born into a gentry family did not necessarily insure that one became a scholar or an official in traditional China.'[3] In his introduction to Fei's book Robert Redfield says that the scholars and the gentry must be discussed together because the former were largely drawn from the latter. 'The scholars were an elite; the gentry, a social and economic class.'[4]

Owning land, but not themselves working it; pursuing a gentlemanly way of life, of which classical scholarship was an important ingredient; forming a 'natural' category of leaders in any community in which they lived—these were the outstanding characteristics of the gentry. The vast social area which this stratum embraced was certainly far from homogeneous in the control of power, in wealth, and in prestige on the national scale; but, however low its standing in the nation-wide power structure, a gentry 'family' was in a position of strength in its home territory.[5] The position of the gentry was economic: drawing rents from land and furnishing credit to the peasantry,[6] the gentlemen exercised control over their social inferiors. Their position was political: not only was the gentry the recruiting ground for the bureaucracy, but it was the stratum from which men could be chosen to speak for their local community on an equal footing with officials appointed from the centre.

It was this indirect relationship between landholding and political status which removed the Chinese imperial system from the realm of feudalism,

[1] *New Light on Chinese Society*, p. 11.

[2] Hsu, *Under the Ancestors' Shadow*, pp. 5f., after accepting Wittfogel's formulation, still maintains a thesis, which he attempts to document, that 'families' rise and fall within the generally stable higher order. His argument is interesting, but I am concerned here only with movement between classes or strata.

[3] Fei Hsiao-tung, *China's Gentry, Essays in Rural–Urban Relations*, revised and edited by M. P. Redfield, Chicago, 1953, p. 17.

[4] Ibid., p. 6.

[5] For differentiation within the ranks of the gentry, see W. Eberhard, *Conquerors and Rulers; Social Forces in Medieval China*, Leiden, 1952, pp. ixf., 13ff., and 122ff.

[6] On the importance of landlords as sources of credit in modern times, see Wu, op. cit., p. 63.

in spite of what is nowadays asserted by Communist analysts. Landowners were not aristocrats whose political status depended without intermediate qualifications on their economic role. Tawney, with characteristic neatness, has said: 'Landlord and tenant are parties to a business contract, not members of different classes based on privilege and subordination.'[1] Certainly, if the landlord was a gentleman, there were, to use a Durkheimian turn of phrase, non-contractual elements in the business contract such that privilege and subordination might enter, but they entered along the path which linked gentrydom with bureaucracy. The Chinese peasant was not a serf.

It is only a superficial paradox that, when a lineage was composed both of peasantry and gentry, the humble peasant had access to the main source of prestige in his society. The members of a community consisting only of peasants were cut off from the honour which flowed through the gentry to their humbler lineage fellows. Imperial graduation and office-holding, while conferring power on only a restricted range of those related to the graduate and the bureaucrat, spread their glory much further afield. It is clear that the poor and the humble could in some sense identify themselves with the men of their lineage who had done great things. The boards recording imperial honours which hung in the main ancestral hall shed their splendour throughout the descent group. Since a particular lineage might span many centuries, the enjoyment of one such honour was enough to afford many people the chance of being endowed with prestige.

Some Western observers, failing to see how social differentiation was linked with a system of pervading honour, have misinterpreted what they saw. Not only did honours won within a lineage confer prestige, but the tracing of genealogical connexions with other lineages was a means of ensuring the flow of glory along diverse agnatic channels. The Englishman Lindley, for example, concerned to defend the leader of the T'ai-p'ing Rebellion against the charge that he was of humble peasant origin, asserted the glory of his line. 'The genealogy of Hung-sui-tshuen's family is one of the most ancient in China. During ten centuries, until the era of the present century, they trace members of their house occupying the most exalted stations in the empire. So far back as the Sung dynasty, A.D. 1000, many of the Hungs were prominent literati; from that time to the Manchoo invasion, numbers of them have been members of the Han-lin College—the highest literary rank in China.'[2] By such arguments, of course, there could have been few peasants in China who could not lay claim to similar connexions. In an agnatic system with a small number of surnames, genealogy widely distributed the benefits of honours individually acquired; so that, in de Groot's words, 'maint Chinois appartenant à la lie du

[1] *Land and Labour in China*, p. 63.

[2] Lin-le [A. F. Lindley], *Ti-Ping Tien-Kwoh; The History of the Ti-Ping Revolution*, London, 1866, 2 vols., vol. 1, p. 32.

peuple peut se targuer de la possession d'un arbre généalogique qui ferait venir l'eau à la bouche aux plus nobles familles de l'Occident.'[1]

Because the bureaucracy was a specialized wing of the gentry class, upward mobility in China could be achieved either by direct entry to the bureaucracy from outside the ranks of the gentry or by assimilation to the gentry class in some other fashion. Recently an extraordinarily detailed study of the Chinese scholastic and official system in the nineteenth century has tried to answer the question of how far newcomers found their way into the bureaucracy and the elite of titled scholars from whom the bureaucracy was recruited.[2] Unfortunately, this book uses the term 'gentry' in a manner different from that in which it has commonly been employed.

The study asserts that the Chinese terms *shen-shih* and *shen-chin*, normally translated as 'gentry', were, in the last centuries of the Ch'ing dynasty, used to name only that stratum of Chinese society which, consisting exclusively of men with educational titles, furnished the bureaucracy with its officers. Dr. Franz Michael, who introduces the study, tells us that we must not be misled 'by the loose way in which the term has been used during the republic to describe what was in the main a group of landlords when the gentry of the imperial time no longer existed'.[3] He dismisses Fei's study of the Chinese gentry as an unjustified interpretation of the past in terms of the present.[4] I suspect that the Chinese terminology was not so rigidly employed in Ch'ing times as Michael and Chang assert, but of course I am not qualified to judge the issue.[5] Even, however, if these two scholars are right in saying that nineteenth-century usage was such that the words we now normally translate as 'gentry' designated only a class of literati, still, from a sociological point of view, it can be shown that, used in a restricted sense, the word 'gentry' must obscure certain important problems in the study of Chinese society.[6] The category of the population which Chang calls gentry (that is, the titled scholars) is, however, precisely that which we must examine in order to study the question of social mobility by means of scholarship and the attainment of office through scholarship.

[1] *Les fêtes. . . .*, pp. 552f.

[2] Chung-li Chang, *The Chinese Gentry, Studies on their Role in Nineteenth-Century Chinese Society*, Seattle, Washington, 1955.

[3] Ibid., p. xviii.

[4] Ibid., p. xviii, fn. 5.

[5] The character for *shen* means a kind of girdle worn by people of high status, especially officials. The terms *shen-shih* and *shen-chin* probably corresponded in their vagueness to much the same range as the English 'notables'. Couvreur translates *shen-shih* as 'les notables et les lettrés'. I am indebted to Mr. O. B. van der Sprenkel for advice on this matter. For the view taken in Chang's study on the linguistic point see note 6 to p. xviii.

[6] Cf. my review of Chang's book in *Pacific Affairs*, vol. XXIX, no. 1, March 1956, pp. 78ff.

To enter the bureaucracy it was necessary either to qualify in state examinations, which was the 'regular' mode of acquiring the status of a literatus, or to buy a literary title, which was the 'irregular' mode. The status of literatus by itself was no guarantee of office, but the acquisition of the status was a necessary preliminary to office-holding.[1] At any time the number of office-holders was much smaller than the number of literati. While in the early part of the nineteenth century the literati, regular and irregular, numbered over a million, and by the later part of the century they had reached nearly a million and a half, there were only some twenty-seven thousand officials, civil and military, in the middle of the century.[2] Since so many literati were out of office, the vast majority of them lived at home or were at least able to live at home if they chose.

The need to pass state examinations or acquire literary status by purchase imposed a brake on mobility. The examinations were technically open to all men other than those belonging to a few and small disfavoured categories (for example, the families of slaves, servants, prostitutes, and entertainers).[3] At some periods in the history of the state examinations artisans and merchants and their immediate descendants were prevented from entering,[4] but this restriction does not appear to have operated during the phase covered by Chang's study. Yet it was clearly difficult for the son of a peasant to compete on equal terms with the member of a 'family' which had already established its position as an official-producing group. Candidates had to be guaranteed by literati; influence, favouritism, and other forms of advantage weighted the system against the humble candidate. More important still, the poor man could hardly afford to provide his son with the classical education on the basis of which he would need to be examined.[5] Candidates were prepared for the examinations either by private tutors or in private schools. It is possible that where schools existed on a lineage or village basis,[6] the sons of the peasantry, having access to them, might succeed in bringing themselves up to examination standards. In I-hsü, Lin writes, 'Even to this day the private school is attached to the ancestral hall; there the private teacher gives instruction and the younger lineage members study. . . .' For Phoenix Village Kulp contrasts the modern situation, in which the severance of the formal link between official appointment and education reduces interest in schooling, with the old position. Phoenix Village was

[1] The complexities of the system are set out with admirable clarity by Chang at pp. 3–32 of his study.

[2] Ibid., pp. 116, 138.

[3] Ibid., p. 183.

[4] See K. A. Wittfogel and Fêng Chia-shêng, *History of Chinese Society, Liao (907-1125)*, Transactions of the American Philosophical Society, New Series, vol. 36, 1946, Philadelphia, 1949, pp. 457, 460.

[5] Chang, op. cit., pp. 182ff.

[6] See above, pp. 11, 13, for lands set aside to finance education.

apparently outstanding in its district for producing scholars in imperial times, and in those days the village leaders saw to it that every boy of ability, rich and poor, was given the opportunity to study. 'A poor boy from any family might find his way to success and official position and thereby raise his family from the depths of penury.'[1] Up to 1911 at least successful scholars met in the so-called Scholars' Hall to instruct the boys of the village.[2] The past, which Kulp had not himself observed, appears in his account in a distinctly rosy light, but even if it approximates to reality Phoenix Village cannot have been a very representative community in respect of the facilities afforded to the sons of the poor.[3] We may scarcely estimate the effective costs of a boy's education simply in terms of the expenses of his training; the sacrifice of his labour during the long years of study must have acted as a major disincentive to his father.[4] Certainly, we have little reason to conclude that any large number of peasant lads raised themselves to high estate by means of the imperial examinations.[5] It is, of course, even more obvious that entry into the stratum of the literati by means of payment was not likely to afford much opportunity to the poor.

In an analysis of 2,146 biographies of literati of the last century Chang

[1] Kulp, op. cit., p. 217.

[2] Ibid., p. 218. See ibid., pp. 216ff. for education in Phoenix Village.

[3] When the New Territories were taken over, with a population of some 100,000, 314 forms were filled in by school teachers. Schools varied in size from 3 to 56 pupils, with an average number of 15-20. The teachers were generally natives of the 'sub-districts' in which they taught and few of them held any literary degrees. 'In a few instances teachers were hired by wealthy families. . . .' See *Report on the New Territory at Hong Kong*, p. 11. Chang, op. cit., p. 186, points out that there was no public education system, candidates for the examinations being prepared by private tutors or in small schools. The *i-hsüeh*, 'charity schools maintained by the local gentry', were in some areas quite numerous, but there is no evidence that they produced many scholars who took part in the state examinations.

[4] Cf. Chang, op. cit., pp. 186f.

[5] Note the cynical proverb: 'Bachelors of Arts [*hsiu-ts'ai*] are not the sons of poverty: Buddhist priests are not the sons of wealth'. Scarborough, op. cit., p. 75. (The proverbial expression of the optimistic view of mobility may be seen in the following expressions. 'Even thatched cottages yield high officials.' Ibid., p. 337. 'Large numbers of the gentry beget sons who die of want: many an ordinary family yields one who becomes a courtier.' Ibid., p. 340.) Liu Hsing-t'ang, op. cit., writes of the Fukien lineages that, although the 'book-lamp-fields', the education lands, helped to produce men who would protect the interests of the lineage as a whole, they 'undoubtedly have in certain places been a keen weapon for exploitation in the hands of some powerful and aggressive families within the lineage, because very few poor families produce intellectuals. They limit the award of scholarships to only those of the rank of *hsiu-ts'ai* or of ranks above that of *hsiu-ts'ai*. This is as much as to say that the poor are excluded. The practice of educating all the young of the lineage free is comparatively fair; since the poor, however, have long looked upon their children as productive forces, how could they let them go to school?'

concludes that 35 per cent of these men were newcomers.[1] By a newcomer Chang means a literatus whose father or (presumably paternal) grandfather was not a literatus before him. A little reflection will show that, on this basis, the percentage of 35 as an index of what Chang calls social mobility is not very impressive. A literatus whose close kinsmen other than father or paternal grandfather were literati would by Chang's definition be classed as a newcomer. However, even were we to accept the figure at its face value, it would still tell us not about social mobility in a general sense but rather about succession in a scholastic system. By calling the literati 'gentry', Chang has obscured the problem of the relationship between the literati and the wider social class within which they stood.

It is clear, at any rate, that the greater part of the movement into the ranks of the literati from outside the gentry class must have taken place by means of money. Not only could the peasantry not generally afford to put their sons forward for the examinations; it was unlikely that the upward social path of a peasant family would follow the line of patient land accumulation and consequent enrichment. In a heavily populated and intensively worked agricultural milieu it was scarcely possible for poor peasants to advance their sons far along the road to officialdom by the sweat of their brow and their agricultural skill. Land, in the words of Fei's peasants, breeds no land.[2] On the contrary, the building up of wealth to set social promotion going had to come from other kinds of economic activity: trade (which was not necessarily legal) and probably such less respectable applications of non-agricultural skill as military activities and banditry (from which soldiering was not always too clearly to be distinguished).[3] Not that wealth was the unique means of rising into the ranks of the gentry; influence built up militarily or otherwise might ultimately promote individuals and their dependants through a system of patronage.

We are, then, faced by the paradox that the gap between the two great respectable orders of Chinese society, the gentry and the peasants, was probably bridgeable in the main only by one of the theoretically non-respectable orders, the merchants. Trade was, in official theory, highly distasteful, but the contemptible business man could, in fact, travel the road to the higher respectable order through his sons, even if he chose not to buy literary status for himself. Despite the power which they might develop as men of commerce, both the ideals and economics of their society drew business men on to convert one type of capital into another:

[1] The total sample of biographies is 5,473, but the data for classifying subjects as newcomers or established literati were available only in the smaller sample. Ibid., p. 214.

[2] 'Peasantry and Gentry', p. 6.

[3] Cf. M. J. Levy and Shih Kuo-heng, *The Rise of the Modern Chinese Business Class* (mimeographed), New York, 1949, p. 5.

money went into land and sons into the examinations. By this process wealth could buy social status and political power; but once power was achieved it in turn brought wealth—a far more respectable kind of wealth, for it was gained in the course of bureaucratic duties.[1] To some extent also, the gap between those whose wealth rested upon business and those whose position was assured by gentry qualifications might be bridged by marriage between them, a fact which should remind us that the official prejudices of Chinese society did not lay down rigid barriers between the classes they presupposed. Chen Ta, discussing the position of rich returned emigrants in Fukien and Kwangtung in the 'thirties of this century and showing that they made desirable husbands, comments that to some extent the gentry also liked to marry their daughters to emigrants, especially when there was a shortage of prospective sons-in-law of good family living in the village. 'The motive here is the old one of creating a bond between the rural landed aristocracy and the rich merchant class. . . .'[2]

It follows from this argument that, while at any time in any particular local community merchants and gentry might be clearly distinguishable in political status and prestige, in time individual business men might pass into the higher respectable order. This order, incorporating the literati, was based economically on landowning and money-lending and socially on landowning and a gentlemanly way of life.[3] We have now to see to what extent the gentry were represented in the life of localized lineages in south-eastern China.

We can establish first of all that the literati were generally drawn from the countryside as well as the towns. This fact emerges from casual observation of the literature, but we can put it on some sort of a numerical basis from the data of a modern enquiry. In *China's Gentry* Fei summarizes some of the results of an analysis made by himself and Quentin Pan of the origin of 915 scholars 'who passed the high-ranking imperial examinations (those above provincial rank)'.[4] Of these 915 men 52·5 per cent came from the 'traditional Chinese town', 41·16 per cent from rural areas, and 6·34 per cent from 'intermediate small towns'. Fei considers the question of the extent to which the fathers of these scholars had held

[1] Ibid., pp. 5, 12.

[2] *Emigrant Communities in South China, A Study of Overseas Migration and its Influence on Standards of Living and Social Change*, London and New York, 1939, p. 134.

[3] The 'gentry' of Chang's study, i.e. the literati, are said not necessarily to have owned land. See especially p. xvii. Certainly, we must recognize that land-ownership by itself was not the only basis of gentry power and status, but it seems equally sure that land-owning provided both a common economic basis for gentry life and a general foundation for gentry prestige.

[4] Op. cit., p. 132. This book does not come directly from Fei's hand and the period to which these figures relate is not explicitly stated. However, T. H. Shen, op. cit., p. 128, cites Fei in the *Ta Kung Pao*, 1947, as saying that the data refer to the Ch'ing dynasty.

literary degrees. In the town sample the ratio of scholars whose fathers had held degrees to those whose fathers had not held degrees was 68 to 33; while the corresponding ratio for the countryside was 64:36.[1] In the Ch'ing dynasty, then, it seems that there was continuous recruitment of literati from the rural areas. Moreover, since many of the town literati must have had ties with the countryside despite their residence in town, the importance of the scholars in rural life is clear.

In the second place we can discover that south-eastern China contributed a fair share to the literati of the nation. Chang estimates that in the pre-T'ai-p'ing period the literati and their immediate 'families' formed 1·1 per cent of the population of Fukien and 1·8 per cent of the population of Kwangtung. The national percentage was 1·3, the provincial range running from 0·7 (Anhwei) to 3·5 (Yunnan). The corresponding series of percentages for the period after the T'ai-p'ing Rebellion was 1·7, 1·8, 1·9, 0·6 (Szechwan), and 5·0 (Shensi and Kansu).[2] We may note that both Fukien and Kwangtung were allotted sizeable quotas in the provincial and metropolitan examinations,[3] the graduates in which formed nearly the whole section of the civil service to be recruited by the 'regular' route. Furthermore, from Zi's analysis of the first three *chin-shih* (metropolitan graduates) in the examinations held from 1646 to 1894 we can see that men from the two south-eastern provinces made a fair showing.[4] I am not sure how far one may draw firm conclusions from the extent to which men from Kwangtung and Fukien appear in the great American compendium of Ch'ing biographies, but I note that

[1] Fei, op. cit., p. 133.

[2] Chang, op. cit., table 32, p. 164. It is interesting to find data on a similar point in one of Ellsworth Huntington's wide-ranging enquiries into human affairs. Arguing the superiority of the southern over the northern Chinese, Huntington investigates the provincial origins of 324 Chinese holding high office just before the 1911 revolution. The 324 men were all those 'graduates', other than Manchus, Mongols, and Bannermen, who appeared in the list of 'the higher metropolitan and provincial officials in October 1910. . . .' In Fukien and Kwangtung the ratio of these officials to population is shown to be above the ratio for the country as a whole. See *The Character of Races*, New York, 1924, pp. 161f.

[3] Chang, op. cit., pp. 123f.

[4] Etienne Zi (Siu), *Pratique des examens littéraires en Chine*, Variétés Sinologiques, no. 5, Shanghai, 1894, p. 221. The first three places were taken as follows:

	1st place	*2nd place*	*3rd place*	*All three places*
Total	108	108	108	324
Fukien	3	6	1	10
Kwangtung	3	3	4	10

321 of the total places went to Chinese in China proper. 116 went to Kiangsu, 74 to Chekiang, and 21 to Anhwei. Fukien and Kwangtung, with 10 each, are not the lowest, ten provinces showing fewer than 10 places. The average provincial showing is 17 places. It is important to note that places gained in Fukien and Kwangtung were not concentrated in particular counties. In each province the 10 places were spread over six counties. Ibid., pp. 222ff.

55 of the 800 or so individual biographical sketches deal with men born in the two south-eastern provinces.[1] Twenty-seven of these 55 sketches concern men who lived in the nineteenth century.[2] Two-thirds of the 27 notables appear to have been scholar-officials of the conventional variety, the remainder being mainly merchants or men brought to prominence by the T'ai-p'ing Rebellion.

We are now left with the question of the distribution of the literati in the two provinces which concern us. They certainly came from many different parts of the provinces, but were they so evenly spread as to give each local community a representative in the prestige-laden sphere of Chinese society? There is no numerical answer to this question, nor indeed can an answer be given on the basis of any wide survey of villages in the area. We have seen that both Phoenix Village in Kwangtung and I-hsü in Fukien boasted their imperial graduates, the former apparently in considerable numbers, and the general literature certainly leaves the impression that there must have been a wide range of local communities which enjoyed the privilege of numbering titled scholars. But of course, all this evidence is biased; for we must surely expect that it is precisely those communities producing scholars which, by attracting the attention of the outside observer or by encouraging their own members to write about them, find their way to our knowledge. We must, therefore, face the probability that an analysis of the south-eastern localized lineage which presupposes that it contained titled scholars is an imperfect one. A similar and even more intractable problem arises when we consider the extent to which localized lineages produced important merchants. In some communities the traders were, at least in agnatic terms, outsiders. We cannot be sure that every lineage developed a body of leaders drawn from the ranks of the gentry and the business men. The general treatment of the lineage in Fukien and Kwangtung must, therefore, be careful to take the possibility of variation in this matter into account.[3]

We should, however, take the question of the uneven distribution of gentry and merchants a step further. We may not assume that, when a lineage boasted its powerful men with important connexions outside the local community, they were to be found evenly spread through the lineage. We have already considered the manner in which intermediate segmentation depended upon economic resources;[4] we must recognize that the class stratification of gentlemen, merchants, and peasants probably received a vertical expression in the relations between segments. There

[1] See A. W. Hummel, ed., *Eminent Chinese of the Ch'ing Period (1644-1912)*, 2 vols., Washington, 1943.

[2] Men who died after 1912 are not included in the collection so far as individual sketches are concerned.

[3] Of the twenty-seven notables mentioned in the last paragraph, at least a third were townsmen, Canton accounting for nearly the whole of this fraction.

[4] See pp. 47ff. above.

was a general glory emanating from those of high status in which ordinary members of the lineage could bask; but, viewed from the inside, the lineage might be a collection of small groups each of which enjoyed a different status on the basis of its scholarly and economic achievements.

8

The Distribution of Power within the Lineage

The bureaucratic system of China sent its officers no lower than the county seat. The *hsien* magistrate was the immediate point of contact between the rural population and the scholarly administrative system.[1] The magistrate was by rule not a local man, for he was not allowed to serve in his own province, and he was frequently moved. Nor was he supposed to marry the daughter of any man in his jurisdiction or to take up land in the area he administered. In theory at least, he was removed from a kinship setting in the course of his duties, for he was supposed not to employ relatives in connexion with his office.[2] If the rules were strictly followed the magistrate occupied a position which encouraged bureaucratic impartiality. Even however if the rules were not fully observed and the magistrate in consequence developed intimate social ties with the people whose affairs he administered, to the vast majority of the inhabitants in his county he was necessarily a remote figure. At the very least, residing in an area which might hold hundreds of villages and in which his *yamen* (office) might be many miles away from most of them, the magistrate was physically remote. In south-eastern China the gulf between the official and the people was made greater by a barrier of language; the inhabitants of Fukien and Kwangtung spoke dialects of Chinese which were unintelligible to outsiders;[3] so that the magistrate in this region must have been in some respects in much the same position as a district officer in a

[1] Owing to irregularities in the administrative structure, the lowest unit in the hierarchy was in some cases not the *hsien* but the *chou* or the *t'ing*. Moreover, some posts were filled by assistant magistrates.

[2] See, e.g. R. K. Douglas, *Society in China*, London, 1901, pp. 36ff. and 70. In fact, kinsmen were sometimes employed. Cf. p. 25 above.

[3] The written language of China is one; the dialects of Fukien and Kwangtung have their special pronunciation of the written characters and their own vernacular words and idioms. On the number and distribution of the dialects in the region see R. A. D. Forrest, *The Chinese Language*, London, 1948, and his Appendix, 'The Southern Dialects of Chinese', to V. Purcell, *The Chinese in South-east Asia*, London, 1951; and Yuen Ren Chao, 'Languages and Dialects in China', *The Geographical Journal, vol. CII, no. 2, August* 1943. In the south-east only scholars and a few other people who had travelled widely knew enough Mandarin Chinese to enable them to converse without difficulty with the magistrate. See, e.g. W. H. Medhurst, *A Dictionary of the Hok-këèn Dialect of the Chinese Language. . .*, Macao, 1832, p.v. The Hokkien dialect is spoken in Amoy and its hinterland.

colonial administration, lacking knowledge of local customs and requiring interpreters and informants to enable him to function.

From his *yamen* the magistrate collected the taxes imposed by the state and supervised the maintenance of public order. These were his chief responsibilities.[1] Provided enough taxes came forward and there was no breach of the peace of which he chose to take notice there was little reason for him to interfere in the government of local communities. He could be appealed to as a judicial person and so become involved in disputes within and between local communities, but the theory of government informing the system within which he worked encouraged him to meddle as little as possible in local affairs. In accounts of the relations between the bureaucracy and the local community considerable stress is put upon official 'do-nothingism'.[2]

There were three kinds of link between the magistrate and the people in his care: his staff in the *yamen*; the petty officials located in the towns and villages; and the local gentry. The first of these categories must be dealt with very briefly. The advisory, secretarial, and other staff employed by the magistrate, nominally out of his fixed allowance, were often locally recruited and could afford the people of the area, therefore, some more or less direct contact with the administration. In fact, sometimes the staff, or elements of it, were a fixture inherited by magistrates in turn. Entrenched in the *yamen* these men no doubt provided a profitable link between certain sections of the population and the *hsien* government, and doubtless some lineages had members strategically situated in this fashion.

The question of the petty officials is a more complicated subject, because there is a conflict in the literature between theoretical and actual systems of local administration. One finds statements that beneath the magistrate the county was organized in a system of units building up from households to *pao* in multiples of ten. Thus Hsieh Pao Chao says that ten households were grouped in a *pei*, ten *pei* in a *chia*, and ten *chia* in a *pao*. (On the assumption that a household held five souls, one *pao* consisted of five thousand people.) The *pao* was headed by a *pao-chang* 'elected by the people independently of the government help or influence'. He was obliged to report to the magistrate all cases of 'robbery, religious heresy, gambling, runaways, kidnapping, counterfeiting, sale and transportation of contraband goods, swindling, organization of secret societies,

[1] Population and land registers were kept in the *yamen*, while in some circumstances education and flood relief were among the magistrate's concerns. On this and a number of other matters connected with the administrative system and the law I have been guided by Sybille van der Sprenkel, *A Sociological Analysis of Chinese Legal Institutions with Special Reference to the Ch'ing Period, 1644-1911*, unpublished M.Sc.(Econ.) thesis, University of London, 1956. I am very grateful to Mrs. van der Sprenkel for permission to cite her thesis, which is the best account I have seen of the interaction between the official and community institutions of modern China.

[2] See Fei Hsiao-tung, *China's Gentry*, chaps. 2, 3 and 4.

unknown and suspicious characters', and he was responsible for collecting census data and for checking transient residents. He organized part of the militia for protecting granaries and treasuries and generally for work against bandits. He helped in the collection of taxes. 'Standing between the governmental agents and the people, his duties were semi-official and his position the cornerstone of local government in China.'[1]

The *pao-chang*, or *ti-pao* as he is more usually called, certainly existed, but it is less certain that he was a kind of democratic worthy presiding over a neat hierarchy of units in a decimal system. Imperial edicts in the eighteenth century enacted the pyramidal *pao-chia* system, but it is far from clear how, if at all, it worked. Fei says that the system was introduced in Fukien in 1933, owing to the spread of Communist influence, to supersede the local self-government measure of 1929.[2] Lin mentions *pao-chia* when he writes of I-hsü in 1936, but all he says is that 'lineage members, for the purpose of common defence, banded together forming a *pao-chia* organization which raised local militia and posted sentries. All these matters were dealt with by the ancestral hall, which thus necessarily became a military headquarters and assembly point for the militia.' The modern, republican, version of the system was, at least in name, a revival. Yet what it revived was probably not implemented in Fukien and Kwangtung in the nineteenth century. Meadows, writing in the eighteen-forties, refers to the system as it was laid down in the penal code and then comments that it did not seem to exist, at least as far as Kwangtung was concerned, except in the code.[3]

The *ti-pao* may not have presided over any actual *pao-chia* hierarchy but he was an important figure in the administration. Meadows's notes on the *ti-pao* in Kwangtung read realistically enough. He was a 'person whose powers and duties resemble those of our constables'. In the countryside his authority and responsibility covered a 'quarter or the whole of a town or village'.[4] He was, 'in short, the chief *informing officer* of the quarter to which his authority extends, being bound to inform against all criminals and suspicious persons. . . .' He derived his income from 'presents from thieves, donations from householders, and fees for affixing his stamp to petitions'.[5] The post was filled by the local householders, and when they were numerous the more influential among them actually decided who would be the *ti-pao*, the magistrate formally confirming the choice.[6] 'The station of a *ti pao* in society is below that of a respectable

[1] *The Government of China (1644-1911)*, Baltimore, 1925, pp. 309f.

[2] *Peasant Life*, p. 112.

[3] T. T. Meadows, *Desultory Notes on the Government and People of China and on the Chinese Language; Illustrated with a Sketch of the Province of Kwangtung. . . .* London, 1847, p. 120.

[4] Ibid., p. 117.

[5] Ibid., p. 119.

[6] Ibid., pp. 119f.

tradesman or a master mechanic, though his influence be more generally felt.'[1]

Ti-pao appointed in the villages and administrative groupings of villages[2] were petty officials who might enjoy considerable power but whose status was pitched low by the very work they did. As runners of the bureaucracy they were in the position of men liable to incur the displeasure of both the rulers and the ruled. Their earnings might be considerable and their post coveted for this and other reasons; but in any differentiated community they were not among its leaders. These leaders were not formally incorporated into the administrative system. Among the leaders the members of the local gentry took their place. They held the prestige, the status, and the knowledge which enabled them to formulate and execute village policy. Enjoying a position in the national system of status they could speak for the village to the representatives of the bureaucracy from a point of vantage. In times of difficulty they, rather than the petty officials, negotiated with the magistrate. Literati had calling rights, and as gentleman to gentleman the local scholar could visit the magistrate to smooth the path of settlement when bureaucratic demands were heavy. The wider connexions of the local gentry in the towns and the capitals sometimes allowed them to get pressure exerted on the county magistrate from above.[3] Kulp writes that the scholars, speaking the official language and able to move among the officials, formed 'a working nexus between the village and the world outside with which the ordinary villager seldom comes into contact'.[4]

The village government within which the gentry played an important part was concerned with a wide range of activities, among which the most significant were defence, the maintenance of internal order, the upkeep of communications and water channels, and the control of common property. The experience and prestige of the gentry enabled them to perform a leading role in the conduct of village affairs. We have, then, to

[1] Ibid., p. 120. The first administrators of the Hong Kong New Territory found that the magistrate of the county of which their new district had been a part had under him about sixty 'runners', who maintained contact with the population at large, and at least two 'constables' in each village. In large villages there were five or six of these constables, the chief one being called *Tipó*, i.e. *ti-pao*. These men were appointed by the village and paid out of contributions made by the villagers according to landholdings. 'Their duty is to keep watch, especially at night. They have the power of arrest, which is deputed to them by the gentry and elders of the village.' See *Papers Laid Before the Legislative Council of Hong Kong 1899*, 'Extracts from Papers Relating to the Extension of the Colony of Hong Kong', no. 9/99, p. 10. On the low status of the *ti-pao* see also Y. K. Leong and L. K. Tao, *Village and Town Life in China*, London, 1915, p. 64.

[2] Lin, speaking of I-hsü, refers to the *hsiang* as a political unit comprising several villages. On the lack of coincidence between *hsiang*, as administrative units, and the local network of social relations cf. Fei, *Peasant Life*, pp. 114ff.

[3] Cf. Fei, *China's Gentry*, pp. 82ff.

[4] Op. cit., p. 112.

look into the relations between leadership springing from the genealogical structure of the lineage and leadership by the gentry. Both the class structure and the lineage system threw up leaders. How were the two types of political person accommodated?

In the segmentary system, except at the household and extended family levels where a primogenitory bias threw weight on oldest sons, the principle of seniority in line of descent was rarely manifested. Sub-lineages were often numbered in order of their seniority (great, second, third, and so on), but their political status was not affected by this order. In the furnishing of leaders on a genealogical basis all segments were normally equal.[1]

We have seen that in I-hsü the heads of segments came to their position by virtue of seniority in generation and age, and that the device of a village head appointed on the basis of age alone prevented difficulties arising when the head of the lineage proved to be immature.[2] The principle of lineage headship on the basis of generation-cum-age status appears to have been common, and it follows that, if all sub-lineages were of equal demographic composition, leadership would be likely to circulate among them. However, major segments of like order were not often neatly balanced in numbers; as Miss Hu points out,[3] the richer segments of a lineage would tend to multiply faster than the poorer, and it is possible that the better-off lived longer than the worse-off. Consequently, social differentiation within a lineage gave the influential members more chances of filling positions of leadership even on a genealogical basis.

Yet the fact that leadership could be ascribed according to kinship criteria, and so sometimes at least promote men who were illiterate and lacking in influence, must arouse our scepticism about the power exercised by genealogical leaders drawn from the humbler levels of the lineage. Miss Hu shows that leadership in lineages which were socially differentiated was likely to be subordinated to leadership resting on other principles.[4] Kulp makes no bones about the importance of the scholars in Phoenix Village, and Lin admits them to the central governing institution of I-hsü. The gentry were not likely to allow kinship rules to interfere with their exercise of power.

Lin discusses the evolution of the ancestral hall association in I-hsü. 'Since ancestor worship was originally performed by the various branches of the lineage separately, the head of the lineage and the heads of the various sub-lineages did not constitute a compact organization. Later, as relationships developed between the lineage and the government and

[1] Cf. Hu, op. cit., pp. 27f.

[2] See p. 34 above. While Kulp makes great play with the notion of kinship status as a traditional basis for leadership, he is vague about the precise kinship qualifications. See Kulp, op. cit., pp. 106ff.

[3] Op. cit., pp. 26f.

[4] Ibid., pp. 28ff.

between the lineage and the neighbouring lineages, contacts were made and negotiations always carried out through the head of the lineage and the heads of the various sub-lineages. In this way the ancestral hall became a diplomatic centre. Furthermore, as the number of lineage members increased, cases were constantly arising which had to be heard—such as disagreements among all members about inheritance, violent conflicts, forcible seizure of property, adultery, gambling, quarrels, and clashes—making it necessary for the lineage elders to come forward to exhort, praise, reprimand, or punish. Thus the ancestral hall necessarily also became the court or organ of internal control for the lineage. Moreover, matters such as allocating shares of taxes to be paid, the collection of contributions for works for the common good, the management of ancestral property, and the distribution of relief grain from the public granary, were all the concern of the ancestral hall. As a result, the hall inevitably became in addition an institution dealing with financial and economic affairs.' And for the purpose of defence a *pao-chia* organization was set up under the control of the ancestral hall. 'To sum up: the more the business affairs of the lineage multiplied and the functions of the ancestral hall increased, the more important became the positions of the lineage and sub-lineage leaders and the greater became their power.

'As a result of the increase in the functions of the ancestral hall, its organization became more complex and strict. The heads of the lineage and the sub-lineages were originally separate individuals who associated to carry out the sacrifices. In order to adapt themselves to circumstances and carry out their functions, they gradually increased the degree of cohesion between them, and from this there arose the ancestral hall association, of which the leaders of the lineage, the village, and the sub-lineages were automatically members, while those of the lineage who held official rank or title were invited to attend by the lineage or sub-lineage leaders. . . . The ancestral hall association has never been regulated by government legislation, although in the past the government encouraged the organization based on the ancestral hall because of its convenience for the collection of revenue. . . .

'The reason why the association has become an influential body is that the whole of the membership is drawn from the powerful elements in the lineage. As regards the heads of the lineage and the sub-lineages, their authority, experience, and reputation are enough to carry weight with the mass of the members; while the former officials and men of education, because they are known for their learning and wealth, are also able to lead.'[1]

[1] What degree of historical reality underlies this account of the gradual centralization of lineage affairs is obscure. We may well suspect that Lin is reciting the lineage's own account of its development and that this version is an ideal one. As the lineage in I-hsü is described for the present, it resembles other lineages in Hu's survey at different periods.

Whatever the precise nature of its formal institutions of government, the Chinese lineage was so organized as to place considerable power in the hands of a controlling group. From one point of view the lineage was egalitarian: theoretically men were promoted to positions of authority according to kinship principles, and all members had equal claims on the property owned corporately by the lineage and on the ritual and secular services which it provided. In practice, access to power and benefits was unequally ascribed. An elite in the lineage wielded much of the power and controlled the distribution of economic and ritual privileges, as we shall see when we examine the management of common lands, the payment of land tax, and the process of ritual differentiation.

Commenting on the nature of social differentiation within the lineage, I pointed out that the unequal distribution of power and status could serve to mark the lines dividing segments. The component units of a lineage, even when they were genealogically balanced, were sometimes unequally weighted in their riches, influence, and numbers. The oppression of weak segments of the lineage by strong ones emerged from statements made to me by Chinese in Singapore, and we may find hints of this phenomenon in the literature. Chen Han-seng speaks of the 'so-called strong branches of the clan' supplying the effective 'clan' officers.[1] Both Phoenix Village and the Hwang Village of *The Golden Wing* were divided into two major groups. While in the former the two groups corresponded to the two sub-lineages of which the community was composed, there is no indication in the case of the Hwang Village how 'the two main groups of families' between which there was 'latent conflict' corresponded with lineage segments.[2]

How far was the formal segmentation of the lineage reconciled with the differences in numbers, power, and status between segments of the same order? This question must lead us to ask in turn about the fate of genealogical justifications, which provided the framework for the alignment of the segments in the lineage, when these segments developed unevenly. Genealogies are usually treated by social anthropologists as statements about present relations between individuals and groups couched in an idiom which purports to deal only with the past.[3] In societies which know no writing there need be little discrepancy between the structure of present relations and the structure of relations cited by genealogies for the past. As the present changes the past changes in harmony with it. In Chinese society, however, writing enters the scene, and we may assume that literacy and records introduced into its past a rigidity which rendered it less amenable to the influence of the present.

[1] *Agrarian Problems*, p. 37.

[2] Lin, *The Golden Wing*, p. 153. If this village and I-hsü were the same, the two factions must have divided fifteen sub-lineages between them.

[3] For a clear exposition of this point of view see L. Bohannan, 'A Genealogical Charter', *Africa*, vol. XXII, no. 4, Oct. 1952.

The written genealogy was clearly an important instrument in the apparatus of the lineage. It defined its membership. It was revised, or at least it was supposed to be revised, about every one or two generations when, by an elaborate and expensive procedure, the accumulated marriages, births, and deaths were added to the information already recorded. I assume that on the whole a genealogy which purported to set out the founding ancestor of a lineage and all his descendants in the male line was likely to be a fairly reliable statement of historical events. All or practically all the data it recorded were probably accurate, although it may well have omitted information which a complete register would have included. It may be that some of the facts recorded were fanciful; the high status given to the founder of the lineage in Phoenix Village may well be suspect, for example, while it is possible that a lineage rising in status and beginning for the first time to keep a genealogy might record its earlier history in an ideal fashion; but by and large people who appeared in the genealogy were probably given in the kinship and status positions they occupied in life. Those who outraged the morals of the community (by committing incest, for example) were likely to be left out of the genealogy or struck off if already recorded, while children given out of the lineage in adoption might not appear.[1] Children who died young were probably also ignored.[2] For the most part, however, any important reshaping of the genealogy to suit present requirements seems to have been ruled out by the care exercised to keep a scholarly check on its integrity.

The same cautious acceptance cannot be extended to those parts of the genealogy which dealt, not with descent within the lineage, but with the links tying the lineage to other lineages. Here was a field in which alterations appear to have been acceptable on the principle that research into the history of the antecedents of the lineage made the record of this remoter past revisable. When lineages of the same surname decided to act together they provided a charter for their union in the upper regions of their genealogies.[3] Hu reports an astonishing case in which one hundred and eighteen local groups in eastern Kwangtung with the same surname, having established a union between them, produced a genealogy which was the fruit of the labour of a staff of forty-eight. One section of the genealogy gave the movements of each of the one hundred and eighteen groups since the Sung dynasty, the dates at which they settled in their present areas, and the places from which they had come.[4] Genealogical statements

[1] Cf. Hu, op. cit., p. 135.

[2] Hu, ibid., p. 44, mentions a few cases in which high fees were charged for the acceptance of the registration of births (on the basis of which the genealogy was later revised). A practice of this kind must have reduced the historicity of the genealogy by a wide margin. I am inclined, however, to doubt the prevalence of such a charge.

[3] Ibid., pp. 45ff.

[4] Ibid., p. 42.

might also be produced for alliances struck up between groups of linked surnames,[1] and even when the co-ordination of local agnatic groups was not sought a particular lineage might seek to prove a link with lineages of outstanding status. Certainly, in the genealogical information on extra-lineage ties we are likely to find ample material to illustrate the manner in which the past is manipulated to justify the alignments and the interests of the present.

If, however, the data concerning descent within the lineage were relatively unchangeable, then it might come about that the size and influence of any group defined as a segment by the genealogy were out of step with those of the other segments of like order. Miss Hu gives a persuasive, if not very well documented, answer to the question which springs to mind. She says that since the various major segments of the lineage 'have a certain responsibility' in regard to ancestral rites and common property they must be fairly evenly balanced. The uneven development of segments resulting in the emergence of 'branches of disproportionate strength with regard to membership and financial ability' sometimes produced a reshuffling in the lineage after deliberation. The lineage of T'an in Kiangsi is given as an example. There, a process of uneven growth in numbers and wealth having taken place, the one sub-lineage (*fang*) which had outstripped all the others was divided into five parts (*fên*), while the remaining sub-lineages were grouped into two parts.[2] In this fashion the fixed facts of the written genealogy could be adapted to current needs by the superimposition of a new system of division.

Mrs. Bohannan, in the article which I have cited, says that a lineage system can perhaps survive only in a non-literate society such as the Tiv of Nigeria, which she is discussing, 'or, possibly, in one which avoids committing its constitution to paper'.[3] The Chinese system is not a lineage system in the sense in which Mrs. Bohannan uses the expression.[4] In the Chinese case the principle of segmental aggregation does not pervade the society. Yet when in China patriliny was brought in to regulate the links between local communities, the genealogical justifications, as we have seen, were produced and varied. These justifications emerged from research, which was often conducted with an impressive apparatus of scholarship, and it therefore seems that the flexibility of purely oral systems may sometimes be achieved in written systems by the academic manipulation of evidence. The Chinese were not necessarily more conscious of 'cheating' or 'falsifying' than Mrs. Bohannan's Tiv.

On the other hand, it seems to have been more difficult in China to

[1] See p. 5 above.

[2] Hu, op. cit., p. 19.

[3] Op. cit., p. 314.

[4] She follows M. Fortes and E. E. Evans-Pritchard, eds., *African Political Systems*, London, 1940, p. 6.

adjust the genealogy to changes in the internal order of the lineage; in this the relative inflexibility of written genealogies is apparent. The kind of one-sided segmentation of which I have spoken earlier[1] would in an oral system have reduced itself to symmetry by providing a new segment with the genealogical justification for considering itself co-ordinate with the segment from which it had emerged. Yet, if we may generalize from the case of the T'an lineage reported by Miss Hu, the rigidity of the written genealogy might sometimes be circumvented by the use of an alternative method of grouping. While, therefore, I am inclined to assent to Mrs. Bohannan's general proposition, I may suggest that the Chinese evidence shows ways in which the inflexibility of written records may be mitigated.[2]

[1] See p. 49 above.

[2] There is a further aspect of the Chinese system which should be noted. Re-arrangement of the past to entail a merging of adjacent generations was excluded by the distinctiveness of the generation particles in personal names. The system of generation names was maintained and fixed by means of a written series. Further, in the ideographic nature of its writing the Chinese system allowed the identity of surnames to be apparent even when they were pronounced in different ways. Certainly, among overseas Chinese the identity of surnames in their written form has allowed agnatic organization to transcend dialect boundaries.

9

Political Power and Economic Control

We have seen that a large area of the cultivable land in south-eastern China was held corporately by lineages and segments of lineages.[1] There were two systems of operating these common lands. In one system the owning group acted as joint landlord, rented the land to tenants, and either applied the rents to group purposes or, in a few cases, divided them up among constituent families. In the second system the land was circulated among component sub-groups, the current holders being charged with providing the wherewithal for the rites of collective ancestor worship. In Phoenix Village the two systems were used in respect of different types of communal land,[2] while the ancestral land of the Hwang Village circulated.[3]

When common land circulated, the rights of weak 'families' appear to have been relatively secure, but when it was managed centrally and exploited on a business basis a number of abuses seem to have arisen to derogate from the rights of those men remote from the locus of lineage power. Even if we find it difficult to accept completely the picture painted by Chen Han-seng of the shabby treatment meted out to peasants by their land-controlling kinsmen in the Kwangtung of the 'twenties, we should be able to agree with Miss Hu when she says that, despite the benefits conferred on the poor of the lineage by common property, it was also the cause of 'considerable tension, the more so as it may be used to further private interests'.[4]

Chen begins his account of the malversation of lineage benefits by pointing out that while 'clan' heads, chiefs, and trustees were selected on the basis of age and generation status, their positions were 'merely honorary'. Real power, he asserts, was exercised by managers, treasurers, and chief-accountants. If men of real power were elected (by the members of a lineage as a whole, by sub-lineages, or by elderly members), then they were in fact drawn from the largest 'branches of the clan'. 'And they themselves are supposed to be "rich and reliable", "learned and rational".'[5]

[1] See above, pp. 11f.

[2] See above, p. 12.

[3] Loc. cit.

[4] Op. cit., p. 90.

[5] *Agrarian Problems in Southernmost China*, p. 37.

The total lineage income, consisting in the main of rent from fish ponds, houses, and land, and from interest on loans, was controlled by the lineage treasurer or accountant, who held what remained after the payment of taxes, religious and secular expenses, and various subsidies for education. In reality he had the free disposal of the lineage money left in his hands. 'The common property of a clan is so manipulated as to become a modified form of private property. The vast sum of clan incomes, representing the fruit of the labor of multitudes, is quietly passing into the possession of a relatively few people.'[1]

Chen's theme is the conversion of the peasant with genuine control over the property in which he shared into the dumb creature of a complicated machine of exploitation. He sees the decline of the 'clan' as a leading symptom of the social disintegration of modern China.[2]

He attributes the leakage of lineage funds into private pockets and the conversion of common property into private property to the gross economic changes taking place at the time he was writing. To blacken the present Chen no doubt idealizes the past, and we may well feel that, whatever his assessment of the evils of the twentieth century, he is probably overlooking the fact that an unequal access to the benefits of common property was a permanent feature of large-scale lineage organization in China.

The control of lineage property was one method by which those standing at the centre of power exercised influence on the community as a whole. Another method was the collection of taxes in such a way as to turn the governing elite of the lineage into a fiscal intermediary between the state and the landowner. The payment of tax was a duty which in theory each landowner owed to the state through the county magistrate and his collectors, but in practice the individual landowner did not always pay his taxes direct to officials. After saying that the lineage 'facilitates taxation' by encouraging its members to pay their taxes at the times due, Miss Hu goes on to point out that the system 'was not without its drawbacks'.[3] She then briefly cites Liu Hsing-t'ang's material on Fukien.

Liu writes[4] that in certain places the government was unable to collect taxes direct from each family. 'Concerning taxation in Chao-an *A Record of Customs* has this to say: "To maintain law and order the government depends completely on the net revenue recorded in the register of households, lands, &c. In Chao-an it is different. [Of many lineages] nobody knows how many thousands of *mow* they possess and nobody knows how many tens of thousands they number. Only one or two principal families are recorded in the government register. . . . The family heads and the head collector manage the taxes in turn. There is also a 'draft register' called the roll of tax-payers according to which the people are taxed

[1] Ibid., p. 38.

[2] Ibid., p. 39.

[3] Op. cit., p. 57.

[4] 'The Structure of Kinship Groups in Fukien.'

annually. In the absence of the family heads and the head collector someone will take up the office on the strength of his seniority. He has the register. It is not difficult to collect taxes family by family. Is this a reliable register? No. There are people who have more fields but pay less tax and those who have fewer fields but pay more tax. Tax is paid when there is no land and many who have land do not pay. The lineage pays tax for families which have no fields and no members, and no one quarrels. When they buy and sell they do it privately, because their tax is paid out of the common land, and the profit of the common land goes to pay the government. Whenever taxes are to be levied on each family, they collect according to the old register. They manage as though they were perfectly innocent and obedient and the Emperor's order has been obeyed without complaint." All government taxes were managed by the lineage. Here they used exactly the same method they learned from *hsieh-tou* [organized fights];[1] they combined many small lineages into a group to avoid being molested by government officials and their subordinates. . . . Though this situation was peculiar to Chao-an, it was a universal fact that the lineages could defy the local government and its officials.'

Liu does not mean that the refusal of the lineage to pay taxes as the state would have it do necessarily implied that the poorer members of the lineage were exploited by the richer. He appears to see the oppression of the weak by the strong rather in the forced collections of money to finance lineage fights.[2] But we may conclude for ourselves that, gathering taxes as it saw fit, the lineage as represented by its leaders probably distributed the burden to the detriment of the weaker members. The lineage officers in Kwangtung who, according to Chen Han-seng, managed common property so much to their own advantage, often acted as the government's agents in the collection of land taxes from the various families.[3]

The possible benefit accruing to lineage members through whom taxes passed does not, however, exhaust the interest of the topic. There is a purely political side to this matter. When we look at the evidence afforded by the first British administrators of the New Territories of Hong Kong we may see that a 'confusion' of rents and taxes on land endowed the powerful elements in lineages with a control over lineage territory and members which surpassed the bounds of simple financial exploitation. The *Report on the New Territory at Hong Kong*, 1900, reveals an interweaving of political and economic power at the village level.

The report says that 'large and influential clans', whose strength rested not only on their numbers but also on their having members of

[1] See below, pp. 107ff.

[2] Loc. cit.

[3] Op. cit., p. 40.

'official rank' who kept them in touch with the magistrate and higher officers, often took small villages and hamlets under their protection. These smaller villages sometimes paid their taxes to the state through the protecting lineages. But most of the land claimed by lineages was never in fact registered with the government, so that tax was not paid on it.[1] 'The most serious matter of all, however, has been the stand taken by the farmers against the clans, their former landlords. The clans and farmers agree that the farmers are absolute owners of the soil in perpetuity, but have been paying money or produce to the clans for generations, which the clans claim to be rent payable to them. The case for the farmers is that the land is and always has been theirs absolutely free from rent, and that the amount paid by them to the clans was the Government land tax, which they [now] claim to pay direct to the Hong Kong Government.'[2] It is not clear from the account to what extent the farmers were themselves members of the lineages which claimed to be their landlords rather than their tax-collectors, but the picture which emerges suggests an agrarian system in which powerful units acted as political protectors in return for 'taxes'; and we may guess that humbler members of lineages as well as outsiders availed themselves of protection in this fashion. The taxes which the Chinese government failed to collect were often tribute to the effective controllers of rural society.

[1] Op. cit., p. 20.

[2] Ibid., p. 23. The Report makes it clear that a similar problem arose in the relations between farmers and individual landlords. What the landlords considered to be rent the farmers looked upon as tax, and when the British administration collected tax directly from these farmers they regarded themselves as absolute owners of their land with no further obligations to landlords. Ibid., p. 8.

10

Ritual Differentiation

The differences in status and power within the lineage which I have sketched depict a system in which those who enjoyed the greater privileges strove to protect them and those who were underprivileged aspired, at least in the long run, to the heights reached by their more successful kinsmen. In principle all men were equal in so far as their generation and age were equal. In real life equality consisted in being able legitimately to hope that one might overtake one's successful neighbours. Both the protection of privilege and the aspiration towards it were reflected in religious life. Those with power and status tried to retain them by building their houses and siting their graves according to geomantic prescriptions. They attempted to underline their social position by assigning themselves special places and roles in the performance of large-scale ancestor worship. The humble, on their side, prayed for riches and hoped that their virtues would find a reward not only in their fate after death but also in the increasing prosperity of their descendants. By studying the social implications of geomantic burial and the stratification underlying ancestor worship in lineage and sub-lineage halls we can see how ritual life throws the differentiation of the lineage community into relief.

No law in China restricted the burial of the dead to specified places. In the south-east graves were scattered over the hillsides and rises, for the most part in plots belonging to individual owners. Sometimes the dead were buried in graveyards established by lineages or segments of lineages. I should be foolish to assert that the evidence on the point is clear and consistent, but I interpret the burial customs common in Fukien and Kwangtung to mean that very often the common graveyards were set up for the poor while the rich dispersed their dead in individual or 'family' sites. The significance of this is that, following the dictates of *feng-shui*, geomancy, the rich strove to site their tombs wherever the conformation of the landscape at a particular time promised to endow the descendants of the dead with the blessings flowing from favourable burial. The geomantic suitability of a grave site could change, either because of a change in the landscape or as a result of a new interpretation by a different geomancer. Moreover, a new site needed to be chosen if an old one had failed to induce the prosperity hoped for and previously predicted by the experts. De Groot tells us that in the neighbourhood of Amoy parties of men headed by a geomancer were to be seen every day wandering about in the open country in search of good sites for graves.[1]

The dead of the prosperous and influential did not lie compactly ordered in cemeteries. The coffins of the poor might be put into the large graveyards provided for them, but with a rise in fortune their immediate descendants would wish to transfer them to more propitious surroundings.[2] Changes in fortune from generation to generation and the constant search for geomantically induced prosperity encouraged people to disperse their dead. A Chinese proverb speaks of the excessive scattering of graves produced by the pursuit of geomantic fortune: 'In the southern mountains to bury the father, and in the northern mountains to bury the mother.'[3]

Prosperity which followed from or confirmed a well-sited burial was often a temptation to the less fortunate; they tried to tap the good influences to their own advantage by burying their dead on or near the sites which had proved favourable. But the tapping of somebody else's good influence was a trespass, and the attempts to poach in this way and the resistance to the attempts involved a vivid playing-out of the rivalry between groups of different status.[4] The literature speaks clearly of the quarrels and fights which were grounded in geomantic practices.[5] The social significance of these conflicts was that in the endless pursuit of riches and high status, as soon as they had managed to get one foot on the ladder, the poor and the humble sought to chase and overtake their more successful fellows; while those who had arrived tried to entrench their prosperity in the magical insurance of 'wind and water'. Geomancy was the 'cause' of dispersed burial. In Chinese theory the burial site determined the prosperity of the living. In reality of course the prosperity and aspirations of the living determined the burial site and asserted the status of the living against other men in their society.

The competition for good grave sites, precisely because these places were not under the direct control of the central institutions of the lineage, reveals only a sketchy picture of social stratification. In the case of ancestor worship conducted in the large halls, on the other hand, the organized influence of lineage leadership was able to show itself in a systematic

[1] *The Religious System of China*, vol. III, 1897, p. 1017.

[2] Ibid., p. 1376.

[3] Plopper, op. cit., p. 123. On this general question see de Groot, op. cit., pp. 831f., 939, 1374ff.; J. H. Gray, *China, A History of the Laws, Manners and Customs of the People*, edited by W. G. Gregor, 2 vols., London, 1878, vol. I, p. 324; H. Doré, *Recherches sur les superstitions en Chine. 1ère partie: Les pratiques superstitieuses*, vol. II, no. 3, Shanghai, 1912, pp. 282ff.

[4] Cf. Hu, op. cit., p. 38, where she states that there were frequent disputes within lineages which sprang from attempts by poorer families to inter their dead near the graves of their more fortunate kinsmen. See also Gray, op. cit., pp. 325f.

[5] Cf. Doré, op. cit., p. 288; de Groot, op. cit., pp. 1035ff. Hsu, *Under the Ancestors' Shadow*, p. 48, shows for a different area how people strive to poach on one another's sites and compete for sites within one graveyard.

fashion. We need to examine two questions in order to see how social status received a ritual expression in this latter context. The first question is that of the admission and arrangement of tablets in the halls. The second question is the extent to which there was unequal participation in ancestral rites conducted in the halls.

When a domestic ancestral tablet came to be about four generations removed from the living head of the household, it could then be replaced by a different kind of tablet to be deposited in an ancestral hall.[1] If all the tablets of remoter ancestors had been placed in one hall shrine and arranged there according to their generation and seniority in birth order, the shrine would have represented a genealogy taking no account of any hierarchy other than that given by kinship principles. It is not likely that a highly differentiated lineage could have tolerated an egalitarian ordering of the symbols of the dead.

The evidence that genealogical principles of arrangement were modified by the social status of the dead and their living descendants is not abundant; the question probably did not occur to many observers; but when the evidence is given it is very convincing. Miss Hu, on the basis of her general survey of the Chinese lineage, says that in many cases the ancestors received the rites on an equal footing, but she provides evidence that, also in many cases, tablets were ordered by their general social status rather than by their position in the kinship hierarchy. She cites the case of a lineage in Wusih which separated its tablets into three groups: the tablets of the first ancestor and the founders of the five sub-lineages; those of men who were prominent on a scholastic or official basis 'or through outstanding virtue'; and those of ordinary members of the lineage 'who had died without a blemish on their characters'. Miss Hu comments that the 'virtuous' might be people who excelled in filial or fraternal conduct but that they also included those who had made contributions to common funds.[2] In the case material appended to Miss Hu's book we find a striking example in a Kiangsi lineage which charged fifty ounces of silver for the admission of a tablet, only the tablets of officials and certain imperial graduates being allowed in without payment.[3]

I cite de Groot for confirmation in general terms of the practice of exacting payment for the admission of tablets. In his discussion of the cult of the dead in south-eastern China he says that the rules of 'clan temples' regulated the entry of tablets by laying down whose tablets were to be admitted and how much money had to be paid for installing them. The tablets could not be accepted free of charge, for otherwise the temples would have been overcrowded. 'Il va du reste sans dire que les fondateurs de l'édifice se dispensent eux-mêmes de tout payement

[1] I give a fuller exposition of this matter in the next section of this essay.

[2] Op. cit., p. 36.

[3] Ibid., p. 126. See also ibid., pp. 166f., 186 and 169–180 for disputes over payment for the installation of tablets.

pour l'érection de leurs tablettes familiales, et qu'ils réservent à celles-ci les meilleures places.'[1] Doolittle, writing of Foochow, makes a similar statement.[2]

The exclusion of the tablets of the non-'virtuous', or at least their assignment to positions of inferiority in the shrines, was only one aspect of ritual discrimination. The economically and politically weak in the lineage were in some cases not expected to attend the periodical rites conducted in the halls,[3] and when they did attend they were given subordinate roles. This form of discrimination could be easily justified: the scholars and the gentlemen knew best the rites and how to carry them out. So it came about that, while the genealogical heads of the lineage, however socially inept, found their place in the rites, the control of the ritual rested with the lineage elite.[4] In one of the cases from Kiangsi documented by Miss Hu, all men taking part in the ancestral ritual had to be men of education or over the age of sixty-five. The lineage and sub-lineage heads participated actively in the rites only to the extent of carrying the tablets of the earliest ancestors from their shrine to the tables in the main meeting hall. When they had done this they retired, leaving the cultivated men to perform the rites.[5] In another Kiangsi lineage money, standing for meat, was distributed to men attending the ancestral rites; but while the ordinary share was expressed as one catty, and old men were allotted small increments, gentlemen received extra shares of between two and eight catties according to the imperial degrees they held.[6] Several passages in Liu Hsing-t'ang's article on Fukien lineages show us that the sacrifices made to ancestors in the halls were made by officials and old men. Ch'ên Shêng-shao wrote of Chao-an lineages: 'Only meritorious officials of the red girdle class and men over 60 with grandchildren are qualified to take part in the sacrifices and to receive portions of the meat offered after the sacrifice, the amounts varying with their rank.'

[1] *Les fêtes. . .* ' p. 550. Cf. de Groot's *Het Kongsiwezen*, p. 97.

[2] J. Doolittle, *Social Life of the Chinese. A Daguerrotype of Daily Life in China*, edited and revised by P. Hood, London, 1868, p. 174.

[3] Cf. Hu, op. cit., pp. 36f.

[4] Cf. ibid., p. 37.

[5] Ibid., p. 117.

[6] Ibid., p. 126.

II

Ancestor Worship and Lineage Structure

The community constituted by the localized lineage was at once a territorial group and a kinship group. As a village it expressed its identity in religious life by maintaining a temple to the earth god. As a group of agnates and their wives it fell into a series of religious units which defined themselves in relation to common ancestors. The lineages of Fukien and Kwangtung offer us the opportunity to study the social setting of ancestor worship in some detail.[1]

Exploring the structure of the south-eastern Chinese lineage we have seen that household-families and extended families, at one end of the scale, and the lineage and sub-lineages, at the other end, defined themselves in terms of the cult of the ancestors. Moreover, if economic resources were great enough, there were probably intermediate segments between the sub-lineage and its extended families which centred upon ancestral halls. Members of households and extended families worshipped their ancestors in shrines which were part and parcel of domestic architecture. Special halls were required for worship by higher segments of the lineage. The existence of these halls, in some cases at least, introduced into their cult units a ritual discrimination between members such that they were afforded an unequal access to the shrines and their associated rites. This provides us with a point of departure for considering the whole range of differences between ancestor worship conducted at the domestic level and ancestor worship practised by higher segments.

There was a difference between the symbols used in the two different contexts of home and hall. Even if we assume for the moment that wooden ancestral tablets were universally to be found in peasant domestic shrines,[2] we must realize that they were of different design from those placed in halls. De Groot, writing of Amoy and the area adjacent to it, says that the tablets used in the 'temples', as he calls them, were bigger than domestic tablets and as decorated as their owners could afford to make

[1] Cf. the definition of ancestor worship given in A. R. Radcliffe-Brown, *Structure and Function in Primitive Society*, London, 1952, p. 163: 'The cult group in this religion consists solely of persons related to one another by descent in one line from the same ancestor or ancestress.'

[2] De Groot, *Het Kongsiwezen*, p. 90, asserts that there was no dead person in China who did not enjoy respect in the tangible form of a tablet.

them.[1] Doolittle, describing the customs of Foochow, writes that the tablets used in ancestral halls were larger than the tablets of the home, but, in contrast to de Groot, he seems to imply that they were generally simpler in construction.[2]

In connexion with the domestic tablets Doolittle says: 'After the third or the fifth generation has passed away, the tablets which represent it are sometimes taken away and buried in or near the graves of the persons they represent, to furnish room for the tablets representing the individuals of a less remote period, every generation furnishing two tablets.'[3] J. T. Addison, in his very useful survey of the general subject, states that the tablets kept in the home were those of 'the deceased father, grandfather, and great-grandfather'. The tablets of the ancestors beyond the third generation (or sometimes beyond the fifth) were burned in some parts of China and in other parts removed to an ancestral temple representing a group larger than the family.[4]

Unless, as sometimes happened, a tablet stood for a married couple, it represented one individual only. Moreover, no other tablet could stand for the same person. The uniqueness of the representation was ensured by 'dotting the soul' in the tablet during the mortuary rites. When the tablet was made one character in the inscription was left without a dot; this dot was applied in red ink, preferably by a man of high status, in the graveside rites, an act which consecrated the tablet and established the unique relationship between it and the soul with which it was associated.[5]

Since tablets remained by right in the possession of the oldest son when family division took place, a domestic shrine could become the ritual centre for a number of agnatically related families. And, because the number of the generations represented in the domestic shrine was limited, these families were those whose heads were related to one another in the *wu fu*.[6] No segment based upon domestic ancestor worship could in theory exceed the bounds of the *wu fu*. From this point of view we may see the uniqueness of the ancestral tablet as a device for encouraging ritual unity among closely connected agnates in different households. The device, however, did not always work, because, while no cadet family was allowed to own a duplicate tablet, it might set up recognized substitutes. De Groot puts the matter in this fashion. Younger brothers wishing to worship their ancestors must go to the house of their oldest brother,

[1] *Les fêtes. . .*, pp. 550f. Cf. *Het Kongsiwezen*, p. 97.

[2] Op. cit., p. 167.

[3] Ibid., pp. 170f.

[4] *Chinese Ancestor Worship, A Study of its Meaning and its Relations with Christianity*, [Shanghai] 1925, pp. 35f.

[5] See, e.g., ibid., pp. 32ff. and de Groot, *The Religious System of China*, vol. I, pp. 213ff.

[6] See above, pp. 41ff.

but often, when a younger brother moved to another locality, he took with him a large board on which were written the names on all the tablets left behind in the shrine kept by the senior brother.[1] Doolittle offers a similar account, saying that on the division of the family the younger sons could erect a kind of tablet which differed in a number of respects from the original kind. This new tablet bore a sentence which showed that it represented or commemorated 'all the ancestors of a family of a certain surname. The person who erects it also, if he pleases, has recorded the names of his male ancestors, beginning with his father, back to three or five generations. . . . In similar manner, he may have recorded . . . the surnames of his maternal ancestors [i.e., the wives of agnatic ancestors]. . . . At his death this [tablet] descends to his eldest son, who has the exclusive right to erect the other kind of tablet to the memory of their [*sic*] father and mother, while the younger sons may each erect the general tablet to the memory of their father and mother, and of their more remote ancestors having the family surname.'[2]

I have earlier tried to show that the extent to which families in several households maintained unity between them on the basis of ancestor worship conducted at the shrine in the senior household was likely to vary considerably but to be in general limited. Family division led to the proliferation of general tablets, as we may call the secondary instruments described by de Groot and Doolittle, and it was before these that domestic rites of ancestor worship were commonly performed. Yet there is still a further step to be taken in the argument by which I am seeking to distinguish between the ritual objects of domestic worship and those used in the halls. It seems to have been too often overlooked that the poor were probably not in the habit of keeping tablets of the classical type. Miss Hu says that, in default of tablets, they might write the names of their ancestors on strips of paper for each rite and later burn them.[3] It would perhaps be unfair to bring forward evidence from the practices of south-eastern Chinese abroad to demonstrate the rarity of wooden tablets in domestic shrines, but at least I may record that in poor villages I have passed through in the Hong Kong New Territories paper plaques were more conspicuous than tablets.

But whether ancestor worship was conducted before plaques or tablets, rites were performed in every house. Uninfluential people had their own immediate forebears to care for at home even though they might be excluded from the rites carried out in ancestral halls. This suggests that it is a mistake to treat Chinese ancestor worship as though it were a unified and undifferentiated system of religion in which the beliefs and practices relevant to all parts of it were of the same order. Hall and house in fact represented different phases of group life and different elements

[1] *Les fêtes. . .*, p. 19.

[2] Doolittle, op. cit., pp. 169f.

[3] Op. cit., pp. 32f.

in the total cult. I propose now to examine three aspects of this question: the relations between the worshippers and the worshipped in the two contexts of domestic and hall shrines; the rites performed in the two settings; and ideas about the roles of ancestors relevant to the two different contexts.

The ancestors tended in the house always included the recently dead who had produced or adopted children. They did not include, at least as individuals, those who were further removed than about four generations from the head of the family. Sometimes plaques were kept which bore general formulae embracing, in Doolittle's phrase, 'all the ancestors of a certain surname'. There was a tension between the principle by which families related within the agnatic *wu fu* were ritually encouraged to come together and the principle according to which they might legitimately conduct their own domestic rites as separate units. When the second principle was dominant a form of ancestor worship appeared which must elude the requirements of a strict definition of what constitutes this form of religion. The members of a family which individually performed rites before ancestors several generations distant did not link themselves by that act with all their agnates in other families sharing the same ancestors. The ancestors in such a case had ceased to be foci for segments in a lineage, and had become beings whose relations with the living stood outside the hierarchy of agnatic units. It is obvious that a man who was worshipped separately in the several households formed by his patrilineal grandsons was the object of a devotion which did not directly relate to the maintenance of kinship unity beyond the range of one family in a household. At the domestic level, then, the rites of ancestor worship appear to have included both rites of kinship solidarity, in which ancestors were used as the defining foci for determinate agnatic units, and rites of what we may call memorialism, in which ancestors were cared for simply as forebears and independently of their status as ancestors of the agnates of the worshippers. We normally define ancestor worship in terms of rites of kinship solidarity, but in the Chinese case these rites appear unaccompanied by rites of memorialism only at the level where the cult moved from the house to the hall. Once an ancestor had been placed in the shrine belonging to a hall he had ceased to be an object of personal devotion and had become part of the ritual centre of a lineage segment.

In a hall an ancestor was endowed with a remoter and less individualized personality. It is true that particular ancestors in the halls might be singled out by special marks. Those who had attained high honours in the state examinations or occupied distinguished office had not only their tablets to commemorate them but also honorific boards on which their glory was set out. But this was not an individualism resting on personal feelings and intimate knowledge on the part of the worshippers. At the domestic shrines, on the other hand, only the more recently dead were tended, and the most recent among them were cared for by people with whom they had had close personal ties in life. Chinese displayed strong interest in their newly dead kinsmen. Intimacy was not immediately broken by death. The dead continued to concern themselves in the affairs of the living, and the living took thought for the welfare of the dead. The survivors sought to provide the dead with the material comforts—housing, money, clothing, and food—which they continued to need in the other world, and in the practice of spirit-mediumship the relations of life might be given a realistic expression after death.[1] In their turn the ancestors participated in the festivities of the home; they received news of important changes in the lives of their descendants (such as births, deaths, betrothals, marriages, and social advancement), gave advice on important matters when it was solicited, and used whatever powers they might have in the other world to bring benefits to those they had left on earth. When personal knowledge of and affection for the dead began to fade, the ancestors were beginning to move forward to the boundary of the domestic shrine. Once past the boundary their tablets were burned or buried. New tablets might then be made for them so that they might find a place in an ancestral hall; but if their descendants did not have the means or the influence to ensure them a new status in this way then they virtually ceased to exist altogether, unless their graves were remembered.

The worship conducted in the halls took on a professional and 'classical' aspect which was lacking in the domestic rites. Some halls had caretakers. They were probably poor members lodged free in a part of the building in return for their services. As part of their duties they opened the shrines and offered incense before them on the first and fifteenth of each month. On the occasions of the great ancestral rites, in spring and autumn, the formality of the procedure was such that the services of the best educated and the most gentlemanly of the members were called for.

The rites performed in the halls were conducted by and in the presence of men; their daughters and wives played no direct part in the proceedings. In the home, in contrast, it is clear that, whatever the theoretical inferiority of women in the sphere of ancestral worship, they occupied a central position in its performance. The women cared for the domestic shrines and probably carried out the ordinary daily rites of lighting incense. Certainly, if the behaviour of overseas Chinese is any guide, it was the women who had prime charge of the ancestors in the home, remembering their death-dates and praying to them in need. There was nothing in Chinese ancestor worship which forced individuals to communicate with the ancestors only through living intermediaries; any member of the

[1] Different forms of spirit-mediumship were practised among south-eastern Chinese. The dead were contacted mainly through female mediums who conducted private family seances. See de Groot, *Les fêtes. . .*, pp. 285ff., and *The Religious System of China*, vol. VI, pp. 1332ff. For the continuation of this system in an overseas settlement see A. J. A. Elliott, *Chinese Spirit-Medium Cults in Singapore*, Monographs on Social Anthropology, London School of Economics and Political Science, no. 14, London, 1955, pp. 134ff.

family might address them in prayer; but it is likely that the senior woman in the house was in practice the main routine link between the dead and the members of the family. Of course, women addressed themselves to their husbands' ancestors, not their own; but they were performing rites at shrines which would in due course house their own tablets and be served by their own sons and daughters-in-law.

In the halls the ancestors were the only, or at least the chief, class of supernatural beings attended to. The gods were concentrated elsewhere.[1] At home, on the other hand, the ancestors were merely one kind of occupant of the shrine. They were, moreover, inferior to the gods with whom they shared the shrine, standing at their right. At any time of rejoicing or suffering the ancestors shared with the house gods the offerings placed before the shrine, but they were the junior members in the supernatural company. In rich households the ancestral shrine might be physically distinct from that of the gods, but it was not the less inferior for that.

Remoter ancestors received periodical rites in the halls and, once or twice a year, at their graves. The immediately dead were not merely closer in time and interest to their descendants, but they presented more facets of their after-life to the attention of the living. Not only were they served at their shrine and at their grave, but their fate in the nether regions imposed demands on their survivors. Apart from the funeral rites themselves the living must perform such rites in the post-funeral period as would ensure the comfort and success of the dead in their early mortuary adventures. This phase of the care of ancestors is unintelligible outside the context of Chinese eschatology, and we need therefore to consider briefly the ideas about life after death.

The conception of the fate of the dead logically required a tripartition of the soul, for there were three different places to which an individual proceeded on death, and in each of these three places he received different rites. He went into his grave; he was established in his tablet by the soul-dotting rite; he passed into the underworld to experience judgment, punishment, and usually rebirth. The threefold division of the soul was in fact explicitly reflected in the ideas expressed by Chinese,[2] although one would doubtless exceed the warrant of the evidence in concluding that a systematic conception of the soul as three distinct entities was present in the minds of all Chinese.

The soul inhabiting the grave was cared for during the yearly or twice-yearly visits to the tombs. It was served with food and drink, of which the living also partook, so that a kind of communion was set up between the dead and their surviving kinsmen. It persisted as long as the grave which housed it lasted or as long as kinsmen paid attention to it. The

[1] Doolittle, op. cit, p. 179, mentions that he saw 'the local god of wealth' and the 'god of literature' in special apartments in an elaborate ancestral hall in Foochow.

[2] See, e.g., Addison, op. cit., p. 34, and Boüinais and Paulus, op. cit., pp. 9ff.

soul which was installed in the tablet remained in the household shrine until it was superannuated from domestic worship; it was then either transferred to a new tablet to be placed in an ancestral hall or it disappeared from human interest. We may note that the souls of the ancestors who were honoured by being represented by a tablet in an ancestral hall manifested their superior social status by surviving longer than the souls of the less favoured dead. The soul which passed on death into the underworld was subjected to judgment in a number of tribunals, punished for its crimes on earth, and was usually reborn into the world in a form which depended on its merits. (Those guilty of heinous crimes on earth might be confined for countless ages in some fearful dungeon, while a few fortunate souls found their way to the Western Paradise, escaping in this way from the cycle of rebirth.) During its sojourn in the underworld the soul needed the aid of the living in the form of both the supply of material comforts and prayers of intercession. These services were provided in the funeral and post-funeral rites.[1]

It is interesting to see that the souls grouped in ancestral tablets and the souls passing through the underworld mirrored, albeit in different ways, two quite distinct foundations of Chinese society: the agnatic kinship system and the bureaucratic state. When tablets were distributed in a lineage in such a manner as to provide ritual foci for a hierarchy of segments, the ancestors formed a kind of pyramid which was in effect a model of the structure of the agnatic system. The souls in the underworld were judged and punished by what coloured prints show to have been officials and *yamen* servants. The money despatched by the living for the dead was to be applied to exercise those pecuniary pressures which were an accepted part of the bureaucratic process. In their mortuary journey the ancestors relived life in a centralized political system. The soul in the tablet and the soul in the underworld, therefore, were not only remote in place; their functions and experience were so different that they could not be united in an undifferentiated entity.[2]

It fell to the immediate descendants to care for the soul in the underworld, and it is in this phase of the relationship between ancestors and descendants that we see the most intense development of the personal ties between them. The duties owed by wives, children, and daughters-in-law were translated into the religious obligations of providing for the comfort and salvation of the dead. At the upper levels of the lineage system the

[1] See, e.g., J. J. M. de Groot, *Buddhist Masses for the Dead at Amoy*, Leiden, 1885. The structure of the underworld is a complex matter made all the more difficult by the interweaving of Buddhist and other elements. Cf. H. Maspero, *Mélanges posthumes sur les religions et l'histoire de la Chine, I, Les religions chinoises*, Paris, 1950, pp. 123, 130ff.

[2] For a treatment of this question in a wider setting see R. Firth, *The Fate of the Soul, An Interpretation of Some Primitive Concepts*, The Frazer Lecture 1955, Cambridge, 1955, p. 45.

ancestors might be glorified but they could not receive the solicitude lavished upon the recently dead.

The ideas which expressed the ties between the living and their ancestors were clearly not uniform in Chinese society. The literature abounds in contradictory statements which, to some extent at least, must reflect regional or class differences in the formulation of how the dead and the living affected one another. Nor, perhaps, were individual Chinese always very clear in their own mind on this question. Of the village he describes in *Peasant Life in China* Fei says: 'Beliefs connected with the relation of living descendants to the spirits of their ancestors are not clearly and systematically formulated among the people.'[1] Yet, in order to bring the ideas about the roles of ancestors into relation with the cult of the ancestors in large-scale lineages, I shall try to arrive at some general statements about certain aspects of this difficult matter.

It is easy enough, in the first place, to show that Chinese of all kinds and in all places saw a close connexion between the tending of ancestors and filial piety (*hsiao*).[2] Chinese owed their seniors a debt for the gift of life and for sustenance. They paid them respect and they supported them during life. To fail in this duty was to them to undermine one of the principles on which their society was based. Their duty in this regard did not come to a stop when death removed their elders from among the living. They must continue to revere and succour their forebears by respecting their graves and their tablets and by furnishing them with the necessities of the after-life. Even in the more sophisticated and agnostic versions of the theory, in which there was no dogmatic statement about the real existence or needs of the dead, there was still a stress put upon the necessity for continuing after death the reverence and respect which children owed to their parents. By taking the sanctions for ancestor worship from classical sources some Christians in China were able to justify its practice, and by going back to the scholarly exposition by Chinese of the function of rites a rationalist anthropologist was able to find his own views on the role of religion confirmed in the Chinese attitude to the cult of the ancestors.[3]

Undoubtedly, however, in popular Chinese thought the dead were somehow dependent on the living for sustenance and support. As a result it was essential that men and women leave behind them offspring, borne or adopted, to serve them in their mortuary needs. If people failed to assure for themselves the satisfaction of these needs they would turn into hungry ghosts roaming the world in search of food, a plague both to other souls and the living. At set times in each month and at grand public rites in the seventh month the Chinese made special provision for the wandering hungry ghosts.

[1] Op. cit., p. 30.

[2] Cf. Addison, op. cit., pp. 50f.

[3] See Radcliffe-Brown, op. cit., p. 159.

There is a sense in which the living were also dependent upon the dead. But as soon as we make this statement we enter, in Addison's phrase, 'the arena of controversy'. Addison points out that if we were to rely upon the evidence of nearly all missionaries and most European and American authorities on China we should conclude that 'the Chinese believe that ancestors exercise a providential care over their descendants. Their spirits are powerful to work good or ill, in accordance with the treatment they receive. The main motive for sacrifice, therefore, is to obtain protection and prosperity, to secure temporal goods, and to avert the calamities which must ensue upon neglect.'[1]

I have shown elsewhere that among Singapore Chinese ancestors may perhaps intervene to the benefit of their descendants, if they have the necessary influence in the supernatural world, but that they do not harm them unless, possibly, they are neglected. The ancestors are not agents of moral control. Moreover, in comparison with the gods, the ancestors are of minor importance in the conferring of blessings and favours.[2] What I have concluded from my experience in Singapore appears generally to coincide with the views of the only Chinese anthropologist to have written at length on the system of ideas associated with the cult of ancestors. In his study of West Town in Yunnan and in his generalizations about China as a whole, Hsu makes a series of points to establish the essential benevolence of ancestors. They do not punish at all, he says. Their descendants do not offend them, 'and they never cause disasters to befall the coming generations'.[3] In his more general treatment he sets out three 'basic assumptions' of Chinese ancestor worship. First, fortunes and misfortunes derive from ancestors in the sense that merits accumulated during the lifetime of ancestors influence the fate of descendants. Further, since the success of descendants is evidence of the virtue of ancestors, it reflects glory back on to them. Second, the needs of ancestors in the after-life must be satisfied by the living lest they turn into 'spiritual vagabonds'. Third, dead ancestors help their living descendants just as the latter can aid them in turn.[4]

[1] Op. cit., pp. 50f.

[2] *Chinese Family and Marriage in Singapore*, pp. 221f.

[3] *Under the Ancestors' Shadow*, p. 241. And cf. ibid., p. 229.

[4] *Americans and Chinese*, pp. 231f. I suspect that Hsu is wrong in ruling out the possibility that a neglected ancestor may afflict his living kinsmen. However, I think that he errs on the right side in countering the notion that ancestors are vengeful beings. I note that in Wieger's collection of Chinese stories (L. Wieger, *Folk-lore chinois moderne*, Sienhsien, 1909), there are three which show the intervention of the dead to help their living kin (item 99: dead husband helps his widow; item 100: dead father helps his son; item 209: dead man helps his agnatic cousin and siblings) and only one in which vengeance is taken; and in this last case (208) a dead concubine avenges herself on her husband's son because he robbed her of her inheritance. Wieger has fifteen other cases in which the dead take or seek revenge on the living but none of these is concerned with descendants. One can

We may consider now several aspects of the interaction between the living and their dead forebears. In the first place, the glory of one party determined that of the other. The virtues of ancestors descended to their offspring who could cast honour back upon their name. Secondly, by tending their ancestors, men encouraged them not only to continue their interest in their affairs but also intervene to their benefit if they were able to do so. Finally, there was a delayed reciprocity for the care men gave to their ancestors in the shape of a similar attention which they derived in their turn from their own descendants. As men did by their ancestors they would be done by by their descendants.

The balancing of duties and privileges in the second and third forms of mutuality was characteristically that inherent in the relations between the living and the recently dead. It belonged, that is to say, to the practice of the cult of the ancestors at the domestic level. On the other hand, the interaction between the glory of the living and that of the dead was a characteristic sanction for the practice of ancestor worship at the higher levels of the lineage. Famous and virtuous ancestors were set up in the halls; their tablets and their boards of honour shed their light on their descendants. Conversely, the successful among the living raised the status of their ancestors by placing their tablets in the halls. Between the living and the remoter forebears there were no personal relationships; these ancestors had no role in domestic affairs; but they were bound to the living in a reciprocating system of prestige.[1]

I have tried to show in this excursion into ancestor worship that, just as the lineage was not the family writ large, so the cult of the ancestors as it was conducted in the higher segments of the lineage was something different from the worship performed in the home. At the domestic level people were involved with the dead whom they had known in life and

[1] I am not, however, denying that the remoter ancestors were also at times thought to be capable of conferring benefits on the living. In an account of 'clan' worship at the tombs, said to be taken from a 'native composition', we find that the 'prayer' offered 'beseeches the shades to descend and enjoy the sacrifice; to grant protection and prosperity to their descendants, that in all succeeding generations they may wear official caps, may enjoy riches and honors, and never become extinct, that by the help of the souls in hades, the departed spirits and the living on earth may be happy, and illustrious throughout myriads of ages.' See 'Tomb of Ancestors', *The Chinese Repository*, vol. I, no. 12, April 1833, Canton, pp. 499ff.

show that there was a formalized expectation of help and protection from the ancestors by citing prayers given in a kind of guide to domestic worship. See 'The Worship of Ancestors among the Chinese: a Notice of the Kiá-lí Tieh-shih Tsih-ching . . . or Collection of Forms and Cards used in Family Ceremonies', *The Chinese Repository*, vol. XVIII, no. 7, 1849, pp. 370, 377, 378f. Note the prayer at the tombs at Ch'ing-ming: 'Prostrate I pray your protection to surround and assist your descendants, that they may be powerful and honored; let every son and grandson in the house receive a happy sign, and become conspicuous over all, their fame rivaling the lustre of their ancestors. Looking up, we pray you to descend and accept our sacrifice.' Ibid., p. 378.

towards whose happiness in the other world they could make some contribution. Ancestor worship in the halls, on the other hand, was essentially a means of group action in which the power and status structure of the community was given a ritual expression. At all levels of the lineage the sentiments required by the kinship system, as Radcliffe-Brown might have put it, were expressed and reinforced in the course of religious acts. These were rites of solidarity. But in the rites conducted in the halls men were not equal; the solidarity which was generated bound together the unequal.

12

Voluntary Associations

Grouping people by their agnatic positions and according to their status in a political and economic system which was flexible but not fluid, the localized lineage limited the range and nature of the relations constructed between individuals. Within the household co-operation was intense. Between agnates in the *wu fu* there existed, at least ideally, a readiness to act together for religious and economic interests and for the maintenance of peace and order. Men with like economic interests and following a similar style of life were expected to associate with one another, and this was probably especially true of merchants and scholars. The relations between men of unlike social position and power were partly regulated through the religious and other institutions which gave expression to, or were at least connected with, the higher segments of the lineage.

But within this framework there was clearly room for *ad hoc* groupings which might both undertake special tasks not catered for in the formal lineage system and regulate the relations between men making a comparatively free choice of their companions. In other words, voluntary associations of one kind and another might appear in village life. We know of Chinese life in the big towns and in the places overseas where Chinese settled that, in the setting of urban occupations and social alignments not resting on traditional principles, associations—some more voluntary than others—were built up to co-ordinate economic activity and provide the groupings within which social life might generally be regulated. We have information on the multiple functions of guilds in Chinese towns,[1] while the studies of Chinese overseas have demonstrated the high degree to which voluntary associations, recruiting on a number of different principles, have ordered both the local and the wider ties of the settlers.[2] Obviously, conditions in the localized lineage of south-eastern China were not such that associations were likely to assume there so important a structural position, but we must be wary of thinking that, because the lineage community appeared stable and bound by rules of kinship and status behaviour, associations could not emerge on any considerable scale.

[1] See, e.g., H. B. Morse, *The Gilds of China*, Shanghai, 1932. Lin, *The Golden Wing*, pp. 100f., gives interesting information on the manifold functions of the merchants' association in Kutien.

[2] The most thorough study of associations among overseas Chinese is that by T'ien, op. cit.

With one large class of associations we shall be concerned when we turn to the place of the secret societies in rural life. We shall see then that clandestine groupings transcended lineage boundaries and organized large-scale opposition to the state. Another type of association found in the countryside is spoken of in the New Territory at the end of the last century; people came together to talk over a scheme, collected funds which they invested in land, and applied the rents they gathered to one of a number of purposes—perhaps the burial of members of the group or the financing of a member to emigrate to California or Australia.[1]

Kulp, whose book is the fullest source for the study of the topic in south-eastern China, lists six different associations in Phoenix Village: the mutual aid club, the parent burial association, the society for the manufacture of sugar, the irrigation club, the boxing club, and the music club.[2]

Of these the first is a type of money-loan association which has been described for many parts of China;[3] briefly, groups of people engaged themselves to pay sums of money at regular intervals, the collections being placed at the disposal of individual members in turn. The sugar-manufacturing society and the irrigation club were straightforward co-operative enterprises founded on the convergence of economic interests. The boxing and music clubs were, as their names imply, groupings for recreation. The structural significance of these associations is not altogether clear from Kulp's account, but he shows us that the money-loan club was essentially characteristic of the poor members of the lineage, the 'rich families' refusing to grant loans 'without sufficient securities',[4] and that in varying degrees the voluntary groupings gave individuals opportunities to exercise leadership and win prestige.[5] The status-making apparatus devised in associations overseas[6] was clearly out of place in a village community where the class system and the power structure were already adequately expressed, but even there individuals were able to manoeuvre their positions within certain limits.

The most interesting of the associations in Phoenix Village is the parent burial society, for it throws light on the divergence between certain rules implicit in the kinship system and the expectations of behaviour on the part of closely related families. Within the *wu fu* agnates were theoretically under an obligation to help one another in the rites of mourning, but Kulp's evidence makes it clear that the handling of the corpse and the recruitment of wailers in fact rested on the contractual obligations between

[1] *Report on the New Territory at Hong Kong*, p. 18.

[2] Op. cit., pp. 188ff.

[3] See, e.g., Fei, *Peasant Life*, pp. 267ff. and A. H. Smith, *Village Life in China, A Study in Sociology*, New York, 1899, pp. 152ff.

[4] Kulp, op. cit., p. 190.

[5] Ibid., pp. 193, 209, 213.

[6] See *Chinese Family and Marriage in Singapore*, pp. 94ff.

people grouped in voluntary associations. It is true, as de Groot points out, that in lineage villages, in contrast to the towns, death rallied fellow agnates,[1] but it did so simply because of the fact that all within the community were kinsmen; the principle by which helpers at a funeral were brought together was not in reality one which sprang automatically from closeness of agnatic relationship.

There were two parent burial associations in Phoenix Village, and, although they are said formerly to have flourished among the poorer people, even the better-off villagers in Kulp's time had found it worth while to join societies of this sort.[2]

The poor needed the financial aid which was a most important part of the funeral association, but both poor and rich alike were faced with the problem of rallying the requisite mourners. The reason for this lay in the great reluctance of villagers to have anything to do with corpses and to wail. A proper funeral with enough wailing to maintain status was therefore organized on the basis of reciprocal services within voluntary associations.[3] Furthermore, the fact that the elaboration of funerals and the expansion of the body of mourners were indices of the status enjoyed by or aimed at by the bereaved family, which we know not only from Kulp's material but also from the general information on Chinese practice, assures us that mourning was not simply an institution set uniformly in motion by the rules governing behaviour between close kinsmen.[4]

Kulp's data will not take us as far as an analysis of the limits beyond which people could not count on their kinsmen for the performance of mourning duties, but we may at least guess that when the families in several households formed what I have called an extended family[5] they could rely on one another. If a family in a household was not linked with other such families and was part of no segment smaller than one which focused upon an ancestral hall, then it probably could depend on nobody other than its own members to behave in a kinsmanlike fashion on the occasion of a death. The *wu fu*, in other words, merely set a theoretical outer limit for the group within which reciprocal mourning duties on a

[1] De Groot says that in the villages of Fukien the dead were carried to their graves by their fellow-villagers while the coffin-bearers in the towns were coolies hired by undertakers. The poor in the towns formed themselves into death benefit associations with a dozen or two members to organize their funerals. See *The Religious System of China*, vol. I, pp. 192f., and 'De Lijkbezorging der Emoy-Chineezen', *Bijdragen tot de Taal- Land- en Volkenkunde van Nederlandsch-Indië*, vol. XVI, 1892, pp. 86f.

[2] Kulp, op. cit., p. 196.

[3] Ibid., pp. 197ff.

[4] In the towns of China and in overseas settlements the hiring of mourners and their recruitment by means of large-scale funeral associations were devices which showed up the connexion between funerals and family status very clearly.

[5] See p. 46 above.

non-contractual basis could develop; and it was very unlikely that this outer limit was in fact often reached.[1]

[1] I am dealing here only with the question of mourners drawn from families related by agnation; mourners were, of course, also derived from the matrilateral, uterine, and affinal kin in other communities, although doubtless the extent to which they rallied depended upon the status of the bereaved house. I deal below, pp. 101ff. with non-agnatic mourning.

13

Relations between and across Lineages

I have so far in this essay tried to explore the structure of the localized lineage and I have referred only incidentally to the relations between lineages and between the lineage and the state. In this section and the one which follows it I shall attempt to deal with the ties which bound the lineage to its society.

In China as a whole villages tended markedly to exchange their women in marriage, but when village and lineage were identified the rule of exogamy made this exchange compulsory. The majority of the women members of the local community were at any one time outsiders in the sense that their original families lived elsewhere. In all societies, except for a very few in which what has been called the principle of complementary filiation has not been used,[1] important social links are set up between intermarrying groups. The ties springing from marriage spin numerous threads across the boundaries between lineages and sometimes link lineages as wholes in regular relations. The first question we must ask about south-eastern China is whether there were any patterns of intermarriage between localized lineages.

In recent years Chinese evidence has been adduced in theoretical exercises on matrilateral cross-cousin marriage, and if we were able to satisfy ourselves that this form of preferential marriage was in fact current in south-eastern China we should be able to draw certain conclusions about the regularities in relations between lineages. Both Lévi-Strauss[2] and Leach,[3] basing themselves so far as modern China is concerned mainly on a paper by Hsu,[4] have appeared to put China among the societies which significantly practise marriage with the mother's brother's daughter. Surveying the field, Hsu says that, with few exceptions, in all parts of China of which he knows the preferred, but not compulsory, form

[1] Cf. M. Fortes, 'The Structure of Unilineal Descent Groups', *American Anthropologist*, vol. 55, no. 1, Jan.-March 1953, p. 33.

[2] C. Lévi-Strauss, *Les structures élémentaires de la parenté*, Paris, 1949, pp. 434ff.

[3] E. R. Leach, 'The Structural Implications of Matrilateral Cross-Cousin Marriage', *Journal of the Royal Anthropological Institute*, vol. LXXXI, 1952, pp. 36f.

[4] F. L. K. Hsu, 'Observations on Cross-Cousin Marriage in China', *American Anthropologist*, vol. 47, no. 1, Jan.-March, 1945.

of marriage is with the mother's brother's daughter and the disfavoured form is with the father's sister's daughter.[1]

Of two Chinese 'community' studies which have been produced since Hsu wrote his paper one certainly strengthens his generalization and the other may just possibly weaken it. M. H. Fried says of Chinese studied in east-central China that there is a tradition of marriage with the mother's brother's daughter, which is favoured, in contrast to marriage with the opposite kind of cross-cousin, which is disliked.[2] M. C. Yang reports of a Shantung village that a man may marry either his father's sister's daughter or his mother's sister's daughter, but that these kinds of marriage are held to be unsatisfactory. He does not specifically mention marriage with the mother's brother's daughter, but he may cover it in the following statement: 'It is frequently observed that the relationship between an aunt mother-in-law and a niece daughter-in-law can be worse than bad. For this reason, far-sighted people disapprove marriages with cousins.'[3]

Another source for the incidence of matrilateral cross-cousin marriage in China is the 1930 official compilation of customary law drawn on by Théry and van der Valk. These two writers mention various forms of cross-cousin marriage in Hupeh. In some districts of this province it was apparently possible to marry all non-agnatic cousins. In other districts cousin marriage was restricted to mother's brother's daughter and mother's sister's daughter. From two or three counties it was reported that matrilateral cross-cousin marriage was practised with the accompanying prohibition of marriage with the father's sister's daughter.[4] In other words, matrilateral cross-cousin marriage of the kind referred to by Hsu, Lévi-Strauss, and Leach was an established but not universal pattern in Hupeh.

For Fukien and Kwangtung the evidence rests on what Lin Yueh-hwa and Kulp have written. Kulp says of Phoenix Village that there was 'a limited sort of cross-cousin marriage' in which a man might not marry his patrilateral cross-cousin. He gives no clear indication of the frequency of cross-cousin marriage, but he nevertheless states—a fact which seems often to have been overlooked—that cousin marriages were second-best.

[1] Ibid., p. 84.

[2] *Fabric of Chinese Society, A Study of Social Life in a Chinese County Seat*, New York, 1953, p. 64n.

[3] *A Chinese Village, Taitou, Shantung Province*, London, 1948, p. 119.

[4] See Théry, op. cit., p. 390; and van der Valk, op. cit., p. 28. Note that although *piao* (i.e. non-agnatic) cousins came within the general prohibition of marriages within the mourning grades according to imperial law, a special dispensation was written into the Ch'ing code in 1729 to make marriage with *piao* cousins permissible. The Ming code had contained a similar licence. See van der Valk, op. cit., p. 27, and Hoang, op. cit., p. 52.

'Mates with no blood connexion at all may be, and theoretically are preferred.'[1]

We derive our knowledge of matrilateral cross-cousin marriage in I-hsü not, strangely enough, from Lin's article, but from a passing reference by Fei to Lin's unpublished monograph on the village;[2] while in still another context Lin himself states that he found this form of preferential marriage in Fukien.[3] In *The Golden Wing* he does not mention preferred marriages, but in the course of the narrative we learn of a number of proposed and effected matches. I have gone through the various marriages and proposals, finding in them no indication that marriage with the mother's brother's daughter was of any importance.[4] Of course, data taken from a work cast in the form of a novel must be inconclusive, but, while I may not make a case simply on the genealogical material extracted from the book, I can at least appeal to the absence from it of any suggestion that a preferential form of marriage was implemented in the Hwang Village. Lin illustrates many important relationships and practices in village life by dramatizing particular instances of them; if mother's brother's daughter marriage were important we should expect to see it indicated in some way.

The negative evidence I have marshalled from Kulp and Lin does not amount to a complete contradiction of the thesis that matrilateral cross-cousin marriage was generally a preferred type of marriage in south-eastern China. But at least I am sure in my own mind of two things: the preference was not universal in south-eastern China, let alone China as

[1] Op. cit., pp. 167f. It seems generally to have escaped notice that in the genealogy given on p. 157 of Kulp's book there appear what may be the surnames of the husbands of four female agnates. These women form two pairs of sisters, one pair being brother's children to the other. Each woman has married a man of a different surname. Since agnates must bear the same surname and all linked matrilateral cross-cousin marriages must lead into the same group of agnates, these data do not speak for the consistent application of the rule of mother's brother's daughter marriage.

[2] Fei, *Peasant Life*, pp. 51f.

[3] Lin Yueh-hwa, 'The Kinship System of the Lolo', *Harvard Journal of Asiatic Studies*, vol. 9, no. 2, June 1946, p. 94.

[4] I set out here the marriages among the agnates of Hwang Dunglin, the protagonist of the story. We do not know the kinship links between spouses before their marriage, but, as in the case of the genealogical data cited from Kulp, the fact that different surnames emerge means that the preferred type of marriage does not occur consistently. Dunglin himself marries a Cheng. His agnatic great-grandfather married an Ou; his own mother was a Pan; his brother married a Lin; while his son's wife was a Chen. Another son was proposed in marriage to a Chang, which was the surname of the husband of one of Dunglin's sisters. Dunglin's other sister is married to a Wang, and his agnatic niece is betrothed to a Hsu. Finally, two agnates of Dunglin, his second cousin (male) and the daughter of another male second cousin both are married to spouses of the surname Ou, which was the surname of Dunglin's paternal great-grandmother. Of three marriages between Hwang and Ou, therefore, two have transferred brides from Ou to Hwang and one in the other direction.

a whole; and in the communities such as Phoenix Village and the village (or villages) described by Lin, where the preference may have existed, it was not implemented on such a scale as to produce a unilateral flow of brides. No system of circulating connubium could have emerged where women, as in the case of the Hwang and the Ou, moved in both directions. Yet, of course, the problem remains: why was marriage with the mother's brother's daughter said to be preferred? It is just possible to argue that, given the inferiority of bride-givers to bride-takers, Chinese thought of 'the brother's daughter following the father's sister'[1] as a means of establishing a fixed relationship between two agnatic groups, even though they rarely in fact made use of the principle. Again, a very few marriages in one direction between agnatic groups might have been considered enough to set up the desired relationship between them.

But if we accept an argument in this form we have then to ask about the nature of the agnatic groups which passed brides in such a way as to regulate the relations between them. Leach has used the expression 'local descent groups' for the units which participate in connubium.[2] A whole lineage in south-eastern China could not have been such a group, despite its local nature, because it is clear that the circle of men controlling the marriage of a particular woman was no larger than that circumscribed by, at most, the extended family. Were extended families and, in their absence, families in single households the operative units in the rare cases in which women were passed according to the pattern of matrilateral cross-cousin marriage? Or, ignoring the criterion of the control over the marriages of women, can we say that some large segment of a localized lineage constituted a unit for the purpose of the stabilizing transfer of brides? The evidence is not very helpful, but, if *The Golden Wing* may be squeezed once again to yield up suggestions, then the fact that there appear to have been a net flow of brides from Ou to Hwang and a quarrel over trees which brought a large group of Hwang into conflict with a large group of Ou[3] may indicate that the people involved on both sides formed groups whose interrelations were in some sense controlled by the marriages between them.[4] I can scarcely say that, with the data now available to us, I can settle the question of the significance in south-eastern China of the stated preference for marriage with the mother's brother's daughter, but

[1] Cf. Théry, op. cit., p. 390 and Hsu, op. cit., p. 84.

[2] Leach, op. cit., p. 24.

[3] See above, pp. 39f.

[4] I have pointed out (see p. 40 above) that the quarrel involved only the men in Hwang who had direct claims on the trees and only the men in Ou who descended from the man who had bestowed rights on his sister's sons in Hwang. One could perhaps argue that the quarrel produced this alignment not simply because the two opposing groups were based on the inheritance of rights in land and trees but rather because the groups they formed on the basis of these rights were also defined in terms of the marriages between them.

at least the structural issues put by Lévi-Strauss and Leach show where we must look if more material is provided in the future.[1]

Whatever else may be in doubt, the low incidence of marriage with the mother's brother's daughter in Fukien and Kwangtung seems very probable. All that we know points to a situation in which the marriage connexions of a particular localized lineage were cast in many directions. It is possible that different segments of a lineage specialized in marrying members of particular segments of other lineages, and the class stratification of the local community must have aided preferences of this order when segments occupied different points on the scale of stratification. Through its multifarious marriage links with other lineages both the lineage as a whole and the families within it were significantly tied to units lying outside the local community.[2]

From the point of view of the family we can show the implications of exogamy by considering the legal and ritual ties created by the movement of a woman from her original family to that of her husband. I have already discussed in the context of the family and the household the extent to which married women were incorporated into their husbands' families and alienated from the families which produced and reared them.[3] To a high degree a married woman was legally locked within her husband's gates. Her own family had no clearly defined right to interfere in her affairs once she had gone out in marriage, although, as I have shown, there were places where, once she became a widow, certain privileges might be vested in her family of origin. The relations set up by marriage between the parents of the spouses were marked by a formality which helped to protect the wife's parents, who were inferior; the rule of no intervention in one another's concerns avoided situations in which the relatively low status of the wife's people might expose them to intolerable embarrassment. Reading the literature on China in general one gains the impression that when unhappy wives ran home their parents were usually concerned to get them back to their husbands before unpleasantness was generated. We may certainly not conclude that Chinese wives were completely abandoned by their own families, but it is clear that the institutional control exercised by these families over their married daughters was very small.

[1] In their book, *Marriage, Authority and Final Causes, A Study of Unilateral Cross-Cousin Marriage*, Glencoe, Illinois, 1955, G. C. Homans and D. M. Schneider attack the problem of matrilateral cross-cousin marriage from a different point of view. They relate the preference for this marriage to a state of affairs in which authority is exercised over a man by his father and indulgence is displayed towards him by his mother's brother. The conditions of Chinese society more or less fit their scheme, but the hypothesis will hardly explain why the preference is not uniform in China, nor does it claim to be able to account for a wide divergence between the ideal preference and the poverty of statistical appearance.

[2] I refer again to this topic at p. 112 below.

[3] See pp. 30ff. above.

I have pointed out that the married woman's incomplete alienation from her old home was ritually expressed in her mourning duties. Once married a woman ceased to mourn for her parents as though she was a daughter in their house, but she had mourning obligations towards them nevertheless. What these duties were in official theory we can see set out in the Ch'ing Code. If we compare the following diagram 'A', which shows the mourning due from a married woman to her agnates, with the diagram on p. 45 above (which is generally valid for an unmarried daughter as well as for a son, married or unmarried), we shall see that marriage significantly reduces a woman's status *vis-à-vis* her own people.[1]

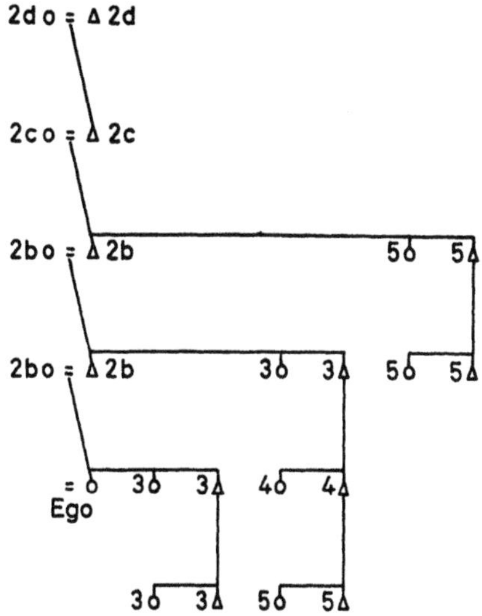

DIAGRAM 'A'

On the other hand, the married woman mourns for her husband's agnates in grades which are in many respects closer to those applicable in the case of an unmarried daughter, as diagram 'B' illustrates.[2]

While the married woman mourns for her own agnates, they in turn have mourning responsibilities towards her. Diagram 'C' shows how a man mourns for his married female agnates and certain of their children.[3] If his daughter, sister, paternal aunt, agnatic great-aunt, agnatic cousin, agnatic great-uncle's daughter, and agnatic second cousin are each married into a different lineage, as is at least theoretically possible, then ego is committed by the mourning rules to a ritual tie with the members of a large number of communities. Moreover, his ritual links with

[1] See de Groot, *The Religious System of China*, vol. II, p. 566, and Hoang, op. cit., Tableaux du deuil, Table III.

[2] De Groot, op. cit., p. 565, and Hoang, op. cit., loc. cit., Table II.

[3] De Groot, op. cit., p. 564.

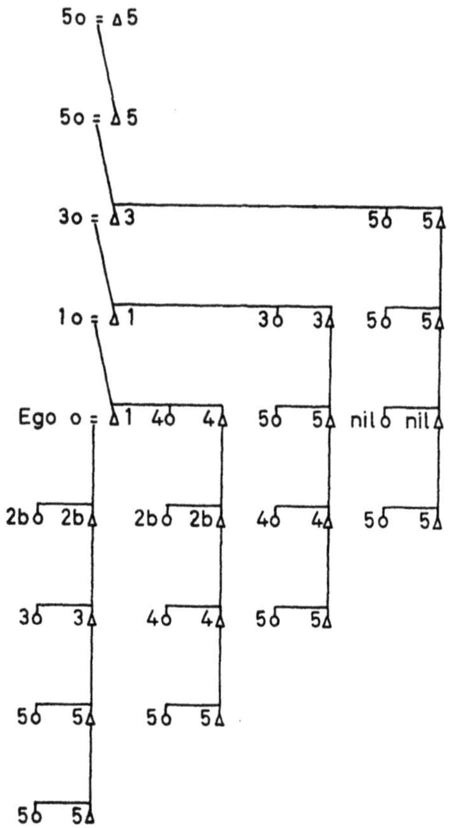

DIAGRAM 'B'

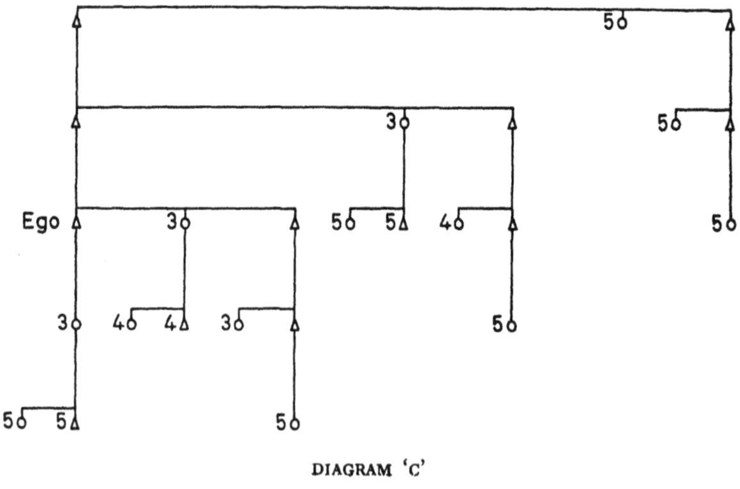

DIAGRAM 'C'

the communities into which his daughter, sister, and father's sister have married are stronger than others by virtue of the obligation imposed on him to mourn for the children of these women.

The official mourning grades show us in this fashion a ritualized structure of relations based on the ties set up by marriage. There remains one further aspect of this structure to be commented upon. Men and women are obliged to mourn for certain of their mother's agnates and for the children of mother's sisters, as diagram 'D' shows.[1] It should be noted that the extension of grade five to cover father's sister's daughter, mother's brother's daughter, and mother's sister's daughter brings these three cousins theoretically within the range of prohibited marriage.[2]

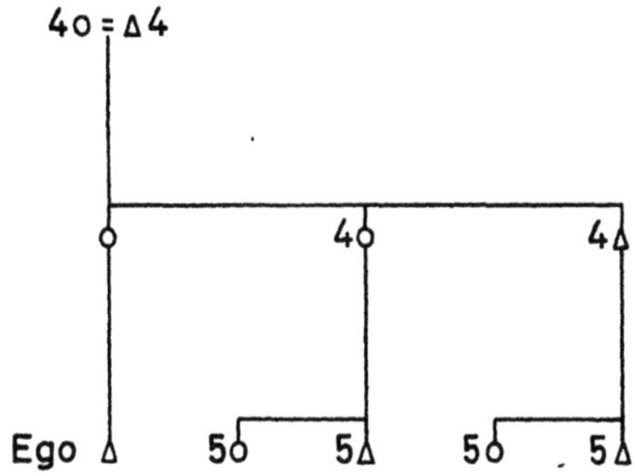

DIAGRAM 'D'

I have shown already that the popular system of mourning by no means followed the official system in all its complexity,[3] but, although we know little of the actual rules by which mourning was conducted by south-eastern Chinese in their villages, we can be sure that certain matrilateral, uterine, and affinal ties were expressed at least on the occasion of funerals. Lin Yueh-hwa describes a funeral in *The Golden Wing* at which the five mourning grades were represented. The dead woman's son and daughters-in-law mourned in the first grade, as did her adopted grandson, because he took the place of his late father who had been the oldest son. Lin says that ordinarily this grandson would have mourned in the second grade. The other three grades (respectively requiring nine months', five months', and three months' observance) were represented by what Lin calls the 'collateral kinsmen, the kinswomen and the relatives belonging to other clans'.[4] In another context in his book Lin says something of the people who arrived to mourn for the death of Dunglin's mother, whose surname was Pan. Her only surviving daughter came, as did 'all the daughters

[1] Ibid., loc. cit., and Hoang, op. cit., loc. cit., Table V.

[2] But see above, p. 97n.

[3] See above, pp. 44f.

[4] Op. cit., p. 106.

married out of the family. . . .'[1] The old lady's original lineage sent seven women and four men, all descended from her father, and each representing 'one of the present families of the Pan connexions'. Lin notes that of these eleven people from the Pan lineage six had never seen the dead woman 'and had as yet no association with the Hwang family'.[2]

Marriage opened up for any family possibilities of social contact with people in other communities when it did not already rest upon a previous set of such relations created by an earlier marriage. From the point of view of the individual man in a lineage the pivot of his relations with his mother's kin was his maternal uncle. We should expect on anthropological first principles that a patrilineal system such as that found in China would bring the mother's brother into a special relationship with his sister's son, and the evidence we have in general confirms this expectation. Although no property rights flowed through married women from the group in which they were born to the sons which they contributed to another group, a mother's brother might, by virtue of the affection in which he held his uterine nephews, make them gifts. Such avuncular indulgence formed the basis of the quarrel over trees between the Hwang and the Ou.[3] At a man's wedding his maternal uncle occupied a seat of honour, presumably symbolizing the continuing interest maintained by a woman's kin in her descendants. In disputes between brothers over inheritance a mother's brother was at least a potential mediator.[4] As far as I can understand the evidence from south-eastern China, the relations between a woman's brothers and her sons were likely to be characterized by affection, although no licensed familiarity could arise between the two classes of men in a society which consistently maintained a barrier of respect between the generations.[5]

The ties between men in different lineages were channelled to a great extent through the marriages linking them together. Whatever the formal limitations on the contacts between a married woman and her original family, she visited them from time to time and took her children with her.

[1] Ibid., p. 130.

[2] Ibid., p. 131.

[3] See p. 39 above.

[4] See Lin, *The Golden Wing*, p. 123.

[5] Fei, *Peasant Life*, pp. 86f., gives a good outline of the role of the mother's brother in a different area of China. The maternal uncle there is the guest of honour at the child's first-month ceremony and chooses a name for him. He accompanies him on his first journey to school. He makes him a valuable gift on his marriage. The sister's son can run to his mother's brother when he is in need. The mother's brother acts as his nephew's protector when his father is harsh. The maternal uncle is the 'formal judge' in the division of family property. I note, however, that Fried, op. cit., p. 95, instances the relation with the mother's brother as one of the ties which are not institutionalized. No doubt the avuncular role in China varies with the intensity of the relations maintained within agnatic groups, and we should expect that south-eastern China would provide a clear picture of the kindly mother's brother standing over against the disciplinary father.

Men were brought into touch with matrilateral kinsmen and affines, and the relations set up on these bases could clearly serve as important foundations for political and economic activity. Mothers' brothers might, for example, exert their influence in bureaucratic affairs on behalf of their sisters' sons, while men linked by a marriage might choose to co-operate in business. The partnership between Hwang Dunglin and his sister's husband, in *The Golden Wing*, is a dramatic example of the potential importance of the ties of affinity.

The strands of marriage criss-crossing lineages linked individuals and families in different lineages. It is possible, as I have argued, that particular segments of lineages were tied in more or less permanent relations with one another. There is also a sense in which marriage expressed the relationships between lineages as wholes. Connubium between two lineages rested on a state of affairs in which, whatever the differences and quarrels between them, large-scale violence had not broken out. If conflict of this kind arose the new relationship of extreme hostility was expressed in a rupture of connubium. An oath was sworn before the ancestors that women would no longer be exchanged with a lineage which had become an outright enemy. Of course, the oath notwithstanding, connubium might later be resumed, but at any particular time extreme enmity and intermarriage were held to be inconsistent. It is at this point that we move over to consider the relations of hostility and dominance through which the lineages in one locality seemed to have formed a system.

The Chinese of Kwangtung and Fukien were notorious for their turbulence. In part this reputation rested on their opposition to the state; trying to collect taxes and suppress seditious organizations the government often found itself face to face with people whose bellicosity earned them a name for barbarism. But the distaste with which officialdom often looked upon the villagers of the south-east was also caused by the frequency and intensity with which local groups took up arms against one another.

Violence often characterized the relations between groups, but it was not necessarily confined to the relations between lineages. Sometimes alignments within lineages developed an intensity of opposition which resulted in open conflict.[1] It is clear, on the other hand, that the tensions generated between opposed groups within one lineage played only a minor part in the general scene of violence. Lineages appear often to have been arranged in sections which sought to dominate and undermine their rivals; the Hwang Village, for example, was split into two opposing groups between which there was friction;[2] but open and organized violence between groups of this kind was rare. Politically and ritually the lineage was a centralized unit within which the peace could usually be kept.

[1] Cf. Hu, op. cit., p. 92.

[2] Lin, *The Golden Wing*, p. 153.

Open hostility between lineages could exist when they were linked by agnation or by the ties of marriage and matrilateral and uterine kinship. In 1899 British administrators in the New Territory noted that a state of feud had long existed between two villages whose inhabitants were patrilineally descended from a common ancestor; many people had been killed in the course of the hostilities, and in one of the villages there was a temple to the memory of those who had fallen.[1] I have seen evidence that in the same area a similar hostile relation exists at the present day between localized lineages bound by common agnatic descent. It is of course possible that organized hostility regulated the relations between lineages which were linked neither by agnation nor marriage; a breach of connubium between two lineages maintained over a long period might be responsible for such a state of affairs; but it seems unlikely that, in a situation in which the marriage net was probably cast very widely, the contacts between lineages were ever independent of either patrilineal descent or the ties resulting from marriage. Hostility, in other words, was generally an aspect of kinship and affinity.

I have already referred to the warlike architecture often found in the villages of south-eastern China and cited observations made on the inter-village fights in one part of Kwangtung.[2] There is evidence that both Kwangtung and Fukien were scenes of constant fighting between local communities. 'At the southern part of Fŭh-Keĕn Province, two families, or, as that word (in Chinese) denotes in its most extensive sense, TWO CLANS, in the Spring of the year [1817], fell out in consequence of some verbal altercation.' The Tsae and the Wang fought each other until eight men had been killed and forty of the houses belonging to the Tsae burned. 'The Police seized a number of the parties; but so bitter was their animosity that the WANG again attacked the other party, and killed several, which obliged the government to call in the aid of the military.'[3] At this same period the Viceroy of Fukien sent the Emperor a long report in which he described the 'disturbed and ungovernable state of that province; arising from the cruel, fierce, and quarrelsome dispositions and habits of the people, who form themselves into armed clans; who fight together, and oppose the ordinary police by force. . . .'[4] The official view of the situation in Kwangtung was no better. 'The governor of Canton issued a proclamation against clans in 1828, in which he says, it is the custom for large clans to seize the best lands and most useful streams for irrigation, at the expense of the smaller clans, whose women they also insult. A little later, the judge puts forward an edict to the same effect. "The Canton people," he says, "pay no attention to the control of the laws. In the

[1] *Papers Laid Before the Legislative Council of Hong Kong, 1899*, 'Extracts. . . ', no. 9/99, p. 6.

[2] See above, p. 8.

[3] *The Indo-Chinese Gleaner*, Malacca, vol. I, no. 3, Feb. 1818, p. 45.

[4] *The Indo-Chinese Gleaner*, vol. II, no. 18, Oct. 1821, p. 229.

conduct of affairs they delight in litigation, and have no regard for the preservation of life. In pursuance of the feuds of the halls of their ancestors, they proceed to collect together a multitude of their own clan's people, and seizing spears, swords, and other weapons, they fight together and kill people".'[1]

References to fighting between 'clans' and villages in the south-east are also to be found for the middle and later parts of the nineteenth century.[2] Miss Hu cites evidence of organized violence in both Fukien and Kwangtung,[3] and in the data she brings forward and the other material available we can discern patterns of events which show us that the hostilities which took place were not random acts of violence haphazardly conducted.

The fights did not of course amount to war, because the units engaged in combat were scarcely independent political units; always potentially and sometimes in reality the state was ready to put a stop to the proceedings. But the fights resembled war in the organization of troops and in the manner in which peace was negotiated or enforced by a victor. The lineages which fought one another were in a state of feud; but the acts of feud might be isolated attacks by small numbers on small numbers in a hit-and-run fashion as well as the pitched battles involving small armies which more readily suggest warfare.

Much of Liu Hsing-t'ang's article on kinship groups in Fukien is taken up with *hsieh-tou*, fighting, and from his historical account we can gather a fair idea of the organizational questions connected with it. It is interesting to see that the prefectures of Chang-chou and Ch'üan-chou were perhaps the most notorious for their belligerence, because it was from these areas that Fukienese migration overseas was heaviest; but the practice of organized violence is shown to have been general in the province. Liu quotes extensively from Ch'ên Shêng-shao's *A Record of Customs*, and from this work we can obtain a vivid picture of the situation, at least from the official point of view.

Ch'ên writes of Chao-an: 'If there is a fight it is due to gain. To be of one mind, one strength, each member of the lineage must pay a share of the expenses. This is called "man and *mow* money". What is this "man and *mow* money"? How much should each man pay and how much should be paid for each *mow*? There are those who draw up the budget,

[1] 'Notices of Modern China. . . ', *The Chinese Repository*, vol. IV, no. 12, April 1836, p. 566. On 'clan feuds' at this time see also ibid., pp. 564ff. and 'Clanship among the Chinese. . . ', *The Chinese Repository*, vol. IV, no. 9, Jan. 1836, pp. 411ff.

[2] See, e.g., T. T. Meadows, *The Chinese and Their Rebellions*, London, 1856, p. 47n.; R. H. Conwell, *Why and How. Why the Chinese Emigrate. . .* , Boston, 1871, p. 86; S. Wells Williams, *The Middle Kingdom*, 2 vols., London, 1883, vol. I, pp. 484f. Conwell, loc. cit., refers, as do other writers, to the 'clan' fights as a source of forced emigrants; prisoners taken were sometimes sold off for export overseas. See also W. H. Medhurst, *China: Its State and Prospects. . .* , London, 1840, pp. 523f.

[3] Op. cit., pp. 92ff.

gather the large sums, collect the small payments, record the income, and record the expenditure; each man has his job and all is in order without any confusion. Then is this quite fair? No. If money is collected according to the number of *mow* of land, the rich pay more and the poor pay less. Even if the poor pay a little it is still unfair. Many families of eight persons are desperately poor; pawning or selling their things they cannot raise enough money. It will not be enough even if they borrow; they have to sell their children. Women and children will weep, holding on to one another. Those who come to collect this forced subscription are hectoring and cruel men; glaring angrily and baring their teeth they will not wait a second. The people of Chang-chou and Ch'üan-chou have dared to refuse to pay taxes to the government, but they dare not refuse to pay this money; they are not afraid of government officials, but they are afraid of these tyrannical bullies. Explosives and weapons come from this money; food for those who take part and other official expenses come from it; the compensation to be paid to the relatives of those killed comes from it. When those shameless rascals hear of an impending fight they jump at the opportunity. The degenerate heads of certain families also take the opportunity of enriching themselves. Those wicked young men of the lineage, without land and wives and children, are glad of such things; they come out when there is gain and disappear when there is danger. All the time the good members of the lineage who have families must suffer the worst. When there is one fight the rich lose their riches; after the second fight the rich become the poor; after the third fight the poor become paupers and they perish.'

Liu notes an imperial edict recorded in the Ch'üan-chou Gazetteer: 'We have heard that the character of the people of Chang-chou and Ch'üan-chou is arrogant and quarrelsome. The large lineages there, because of their superiority in numbers, oppress the poor and weak lineages. Often for a trifle they will gather their members together and engage in fighting against others. . . .'

Violence occurred as a result of the activities of sworn brotherhoods and bands of thugs in some areas, but in the countryside, Liu comments, the fighting usually took place between lineages. Fighting was often on a large scale, with several tens of people killed at each encounter. 'Some bred a hatred that was to last for many generations. After an encounter, when one side was defeated, they might agree to a truce through the good offices of government officials and eminent members of neutral lineages. But the defeated would not rest long. A trifle would again set off a full-scale conflict.'

Liu discusses the various *casus belli*. In most cases he sees the exploitation of the weak lineages by the strong as the root of the trouble. Sometimes fighting broke out during religious festivals. Ch'ên Shêng-shao mentions disputes over the boundaries between fields and graveyards and quarrels over the use of lineage lands. Fighting broke out not only when the interests of a whole lineage were at stake but also when one of its members was attacked, for he would be supported by his fellows.

Fighting could lead to alliances which spread the area of violence. In Chao-an, Ch'ên says, powerful lineages united many weak lineages with them to form strong units. On the boundary between Fukien and Kwangtung conflict sometimes broke out which produced a confrontation of provincial parties. 'There were fierce clashes and prisoners were taken.' The news spread. 'Huge crowds gathered, blocking various passes. People made their hedges dense with bamboo, and all the roads were blocked with people moving away and carrying their possessions. The wicked, availing themselves of the confusion, burned down houses and robbed them of their household goods. Weeping was heard throughout the countryside and fire lit up the sky. They fought and the dead covered the fields.'

Miss Hu adds to Liu's material on Fukien from other sources. She says of one area that when each side in a fight had lost about the same number of men they separated, each side taking away its dead and its prisoners. To drive home the truth that lineages were more concerned to settle their quarrels in their own way than have the government interfere, she cites the case of a lineage which was in dispute with a community of mixed surnames over water supply. They agreed between them not to bring the case before the magistrate lest he cause them greater harm than they could do to themselves by fighting. And Miss Hu says, perhaps ironically, in this case only a few men were killed.[1]

Across the border in Kwangtung the organization of fights seems to have followed similar lines. An eighteenth-century memorial significantly enough traces the large-scale violence to the accumulation of wealth brought about in large and powerful lineages by the investment of profits from ancestral lands. This wealth led the rich and the numerous to oppress the poor and few. If one lineage took on another whose strength was so near its own as to leave the issue of the struggle in some doubt, then its members were summoned to the ancestral hall where they were assured that the wounded would be amply rewarded, the dead honoured with ancestral tablets to be placed in the hall, and the widows and children given land for their support. The income from the ancestral lands was to be drawn upon for these rewards. If any of the opposing lineage was to be killed and individual men of the home lineage were prepared to take responsibility for the homicides on their own shoulders *vis-à-vis* the government, then these substitute 'criminals' and their dependants were to be treated as though their death had occurred as a direct result of the fighting.[2]

This last device for making good to the state the deaths inflicted on the enemy is mentioned by other writers. The author of 'Clanship among

[1] Hu, op. cit., p. 93.

[2] Ibid., pp. 186f.

the Chinese . . .' in *The Chinese Repository* of January 1836, after expounding the general theme of lineage conflict in the neighbourhood of Canton, goes on to say that where the villages were close together and no natural boundary protected one against the other, 'the management of feuds is reduced to a system, and the hostile families are ready armed with spears or bludgeons to enter these not always bloodless broils. Where the hostile parties live within a short distance, and carry on their labors and pursuits, each under the eyes of the other, occasions cannot long be wanting to call forth their cherished hatred. If one turns away the water-course from his enemy's little field to his own, and is too strong or obstinate to make reparation or be compelled to do justice, then not unfrequently the signal-gong sounds, the two parties marshal their hostile forces, and the whole of two villages are arrayed against each other in conflict. When numbers and advantages are equal, the quarrel lasts for two or three days, each party in turn pursuing and pursued. But when the contest ends, all parties return to their business as before. It sometimes, however, happens that death is the consequence to one or more persons, and the result has been known of four people actually killed and more than twenty wounded in one affray. When such is the case, it is the general interest to hush up the matter, and the murders are not reported to government. But if complaint is made and an investigation becomes inevitable, the case is by no means hopeless for the guilty, as might be expected where the laws against murder are so strict as in China.

'In each of the villages in the vicinity of Canton and Whampoa, where these feuds are so common, a curious provision has obtained by custom to meet such exigencies. "A band of devoted men" is there found, and a list of them kept, who have voluntarily offered themselves to assume such crimes and to take their chance for life. When complaint is made, therefore, so many of the first on this list as are necessary come forward, confess themselves the perpetrators of the slaughter, and surrender to the government.' Sometimes these men managed to get themselves acquitted, sometimes they were executed, but more usually they were transported or fined. 'The compensation which tempts to the formation of the devoted band, is security for the maintenance of their families in the case of suffering capital punishment, and a reward in lands or money, sometimes to the amount of $300. This sum is raised by the voluntary imposition of taxes on the inhabitants of that village; and these taxes, said our informant, are no small burden to the poor, who can neither avoid nor easily pay them.'[1]

Now it is of course true that most of the accounts we have of these bloody affrays come from a disapproving officialdom whose members, while they sometimes sought to conceal the unrest in their jurisdiction, at other times no doubt exaggerated the unruliness of their charges in order to justify their own helplessness. We may certainly not conclude

[1] Op. cit., pp. 412f.

that the whole of south-eastern China was all the time in a state of armed belligerence. Yet the evidence undoubtedly suggests that the system of relationships between localized lineages in Fukien and Kwangtung rested on a readiness to settle differences between them as much by recourse to violence as by appeal to the legal machinery of the state. Moreover, although the details are by no means clear, it seems that there were general expectations on the part of the belligerents about the course a particular fight was likely to take and the time and casualties it could fairly be thought to demand. At least when the parties were more or less equally matched, a single engagement was an attempt to keep the balance of an account stretching back over a long series of engagements.

However, some of the fights took place between parties which were not equally matched, and in this kind of violence we see the exercise of force by the powerful community on the weak. Liu Hsing-t'ang finds 'feudalist' exploitation less in the oppression of the poor by the rich in the same lineage than in the subjection of the poor lineage by the rich lineage. And clearly there is some substance in his view of the matter.[1] In several parts of Kwangtung and Fukien, even if the phenomenon was not general, poor families, groups of families, or groups amounting to lineages were brought within the political and economic control of their more powerful neighbours. It is often difficult to see whether the subjection was of lineage to lineage or of individual family in one community to individual family in another community. Chen Han-seng refers to hereditary tenants in parts of Kwangtung who were known, in his term, as servile families. These 'families' regarded the 'clans' which kept them as their masters and, apart from farming the land they held in tenancy, gave unpaid service as labourers, servants, and watchmen.[2]

Liu quotes Ch'ên Shêng-shao as saying that in Chao-an the cultivated

[1] Liu apparently wrote as a Marxist. The more orthodox Chinese Marxist view seems to be that the lineage was a means by which the rich oppressed the poor among their own agnates. At least, this view emerges from Mao Tse-tung's account of his enquiries into the peasant movement in Hunan in the late 'twenties. He says that in China a man was 'usually subjected to the domination of three systems of authority': the state government, 'the system of the clan (clan authority), ranging from the central and branch ancestral temples to the head of the household', and 'the system of gods and spirits'. These three systems together with the authority of men over women were 'the four great cords that have bound the Chinese people and particularly the peasants'. Where the peasants organized themselves, 'the clan elders and administrators of the temple funds no longer dare oppress members of the clan or embezzle the funds'. The 'bad clan elders and administrators' had been overthrown, while the 'ancestral temple' no longer dared inflict 'cruel corporal and capital punishments like "beating", "drowning", and "burying alive".' The exclusion of women and peasants from the 'ancestral temple' became impossible, and at one place 'the poor peasants, not admitted to the banquets in the temples, swarmed in and ate and drank their fill, while the frightened local bullies, bad gentry and gentlemen in long gowns all took to their heels'. Mao Tse-tung, *Selected Works of Mao Tse-tung, Volume One*, London, 1954, pp. 45f.

[2] *Agrarian Problems*, pp. 57f.

fields of a small lineage situated near those of a large lineage had to be looked after by some member of the latter community or they would not be safe from depredation. One-thirteenth to one-tenth of the harvest had to be paid for this protection. Liu goes on: 'First, members of a small lineage had to be careful to humour the others. If there happened to be the slightest carelessness they would be vilified. They had not the power to defend themselves and there was no guarantee for their personal safety. Second, there was no guarantee for their property, which might be encroached upon or plundered. There was no other way to appease the powerful lineage than to give them one-thirteenth to one-tenth of their produce. Otherwise they could not exist. This brought servant lineages into being, and there was tribute to pay.' In a later context, however, Liu points out that the tribute paid in this fashion was not passed from one lineage to another but from a weak family of one lineage to a particular dominant member of a large lineage.

Again, the *Report on the New Territory at Hong Kong*, 1900, speaks of the centuries old fights between 'clans' and the common practice of combining groups of villages for offensive and defensive purposes;[1] and mentions that small villages or hamlets often placed themselves under the protection of 'large and influential clans' to which they referred all their complaints and looked for assistance if they were attacked, robbed, or involved in lawsuits. Sometimes the smaller villages paid their land tax through the influential lineages.[2]

Perhaps the most interesting aspect of the dominance of some lineages by others is the kinship ties between them; but on this question the literature I have read is silent. Did the powerful assert their status by taking wives or 'concubines' from the groups over which they sought to maintain control? Were servile families and inferior lineages always of different surnames from their masters? If agnation was usually absent from the tie between the dominant and the dominated groups then perhaps this was precisely the kind of situation in which a regular transfer of brides in one direction was most likely to be found. One can imagine a system in which the powerful group, while both giving their women to and taking women from other groups of equal status, contracted a series of marriages of the mother's brother's daughter variety with their subordinate groups which put these latter groups, as it were, doubly in the role of the inferior. But this is the purest speculation.

Miss Hu has pointed, however, to one type of situation in which the weakness of small lineages did not necessarily prompt them to seek protection through marriage, for she has shown how certain of the alliances based on linked surnames might be effected between the strong and the weak. At least, her example of the weak lineages of Hu and Yüan in Kwangtung joining 'with the widespread *tsu* of Ch'ên' on the basis of

[1] Op. cit., p. 4.

[2] Ibid., p. 20.

their common descent from the Emperor Shun[1] may indicate an alliance of this kind. On the other hand, rather than ally themselves either by marriage or agnation to strong communities, the weak might band together on the basis of linked surnames to confront their enemies. Miss Hu instances the lineages surnamed Chang, Kuan, Liu, and Chao in Kwangtung which organized common ancestral halls by virtue of descent traced from the four heroes of the Three Kingdoms, and by this means were able to withstand their more powerful neighbours.[2]

The far-flung tracing of agnatic descent, either through one or several linked surnames, and the wide casting of the net of marriage are aspects of the local system of south-east China which obviously pose another set of questions we cannot answer at the present. With how many other local communities was a particular lineage linked and over what geographical area did the social relations of individuals spread? Clearly, the widespread relations of marriage and no-marriage, sometimes defined by elaborate genealogies which covered a vast range of territory, were not likely to have come into being unless in fact the relations between lineages as such and between individual members in different lineages were effectively set within a very broad framework. But the dimensions of this framework remain obscure. At this point I may refer again to the fact that there appear to have been one or two local exceptions to the rule forbidding marriages between all bearers of one surname;[3] it is possible that in such unusual cases, in which the exogamous boundary was drawn at the localized lineage, marriage was called in to regulate the alliances between agnatically related lineages when the fact of agnation by itself was considered insufficient for this purpose. But, once more, in default of fuller information we cannot push the analysis further.

[1] Op. cit., p. 51.

[2] Ibid., p. 94.

[3] See p. 4 above.

14

The Lineage *vis-à-vis* the State

Some lineages, as we have seen, numbered among their members men who were actually or potentially officers in the bureaucracy. Across this bridge between lineage and state there passed a flow of influence which at once favoured the position of the lineage in its dealings with the government and secured the position of the gentry within the lineage in the face of their humbler agnates. But whether or not there were gentlemen in the lineage, the structure and ideology of government in China encouraged the exercise of local autonomy in the sense that, provided enough taxes were delivered up and violence and sedition were not apparent, the local community was expected to look after its own affairs. The low ratio of bureaucrats to population would have made it a virtual impossibility for the state to intervene effectively in a wide range of local affairs, even if the theory of government had promoted such an intervention. In fact, bureaucrats were discouraged from meddling in the life of the communities in their charge.

The construction of the legal system shows us clearly enough how, with the support of the state, a localized lineage was normally the largest unit within which disputes between its members were settled. The *ti-pao* was in theory charged with the duty of reporting certain serious offences committed in his community, but neither he nor the county magistrate was likely to be eager to draw attention to events which by their very existence demonstrated a breach of the harmony for which individual political persons were held responsible. In his judicial capacity the county magistrate constituted the lowest court in the official legal system, but the evidence shows us that only special cases which started in local communities actually found their way to his hearing.[1]

In the first place, the procedure in the official courts was burdensome and dangerous, the method of conducting a trial being calculated to frighten off the innocent as well as the guilty. Indeed, the unpleasantness of court procedure was well attuned to the official view that litigation was a bad thing and ought to be discouraged. Mrs. van der Sprenkel cites the reply of the K'ang-hsi Emperor to criticism of the courts: good citizens, he says, will refer their differences to some elder of their community; but as for those 'who are troublesome, obstinate, and quarrelsome, let

[1] As I have already indicated, I owe a great debt to Mrs. S. van der Sprenkel for guidance on the legal system.

them be ruined in the law-courts—that is the justice that is due to them'.[1]

In the second place, lineages were eager to guard their internal quarrels from the gaze of the world outside, and in attempting to keep their own peace in their own way they were abetted by a judicial system which, while in theory it might treat the individual at law on the merits of his case, in practice would normally be willing to accept the opinions of his influential lineage fellows against him in his suit. In this fashion the magistrate's court was a mechanism which the lineage could use as a sanction against its recalcitrant members, either by invoking its direful judgment in an extreme case or by withholding its own support from a member who, against its wishes, went to law.

'The lineage' was in this sense, of course, its political arm, a central body of men consisting of elders and influential individuals. Doubtless, the constitution of this body differed from community to community, but whenever a lineage was differentiated to the extent of numbering well-to-do merchants and gentry these men provided a locus of authority which accommodated, if it did not supplant, the authority of lineage and sub-lineage elders. The framework of political and judicial action being shaped to a central governing body within the lineage, it was not likely that quarrels and disputes would rise in an orderly fashion through the hierarchy of segments[2] or that private mediation would always successfully prevent important differences from finding their way to the apex of the system.[3] Moreover, the political function of the lineage's central body impelled it to take cognizance of offences such as violence and filial impiety which were regarded as infractions of public morality. The sanctions which lineage courts could bring to bear against offenders ranged from fines and corporal punishment to the stripping away of individual rights and privileges in the lineage; such sanctions could be enforced and entail serious consequences for the status of delinquents.

As we have seen illustrated in Lin's *The Golden Wing* for the modern period, disputes might be brought to an official court of law.[4] But we may suppose that disputes between parties belonging to the same lineage were less likely to gain a public hearing in this way than those between individuals or groups drawn from different lineages. However, in all kinds of cases the courts of the state were likely to be unpleasant to both sides to a dispute, and we may guess that the balancing of rights and duties between

[1] The source is T. R. Jernigan, *China in Law and Commerce*, New York, 1905, pp. 191f.

[2] Cf. above, p. 39.

[3] Miss Hu in her general survey says that 'official' trials by lineage heads were rare, mainly because of the intervention of 'unofficial arbitrators'. Hu, op. cit., p. 59. I suspect that the 'arbitrators' were themselves spokesmen for the lineage as a whole and that their success rested largely on the lineage authority which stood behind them.

[4] See above, pp. 39f.

members of different lineages was as much an aspect of their armed hostility or their concerted alliance as it was an aspect of a formal legal system.

The magistrate, who was of course both administrator and judge, had militia at his disposal to enforce the law; but this official arm was applied less to the support of individual or group claims to justice than to the control of outbreaks of violence directed against the state as such. From the very beginning of the Ch'ing dynasty in the seventeenth century the inhabitants of the provinces of Fukien and Kwangtung had shown themselves particularly resistant to the new central authority, and throughout their rule the Manchus had cause to be wary of the systematic opposition which manifested itself in the south-east. The turbulence for which this region was notorious arose not only from recurrent inter-lineage fights but also from the rebellious acts by which, from time to time, men of Kwangtung and Fukien sought to overthrow the dynasty occupying the throne.[1]

Over a long period of Chinese history rebellion was associated in fact or was thought by officialdom to be associated with certain forms of religious practice and organization. There was of course in China no established church with fixed dogmas against which the deviance of heretics could be measured; but there was, nevertheless, in the ideology of Confucianism a body of religious beliefs which were looked upon as expressing the ideal view of man in society and of society in nature. These beliefs in effect constituted a kind of official religion, which was ritually supported by imperial acts of worship and the maintenance of a system of Confucian temples at which administrators in office were obliged to attend. Embodying a national and bureaucratic view of society and its needs, the official religion was the religion of China *par excellence*; but neither its beliefs nor its practitioners were exempt from the influence of other religious elements. Taoism and Buddhism, whatever the view which might be taken of them officially from time to time, contributed to the ideas of men high in Chinese society and were freely drawn upon for the services of their priests. The institutions of these two religions were subjected to certain limitations by the state, while their ideas, practices, and clergy might often be the butts of purist Confucian criticism. Yet, although in a certain sense Taoism and Buddhism were unorthodox, they were a normal and expected part of the Chinese religious scene.[2]

[1] A further source of trouble in Kwangtung was the conflict between local Cantonese (Punti) and Hakka. The so-called Hakka-Punti war took place in the 1860s.

[2] Anybody who has read in the vast literature on the subject will know that brief statements on the constitution of Chinese religion are very difficult to draw up. In characterizing the 'official religion' and its relations to other systems I have been largely guided by M. Granet, *La religion des Chinois*, 2nd edn., Paris, 1951, especially chaps. III and IV. See also 'L'Esprit de la religion chinoise' in his *Etudes sociologiques sur la Chine*, Paris, 1953.

It was otherwise with the religious movements and groupings lying outside the tolerated institutions of Buddhism and Taoism. Despite the fact that its religious conceptions were often those of Buddhism and Taoism, sectarian religion failed to enjoy the benefit of governmental indifference. Heterodoxy was seen as a political threat to the authority of the state and accordingly persecuted. Whether or not officialdom was always justified in thinking that sectarian activity was aimed at its subversion, a sign that heterodox practice was afoot was likely to lead to official acts of repression. We know that much blood was shed in the putting down of religious groups which aroused the animosity of the state.

In Fukien and Kwangtung the government fought its main campaign of repression against secret societies the professed aims of which were the overthrow of the Ch'ing dynasty, but it also engaged in rooting out religious sects whose ostensible purposes at least were not directly concerned with political defiance. Indeed, we may say that clandestine activity in the south-east ranged itself along a continuum from quietist and contemplative sects at one end to violently anti-government societies at the other; but all such bodies found themselves in the displeasure of officialdom.

The secret societies, both because of their dramatic political importance and as a result of their export to European-controlled territories, have left a considerable literary trace behind them. The more strictly religious organizations, however, are poorly documented. J. J. M. de Groot, who strove hard to collect material on all aspects of Chinese religion during his stay in Fukien in the late nineteenth century, was able to make contact with heterodox sects only in consequence of an accident; he had heard of the existence of three sects in the south-eastern part of the province, but it was only in 1887, when the Prefect of Ch'üan-chou issued an order for their eradication, that material came into his hands. One of the sectarians confided certain documents to him for safekeeping.[1]

The three sects fell into two groups, both of them tracing their origin to the same founder and both pursuing salvation; but in their practices they differed. The founding patriarch had been born into the world (in Shantung) to show suffering humanity the path to salvation. He found himself at first persecuted by the government but finally received honours from the Emperor for, among other things, defeating a Tibetan theologian in disputation. He died in 1647.[2] The Sien-t'ien sect was essentially non-ritualist and domestic, small groups of one sex only congregating in their homes to practise a religion leading individuals to Nirvana. Their members

[1] *Sectarianism and Religious Persecution in China, A Page in the History of Religions*, Verhandelingen der Koninklijke Akademie van Wetenschappen te Amsterdam, Afdeeling Letterkunde, New Series, Part IV, nos. 1 and 2, Amsterdam, vol. I 1903, vol. II 1904 (pagination continuous), pp. 170ff.

[2] Ibid., pp. 180ff.

seem to have been drawn mainly from the well-to-do and the notable.[1] The Lung-hwa sect, of which the third sect was a branch, formed 'vegetarian halls' in private houses and practised an elaborate ritual. It incorporated a hierarchy of dignitaries, each higher rank representing 'a higher stage on the road to salvation'. By initiation men and women were changed into Devas.[2]

De Groot protests, and is perhaps correct in protesting, that sects of this kind were not connected with anti-dynastic activity.[3] Yet it was probably true of the Fukien sects, as it was true generally of cognate and similar sects in China at large, that their messianic and salvationist elements implicitly rejected orthodox principles of social organization and could serve as rallying points for men and women who were in some way dissatisfied with the society about them.[4] Of the precise nature of this dissatisfaction it is difficult to get a clear picture, nor can we see whether the Fukien sects were especially associated with town life and particular social layers of the population. De Groot's slender data will not take us far towards an analysis of this kind. On the other hand, what we know about the interplay of religious and rebellious activity in south-eastern China in modern times indicates that it was the organizations of the secret society type which commanded the largest followings and produced the greatest and most widespread upheavals in both town and countryside.

In the West we are inclined to think at once of the T'ai-p'ing Rebellion when we turn our minds to the great disturbances of the peace in the China of the nineteenth century. Although most of his following was later to come from people outside his native province, the leader of the rebellion was a Kwangtung Hakka whose background in society and ideas was precisely that which concerns us in a study of south-eastern China. Yet, although the T'ai-p'ing Rebellion was the most successful rising of its time and came near to unseating the Ch'ing dynasty a couple of generations before it finally fell from power, it in fact lay askew from the main line of secret society activity. Despite its conventional name it was in fact a revolutionary movement which sought to remake Chinese society according to new principles.[5] The secret societies, in contrast, did not

[1] Ibid., pp. 185ff.

[2] Ibid., pp. 197ff.

[3] Ibid., p. 252.

[4] On the White Lotus and other clandestine religious sects in China in general see, for example, de Groot, op. cit., passim; Chan Wing-tsit, *Religious Trends in Modern China*, New York, 1953, pp. 156ff.; K. W. Reichelt, trans. J. Tetlie, *Religion in Chinese Garment*, London, 1951, pp. 165ff.; B. Favre, *Les sociétés secrètes en Chine, Origine—rôle historique—situation actuelle*, Paris, 1933, pp. 78ff.

[5] See especially G. E. Taylor, 'The Taiping Rebellion: Its Economic Background and Social Theory', *The Chinese Social and Political Science Review*, vol. XVI, no. 6, Jan. 1933; Teng Ssu-yü, *New Light on the History of the Taiping Rebellion*, Harvard University Press, Cambridge, Mass., 1950 (mimeographed); and Vincent Yu-chung Shih, 'Interpretations of the Taiping Tien-Kuo by Non-communist Chinese Writers', *The Far Eastern Quarterly*, vol. X, no. 3, 1951.

manifest themselves in a unique outburst, were ideologically rebellious in the sense that they proclaimed their aim to be the restoration of the Ming dynasty to the throne, and never succeeded in establishing a thoroughgoing alternative government over a wide area.

In the south-east the secret society scene was dominated by the organizations usually known collectively as the Heaven and Earth League or the Triad Society. This group of societies is definable by its standardized ritual, of which we have a number of records. Alongside the Triad there were probably other secret societies ritually distinct, but the concentration of the literature on the Triad apparently reflects the supreme position which this group of organizations enjoyed.[1] Of the origin of the Triad we know very little, and while it is possible that it came into being before the Ch'ing dynasty, its activities are recorded only well after the time indicated by its motto 'Overthrow Ch'ing, restore Ming'. In the myth-history of the Triad, which plays a major role in its initiation ritual, the founding of the society is traced to events taking place during the early years of the Ch'ing dynasty, when the monks belonging to a monastery in north Fukien were treacherously turned upon after they had rendered help in battle to the ruling emperor. The five monks who survived the destruction of the monastery set up the anti-Manchu organization founding five lodges in Fukien, Kwangtung, Yunnan, Hukwang (that is, Hunan and Hupeh), and Chekiang. Certainly Fukien and Kwangtung appear to have been the centre of Triad activities. When the 'censor' of Hukwang memorialized the emperor in 1841 he reported

[1] The English words league, brotherhood, and so on, which appear in the various names for the Triad are all translations of one Chinese word, *hui*, which bears the general meaning of an association. The main sources on which I have drawn for data on the secret societies in Fukien and Kwangtung are as follows: T. J. Newbold and General Wilson, 'The Chinese Triad Society of the Tien-ti-huih', *Journal of the Royal Asiatic Society of Great Britain and Ireland*, vol. VI, 1841; G. Schlegel, *Thian Ti Hwui, The Hung League or Heaven-Earth-League*, Batavia, 1866; W. A. Pickering, 'Chinese Secret Societies', *Journal of the Royal Asiatic Society, Straits Branch*, Part I, no. 1, 1878 and Part II, no. 3, 1879; C. Gutzlaff, 'On the Secret Triad Society of China, chiefly from Papers belonging to the Society found at Hong Kong', *Journal of the Royal Asiatic Society*, vol. VIII, 1846; 'Oath Taken by Members of the Triad Society and Notices of its Origin', *The Chinese Repository*, vol. XVIII, no. 6, 1849; [A. Wylie] 'Secret Societies in China', *Shanghae Almanac for* 1854 *and Miscellany*, Shanghai, 1853; W. Stanton, *The Triad Society or Heaven and Earth Association*, Hong Kong, 1900 (reprint of articles in *China Review*, vols. XXI and XXII); G. Hughes, 'The Small Knife Rebels (An Unpublished Chapter of Amoy History)', *The China Review*, vol. I, no. 4, 1872/3; S. Couling, *The Encyclopaedia Sinica*, Shanghai, 1917; H. M. Cordier, *Les sociétés secrètes chinoises*, Paris, 1888; J. S. M. Ward and W. G. Stirling, *The Hung Society or the Society of Heaven and Earth*, vol. I, London, 1925; J. S. M. Ward, *The Hung Society. . .*, vols. II and III, London, 1926; P. Pelliot, 'The Hung Society' (Compte-rendu of Ward and Stirling, *The Hung Society*), *T'oung Pao*, vol. XXV, Leiden, 1928; de Groot, op. cit.; Favre, op. cit.; J. Hutson, 'Chinese Secret Societies', *The China Journal*, vol. IX, nos. 4, 5 and 6, Shanghai, 1928.

the head lodge of the Triad to be in Fukien and the second in Kwangtung.[1]

It may be that the organization of the Triad into five provincial lodges was purely notional and ritual. All we know for a certainty is that from the end of the eighteenth century onwards Triad groups made their opposition to the state felt. The first Triad rebellion seems to have broken out in 1787 in Formosa, and from that date until 1856 there were uprisings attributed to the Triad in Formosa, Kiangsi, Kwangtung, Kwangsi, and Fukien. After the end of the T'ai-p'ing Rebellion, during which Triad groups brought off their greatest coups, secret society activity of an open kind seems to have waned, and it appears just possible that, if the various Triad groups were co-ordinated, the centre of their organization had by this time shifted out of China itself to Singapore, where a Chinese settlement composed of emigrants from Fukien and Kwangtung conducted its own affairs independently of the British administration and by means of Triad lodges.[2] However, the decline of Triad rebelliousness in the later part of the nineteenth century by no means evidences a falling away in its membership and influence. The British found Triad groups in the piece of Kwangtung they took over at the end of the century,[3] and there is little doubt that the inhabitants of Kwangtung and Fukien continued their secret society organization into recent times.[4]

Triad groups must have been widely spread through the south-east, and, at least in the heyday of their power, able to call upon large numbers of

[1] Wylie, op. cit. Note also the language of the Ch'ing penal code in the Appendix on Rebellion and Renunciation of Allegiance in Staunton, op. cit., pp. 546ff. 'All persons who, without being related or connected by intermarriage, establish a brotherhood or other association among themselves, by the ceremonial of tasting blood, and burning incense, shall be guilty of an intent to commit the crime of rebellion. . . . The punishment of the brotherhood associated by the initiation with blood, which exists in the province of *Fo-kien*, shall be conformable to the aforementioned regulations. . . . All those vagabonds and disorderly persons who have been known to assemble together, and to commit robberies, and other acts of violence, under the particular designation of "*Tien-tee-whee*", or "The Association of Heaven and Earth", shall, immediately after seizure and conviction, suffer death by being beheaded. . . .' See also Wylie, op. cit., who says that in 1810 a clause was inserted in the penal code stating that 'the lawless banditti of Fuk-kien and Kwangtung are forming plots and have resuscitated the . . . *Teen te hwuy*. . . .'

[2] Cf. H. A. Giles, *Freemasonry in China*, Amoy, 1880, p. 27. On the various Triad uprisings in China see de Groot, op. cit., pp. 340ff.; Couling, op. cit., p. 572; and Wylie, op. cit. Stanton, op. cit., pp. 10ff., has similar data, but, in addition, lists Triad incidents in Kwangtung in 1886 and 1892.

[3] See *Report on the New Territory at Hong Kong*, 1900, p. 13.

[4] The Hung League, which is another name for the Triad, ramified to all parts of the world in which Chinese from the south-east settled. A world congress of the League is said to have been held in Shanghai in July 1946 at which a decision was taken to organize the Hung League Democratic Party. See C. Glick and Hong Sheng-hwa, *Swords of Silence, Chinese Secret Societies—Past and Present*, New York, 1947, p. 261.

followers. In the turbulent time of the T'ai-p'ing Rebellion in the middle of the last century Triad forces took and held for some months the cities of Shanghai and Amoy, and captured some smaller cities near Canton.

We have now to ask what the relation was between secret society grouping and the kind of lineage organization existing in the area where the Triad flourished. In a famous work which, for all its sinological shortcomings, continues to impress students of Chinese society, Max Weber asserted: 'To the present day, a considerable proportion of all politically dangerous "secret societies" has consisted of sibs.' Weber based his generalization on slender evidence, confusing the T'ai-p'ing Rebellion and its relation to the village of its leader with secret societies.[1] In fact, the evidence suggests that secret society not only cut across lineage organization but also tended to mark the line dividing the rich and influential from the poor and weak in differentiated lineages.

Teng Ssu-yü writes of the secret societies 'representing rural poverty-stricken peasants and urban unemployed workers and scoundrels'.[2] His characterization may be overdrawn, but it at least has the merit of showing us that some sort of solidarity was expressed in Triad activity which did not chime with the solidarity of lineages standing opposed to one another. It is true that European observers sometimes thought the secret societies to involve a very wide span of the class structure. Writing in the 1840's, for example, two such observers stressed the inclusiveness of Triad membership. 'It is known,' one of them said, 'that the Society includes among its members persons in almost every rank of official and private life throughout the provinces. . . .'[3] The other asserted: 'All classes are permitted to join; and amongst the Triad Society, there are at present mandarins of low degree, police runners, soldiers, merchants, brothel-keepers, gamblers, and needy characters of every description. . . .'[4] Moreover, it is clear that there were troubled times when gentlemen did not hold themselves aloof from the rebelliousness to which by ideology

[1] *The Religion of China, Confucianism and Taoism*, trans. and ed. H. H. Gerth, Glencoe, Illinois, 1951, p. 86. A number of earlier writers were under the impression that there was a close association between the Rebellion and the Triad, but, although the secret societies may have paved the way for the Rebellion and some Triad groups been in touch with the army of the Heavenly Kingdom, there was no formal co-ordination of their activities. Ritually and ideologically the Rebellion and the Triad were distinct and opposed. For a summary of the evidence on this point see Teng Ssu-yü, op. cit., pp. 26ff.

[2] Ibid., p. 28.

[3] 'Oath Taken by Members of the Triad Society. . . .', p. 36.

[4] Gutzlaff, op. cit., p. 364. Cf. Stanton's version of one of the Triad initiation oaths, p. 62: 'After entering the Hung doors, whether industrious labourers, diligent students, scholars, farmers, mechanics, merchants, physicians, diviners, astrologers, geomancers, physiognomists, actors, singers, executioners, lictors, Confucianists, Buddhists, or Taoists, you must not get drunk and by fighting and riotous conduct cause trouble.'

and interest they were normally hostile.[1] I do not say, therefore, that the data are unambiguous, but I think on balance it is right to conclude that the secret societies were essentially movements which, while they may have found some of their leaders among members of officialdom and the gentry, expressed an opposition to the state characteristic of the poor and the peasantry.

In the account of the so-called Small Knife Rebels' attack on Amoy in 1853 we certainly can see the class elements involved. This secret society, which was a branch of or connected with the Triad, was established in Amoy, some five years before the attack, by a Singapore Chinese who was a comprador in the service of Jardine, Matheson and Co. Alarmed at the rapid growth of the society, the provincial government sought to put it down. Tan, the founder, was arrested and tortured to death. The leadership now passed to a man of low extraction who managed to bring over to his side a merchant, 'once possessed of great wealth', who was being squeezed by officialdom. Some two thousand members of the society rose under their new leader in his native village and marched to Amoy. There they found eight thousand fellow members under a council of six men, three of whom were Singapore Chinese. This army succeeded in taking over and holding Amoy against the government for several months. Apart from their prominence in the supreme leadership of the uprising, Singapore Chinese were found also among the holders of subordinate positions, and we know enough about overseas Chinese at this period to say that these Singapore leaders could hardly have ranked as gentlemen.[2] Furthermore, the general support enjoyed by the Amoy rising appears to have rested on the common people.[3]

[1] Wylie, op. cit., says that troops and officials concerned in the suppression of the Yao rising in 1831 were found to be connected with the Triad, and that in the Triad capture of Shanghai most of the government officials seem to have been similarly connected. During the crisis in imperial affairs from the time of the T'ai-p'ing Rebellion onwards some of the literati shifted their allegiance back and forth between government and rebels. Cf. Chang Chung-li, op. cit., p. 70. For what seems a greatly exaggerated picture of secret society influence in high places see P. d'Enjoy, 'Associations, congrégations et sociétés secrètes chinoises', *Bulletins et Mémoires de la Société d'Anthropologie de Paris*, Series V, vol. V, 1904.

[2] This summary of the 1853 Amoy rising is based on Hughes, op. cit. Note that the attack on and capture of Shanghai in the same year seems to have been connected with the same type of secret society (Hsiao Tao Hui) and to have displayed a prominence of men from the south-eastern provinces. See Hummel, ed., op. cit., vol. 1, pp. 118f. (The leader of the Hsiao Tao Hui in the Shanghai adventure was a Kwangtungese who had been for a time an interpreter to Western merchants. The role of the comprador element in the uprisings of this period and the significance of class changes in urban society for an understanding of the whole question of resistance to government are important matters which, however, lie outside my present enquiry.) Stanton, op. cit., p. 16, speaks of Shanghai as having been taken in the first place by men from Fukien and Kwangtung.

[3] Lin-le (Lindley), op. cit., vol. I, p. 166, says that the rebels were greatly supported by the ordinary people from the surrounding villages, but 'the wealthy classes remained aloof from both contending parties. . . .'

Opposition to the state and the ties across kin groups entailed by this alignment are evidenced very clearly for us in the oaths which formed part of the ritual of Triad initiation. By this initiation unrelated men were turned ritually into brothers, and becoming brothers in this fashion they then assumed in respect of one another many of the obligations of agnatic kinship. Perhaps the most striking of the consequences of membership was the inability to marry or have sexual relations with the widow of a fellow member;[1] the widow of a ritual brother, like the widow of a true agnate, was traditionally forbidden.[2] The incest rules applicable to agnates appear generally to have been invoked to control the relations between members and the daughters of their fellows,[3] the bar clearly being an aspect of the solidarity ideally required of men bound in ritual brotherhood.

The Triad initiation, of which we have several versions, must have been a highly dramatic performance calculated, by means of its religious acts, to impress upon new members the nature of the step they had taken.[4] There has been considerable speculation on the meaning of the various parts and symbols of the ritual,[5] but perhaps Sun Yat-sen, whose contact with it was highly professional, comes closest to seizing its essential character when he says that the 'initiation ceremony of the Hung League was cast in the form of a play. . . . By means of a play, deeds of injustice could be portrayed and a sense of revenge could be aroused'.[6] Now it was not likely that such a religious performance, heterodox and seditious, would attract men whose gentry status, quite apart from their personal feelings, directed their ideas and their political interests towards the

[1] See Ward and Stirling, op. cit., p. 67, and Stanton, op. cit., p. 64.

[2] See above, p. 31.

[3] See Stanton, op. cit., p. 61: 'After entering the Hung doors, your brethren's parents become your parents, and your brethren's wives and daughters become your sisters-in-law and nieces'. See also ibid., p. 67: 'He who commits adultery with a brother's wife, or fornication with a brother's daughter, shall be put to death without mercy'. The sisters of fellow-members are not mentioned, and it is clear that there was no attempt to extend widely the agnatic prohibitions. In Stanton's version of the Thirty-Six Oaths the last one reads: 'After entering the Hung doors, you must not marry, commit adultery with or kidnap and sell deceased brothers' widows, so that, in after days, your children and grandchildren may marry with theirs according to propriety, and be fortunate, prosperous, and ever rich and honourable, with prosperous children and grandchildren to succeed them'. Ibid., p. 64.

[4] These versions set out the ritual but are not necessarily accounts of what actually ever took place. However, we have two eye-witness accounts of initiation among overseas Chinese in the Straits Settlements in the nineteenth century. See the description given by Abdullah Munshi (Raffles's Malay teacher) of the rites he saw in the 1820's: A. H. Hill, 'The Hikayat Abdullah, An Annotated Translation', *Journal of the Malayan Branch Royal Asiatic Society*, vol. XXVIII, part 3, pp. 184ff. Pickering saw an initiation in the Straits in the 1870s; op. cit., Part II.

[5] See especially Ward and Stirling, op. cit.

[6] Quoted in Glick and Hong, op. cit., p. 55.

maintenance of the official systems of beliefs and authority. The secret societies were not only a challenge to the security of Manchu rule but also, by drawing on the general fund of forbidden religion, constituted a threat to the religious ideology officially, if not personally, embodied in members of the gentry class.

Important as the religious elements may have been in the secret societies, they seem to have provided them less with a driving force than a solemn apparatus for sanctifying rebellion. It may well be that the fact that we have records of the ritual of initiation only is a mark of the secondary importance played by religion in secret society activity. The sects on the other hand approached the sociological model of the deviant religious movement, even though what they deviated from was less than a highly organized church with a clear-cut body of doctrine. They were groups of freely adhering devotees concentrating on problems of salvation which the pursuit of ordinary religious practices was inadequate to tackle. Leadership in both secret societies and clandestine sects must not only have cut across the group lines drawn by the conventional structure of society but also have thrown up individuals whose spiritual or political qualities overrode the principles of authority enshrined in the agnatic and class systems. If sects and 'lodges' of the secret societies were found in highly differentiated lineages we may suspect that they gave expression to the latent opposition of the common people to the representatives within their communities of the centralized government.

In south-eastern China, therefore, there would appear to have been two alignments of conflict which cut across each other. In some contexts lineages were ranged against lineages; in other contexts lineages, or class sections of them, were united in their common hostility to the state. It may be that the disturbances in Fukien and Kwangtung in the nineteenth century were less productive of general chaos than they might have been precisely because this twofold alignment of conflict prevented *la guerre à outrance* in either direction. John Scarth, whose observations on the 'anarchy' of northern Kwangtung in the 1850s I referred to early in this essay,[1] comments: 'Strange as it may appear, this desperate state of clannish anarchy has proved to be the sole safety of this part of China from worse anarchy at the hands of the rebels. The people were so given to quarrelling that they would not agree to fight.'[2]

The provinces of Kwangtung and Fukien were remarkable in China for three things: large-scale lineage organization, inter-lineage fights, and secret societies of the Triad type. We may well suspect that these phenomena were not randomly associated, but that in fact they were functionally connected. Alliances against the state formed by the secret societies counterbalanced the opposition generated between lineage communities when agnatic organization was carried to a high pitch. To test this

[1] See above, p. 8.

[2] Op. cit., pp. 52f.

hypothesis we should need to look in detail at the way in which both large-scale lineages and 'lodges' of the Triad were distributed through the two provinces. If we could establish that these two types of organization flourished together we should be much nearer an understanding of the importance of the Triad in the south-east.

The violent opposition to other lineages and to the state was merely a phase of the system by which a particular lineage was bound to its society. By acts of hostility it could from time to time assert its independence in a world where in fact it could enjoy no lasting independence. It needed the women from other lineages and, in the last resort, whatever its truculence, it was tied to the state. It is precisely in the ambivalence towards the state that we see the crucial position of those lineage members who were also members of the gentry. They could act to moderate and restrain open hostility; they could mediate and soften the demands for taxes and reprisals made by the state upon their communities; they could bring the prestige of the bureaucratic system into their lineages and yet strengthen them against the system. The differentiated lineage was not autonomous, not simply because it was part of a centralized polity, but also because actual and potential agents of bureaucratic control were incorporated into its community. The ideas and authority represented by the lineage gentry might be resisted, but the gentry were at the same time sources of general benefit. Acts of defiance by the lineage directed against the state in one sense weakened the lineage gentry; yet in another sense these acts enhanced their strength, for the protection which they could afford had in the long run to be called into play.

15

Discussion

It would be as well if, having by now set out a number of facts about lineage organization in Fukien and Kwangtung, I repeated the warning I gave in the Preface to this essay. Many of these facts are drawn from sources which describe only a very few localized lineages; and in the vast area covered by the term 'south-eastern China' they may possibly be unusual. Only a much more ambitious piece of research than I have undertaken will be able to show the extent to which the composite picture I have put together corresponds to something we might fairly call representative and typical. On the other hand, since my purpose has not been merely to detail a collection of interesting facts but rather to come to some general conclusions about the nature of rural society in Fukien and Kwangtung, I propose to put caution aside and try to make some suggestions which may serve partly to explain what we appear now to know and partly to provide lines for further study. The usefulness of armchair anthropology lies not simply in its collation of existing knowledge but also in its questioning and its forward-looking suggestions.

Slender as the data are, they furnish in the first place an hypothesis on the interconnexions between social differentiation and the scale of the localized lineage. It seems on the whole that the larger lineages were the more highly differentiated internally in terms of social status. Now, this is not merely to say that as a lineage grew in numbers its members were likely to differentiate themselves progressively; what probably happened in essence was that social differentiation and growth in numbers were constantly reinforcing each other. Increasing differentiation in status brought benefits to the lineage as a whole which provided incentives for people to stay within it. Growth in membership created the possibility of adding to the corporate resources which furnished the basis for further social promotion.

It has been pointed out that the higher rates of tenancy in the rice areas of China may be due in part to higher productivity.[1] Where people produced a surplus they invested in more land, a commodity attractive of course not only for its security but also for its prestige. Agricultural conditions in the south-east seem to have favoured a form of this process. Invested surplus deriving from a generally fertile terrain concentrated

[1] Cf. Buck, *Land Utilization in China*, p. 196.

land-ownership in a relatively small number of hands, while the growth of the treaty ports in the nineteenth century tended to accentuate the process by bringing urban capital into the rural area. In modern times only some third of the farming households of Fukien and Kwangtung owned all the land they worked; in the Canton delta some 85 per cent of the farmers were said to be tenants.[1] As Fei and Chang rightly argue in their Yunnan study,[2] there is no simple and direct relationship between the productivity of the soil and the concentration of land-ownership, but at least the south-eastern rice economy appears to have been one in which the possibility of creating and investing surpluses in land was well realized.

Yet the high rate of tenancy in the south-east is not, for the present argument, the crucial fact. Landlordism by itself would not explain why large lineage communities held together. The essential feature of land tenure in Fukien and Kwangtung was the important role ascribed to the corporate holdings of lineages and their segments. When the landlord was often the agnatic group of which the tenant was a member, and when being a member of such a group meant having a prior right to tenancy, the poorer people had every reason to stay in the community rather than go to try their luck elsewhere. In other words, the surplus economy of the region, mediated by the institution of collective ownership, created a fund of property which tended to keep lineage members at home. When corporate land was either rented out to members of the corporation or circulated for use among them, the privilege proved a centripetal force.

The benefits derived from corporate property were not, as we have seen, equally distributed. The elite of a lineage, exercising its power, probably pocketed more than its fair share. Yet the humble member of a lineage owning large corporate resources was still in a better position than his analogue in a poor lineage, for he had greater security, greater prestige *vis-à-vis* the outside world, and at least the hope that in time he and his descendants might make their way closer to the central position from which benefits were controlled. We thus have the economic facet of the paradox by which the contrast between high and low status reinforced the integrity of the lineage. It may be true that in the popular sense the poor were exploited by the rich; but even as they were exploited they enjoyed privileges important enough to make their continued residence worth-while.

Not all lineages owned corporate property and some had little. Perhaps they were unfavourably situated from an agricultural point of view and could never produce important surpluses. Perhaps even when the surpluses were produced the first step in the reciprocating system was, for some reason beyond our knowledge, never taken, so that increasing population and increasing corporate property were not set going in a series of

[1] Tawney, *Land and Labour in China*, p. 37.

[2] Fei Hsiao-tung and Chang Chih-i, *Earthbound China, A Study of Rural Economy in Yunnan*, London, 1949, pp. 6f., 305f.

mutually promoting events. The small, relatively undifferentiated lineage was one characterized not only by an absence of rich people but also by a lack of lineage property.

In the period we have been examining there could have been little new land to take up, except in the hilly area which in any case was not of great value for cultivation. If men in poor lineages sought their livelihood elsewhere they must have emigrated to the towns or overseas, married without dignity into better-off households in other villages, gone to work as labourers in other communities, or perhaps managed in some cases to rent land elsewhere. Except possibly from overseas remittances, capital was not likely to flow back into a poor lineage in any considerable quantity. A lineage with corporate resources large enough to keep its members in the village might, of course, stimulate the growth of its population to the point where increasing numbers outpaced the accumulation of common property; there was presumably some optimum size beyond which benefits decreased to the point of promoting emigration. Yet of course a rich lineage was one which did not rely solely on agriculture for its investable income, and population pressure on the land would not necessarily limit its ability to provide attractive benefits. Trading, usury, and bureaucratic office were sources of money which could reinforce the position of a lineage by bringing capital into the system from outside. It is important to distinguish between the improbability of the poor members of such a lineage making much headway in accumulating wealth, and the possibility that the lineage as a whole grew richer through the activities of its elite. Land, as far as the latter-day poor peasant was concerned, may have bred no land, but a corporate holding of land and other property by his lineage gave him an advantage over the member of a lineage without such common resources. Indeed, we should say that what is really important in classifying lineages for the purpose of this argument is not the average level of wealth as measured by the resources controlled by individual households, but the total sum of corporate property from which these households actually or potentially drew benefit.

In order to explain why some lineages rather than others managed to hold their members together I have adduced the factor of common property. We may well wonder why rich individuals should place their wealth at the disposal of their lineage or one of its segments instead of leaving it to be enjoyed exclusively by their immediate descendants. Chen Han-seng assures us that the 'sense of family responsibility' is such in China, and especially Kwangtung, that while 'the individual family likes to enjoy the prestige of a big land owner, it considers it just as important to strengthen the economic status of the main stem of the family, that is the clan, as to bolster up the security of the direct descendants'.[1] Doubtless part of the answer to our question is to be found in some such statement as this. There is an initial assumption in the system that the lineage as a whole

[1] *Agrarian Problems*, p. 30.

must be protected and provided for, and that those who are rich are morally right to divert from their sons a portion of property which will serve the community. But I do not think that this explanation by itself takes us far enough. In the discussion on ancestor worship I pointed out the intimate connexion between the endowment of ancestral halls and lineage segmentation: a new segment came into being when property was set aside to finance a hall for it. At the same time I argued that lineage segmentation in this fashion was an aspect also of social differentiation, in the sense that any section of a segment which wished to mark a new identity for itself on the basis of its superior status *vis-à-vis* other sections could turn itself into a sub-segment by establishing a hall. Property vested in the new genealogical unit and added to the fund in succeeding generations was, therefore, not so much directed to the support of the 'clan' as to the maintenance of what, in the first place, was a small unit in the 'clan'. As time went on, of course, the numbers of people deriving benefit from the property might grow, and a later observer might conclude that the common property was intended to bolster up a very large segment of the lineage; in fact, from the point of view of those who established or donated property to the fund, the benefits were to go to their immediate agnates and not to a large section of the community. If men added to the property held by the lineage or its sub-lineages they were doubtless doing what Chen had in mind; they were strengthening a major group in their society. If they endowed segments lower in the hierarchy they were more concerned with their own status and that of the restricted range of agnates with whom they identified themselves closely.

The argument that in the south-east the existence of large-scale localized lineages partly depended upon the maintenance of corporate property and that this property was probably made possible at an earlier stage of settlement by the relatively high productivity of the land, is one which may have a bearing on the more general problem of the uneven distribution of large localized lineages in China. Fukien and Kwangtung especially and, to a considerable extent, central China displayed a system in which villages tended to be composed of the members of single lineages. Elsewhere in the country there was no marked incidence of the large-scale single-lineage community. Naturally, there may have been at work a very complicated set of factors to produce this distribution, but we should perhaps consider as important among them the possibility of accumulating corporate property on the basis of an agricultural economy in a favourable milieu. Large-scale localized lineages by no means appear throughout the rice-growing areas of China, but it may be that the cultivation of rice was one of the conditions predisposing local communities of agnates to build themselves into large settlements. Of course, measured against the other sources of wealth drawn upon during the history of a successful localized lineage, the surplus from agriculture may seem unimpressive; all I am suggesting is that it may have been the surplus accumulated in a highly productive rice economy in the first place which helped to set going the system of corporate property which in turn promoted the development of large agnatic communities.

The benefits to be derived from membership of a differentiated lineage in the south-east were not, of course, only economic. Carried to its full extent differentiation in status created and retained within the community men whose social position as scholars and bureaucrats conferred prestige and power upon their lineage as a whole. Not only, therefore, could the lineage accumulate tangible property in which the humbler men shared to some extent, but it might also build up a collective reputation for learning and gentility which was in fact based on the activities of very few members but which spread its light over all the others. Seen from the outside a lineage was a corporate group which, at least in certain circumstances, was taken to be undifferentiated. Facing his glorious agnates the poor tenant farmer deferred and was humble; facing the outer world he might stand as a member of a group endowed with general prestige and general influence. In a lineage which contained only poor farmers and small traders an individual was humble not only in his own right but also by virtue of the meagreness of the status of the lineage as a whole.

There were legal and political benefits to be derived from remaining a lowly member of a powerful lineage. In theory the state dealt with its individual citizens or their closest kin, but in practice it treated them as members of organized local communities. If in the conduct of lawsuits and administrative and fiscal matters the lineage could be spoken for by gentlemen, then the peasant enjoyed a protection and advantage which he was not likely to want to forgo. As long as the administrative system was borne by a small corps of officers who had runners rather than representatives in the villages, and as long as the bureaucracy recruited its officials from a class well established in the countryside, the relations between magistrate and village leadership were more profitable to the members of strong lineages than to those of weak lineages.

Of course there were losses as well as gains to the poor and uninfluential member of a highly differentiated lineage. Because he stood away from the centre of power his benefits tended to be residual and his effective control of the property of which he was a nominal owner was slight. The very property in which he had rights might be used to increase the personal wealth and status of those already in power; land, for example, which had been set aside to finance education might in practice serve only to school the sons of the lineage elite, while the income from common property, both by subterfuge and through a system of ritual preferences, might to a large extent find its way into the pockets of the influential. Yet the unity of the lineage *vis-à-vis* the outside world rested precisely on the strength which this concentration of power promoted. It was better to be a little fish in a big pond than a little fish in a small pond.

The advantages of being a member of a strong lineage lay not only in the dealings with the state but also in the relations with other lineages. We have seen that organized violence between lineages appears to have been recurrent. It was clearly better to remain within a community which had the advantage of manpower and economic resources for weapons and fortification. The small and weak lineages could hold their own only by banding together or placing themselves for a price under the protection of strong neighbours.

I have spoken earlier of drawing a composite picture of the lineage in Fukien and Kwangtung, but in fact the trend of the present argument suggests that, in order to seize the totality of rural society in these two provinces, we require not a single picture but a variety of pictures. If we had more and better data we might be able to give a number of examples of localized lineages arranged on a scale from least to most differentiated in social status. As it is, we can express this range of variation only by means of models of the polar opposites of the scale. Let us attempt to set out the characteristics of two extreme types, A and Z, of the south-eastern Chinese lineage. In contrasting them we shall see how wide the variation might be and how, knowing a few facts about a particular real lineage, we could guess at where to place it along the continuum from A to Z.

Lineage type A is small in numbers, with a population of two or three hundred souls. Apart from one or two small shopkeepers and a few craftsmen, its members are cultivators of small pieces of land which they own outright or rent from external landlords. Their general level of income is low. They own no common property except for a plot of land which is the grave site of the founding ancestor. Any increase in the pressure of population on resources leads either to a failure to marry and have children or to migration in search of work, petty trade, a berth in a strange village as a married-in son-in-law, or membership in the army or a bandit gang. In order to protect itself from the assaults and insults of other lineages and to mediate its contacts with the state it places itself under the dominance of a strong lineage; for this protection its pays in services or 'taxes'. Apart from domestic ancestor worship, which is conducted before the simplest of instruments, and annual rites at the tomb of the founder of lineage, there is no ancestral cult. There is no recorded genealogy, individual men being placed in the system merely by their generation (which is indicated by their personal names) and their ascription to one or other of the sub-lineages which trace their origin from the sons of the founder. No genealogical unit stands between the sub-lineage and the household, nor is there any tendency for groups of closely related households to co-operate economically and ritually. Headship of the sub-lineages and the lineage passes to the oldest men in the senior generation of these units, no other formal leaders being recognized. Disputes are brought before sub-lineage and lineage heads, but when they cannot be resolved a gentleman from the protecting community is brought in to try to reach a settlement. In this model of type A only the last statement is pure guesswork; the other statements are based, at most at one remove, on facts set out in the main body of this essay.

Lineage type Z numbers two or three thousand people, among whom there are retired bureaucrats, the families of bureaucrats in office, and gentlemen aspiring to officialdom. There are also some well-to-do merchants, a proportion of small traders and craftsmen, and a mass of cultivators, the greater part of whom work land held in the name of the lineage or its various segments. The majority of the members of the lineage are poor, but the lineage as a whole is corporately rich in land, ancestral halls, and such other items of property as rice mills. Men tend to stay within the community, and even if they go out of it in order to take office or engage in business they leave their families behind, return when they are older, and send money back. There is a hierarchy of ancestral halls, but it is not symmetrical; that is to say, some sub-lineages are more segmented in respect of halls than other sub-lineages, while some branches of one sub-lineage are more segmented in the same fashion than other branches. This asymmetry corresponds to an uneven distribution through the lineage of men of high status and wealth. The written genealogy plays an important part in the system, both linking the lineage to other lineages in connexions which bring prestige and useful alliances, and showing the membership of property-owning segments. Regular rites of ancestor worship in the halls express the existence of particular segments, and at the same time, by segregating tablets and discriminating among the worshippers, underline the status differences in the community. As in type A, genealogical headmen are appointed, but here their position is overshadowed by that of the gentry (if they are not themselves gentry) who constitute, with help from the richer merchants, a central government of lineage affairs. Despite the existence of a hierarchy of segments, disputes tend to be referred to mediators drawn from the lineage elite, while in extreme cases the elite and the genealogical heads may sit as a court in formal judgment. The statements in this model of type Z will clearly be recognized as the facts to which the greater part of this essay has clung.

I have spoken of A and Z as models. Neither is a statement of an average of all the lineages of one type which I have been able to examine. They are rather summaries of characteristics which I imagine we should find if we were able to study extreme cases. They are explanatory models in the sense that, by implication, they show the interconnexions between elements; in A smallness of scale and a rudimentary genealogical segmentation go with a low level of corporate property and a lack of social differentiation, while in Z the complementary correlations are shown. Now these polar models may never have had their analogues in reality, but they express what we may assume would have happened if certain conditions had been taken to extremes. It may be that if we built a kind of compromise model M, which was intermediate in characteristics to A and Z, we should in fact be closer to general historical reality; but by beginning with A and Z, as sharply delineated contrasts, instead of some more 'realistic' model, M, we are able, I think, more clearly to set up a mental framework within which we may accommodate the stretch of reality when we come to know it from a whole series of concrete cases.

A and Z are constructs standing above some cruder appreciation of reality—or rather they would be if we had a better knowledge of reality. Because this essay is based on slender material, it can be fairly urged against me that the constructs are more works of imagination than abstractions from real life. But I think that even if we had at our disposal a body of good historical and field material on south-east China, the method I have used here would still be justified and useful at some stage. A vast compendium of documents on, say, fifty localized lineages in Fukien and Kwangtung would need to be digested into simplified statements before we could grasp its significance. To make an average picture of the data might obscure the interrelations between the crucial elements involved. Certainly, the lineages of south-eastern China were not all of one kind and were ranged in scale and morphology along some sort of continuum. Models such as A and Z should help us grasp the nature and implications of the continuum. I admit the possibility that the more facts we come to know the greater may be our reluctance to build and use simple models such as I have constructed here, and as a result this essay may have justified itself by a queer reversal of procedure: it may explain much because it knows so little. But in the long run anthropologists will have to get more and more accustomed to making and manipulating models which from one point of view do extreme violence to the richness of the material they collect.[1]

I turn now to the more general question of the way in which the study of the south-eastern Chinese lineage fits into the anthropological theory of unilineal kinship organization. Although at long last the investigation of non-unilineal kinship systems seems to be coming to the fore in anthropological writing, it is still true to say that the best descriptive and analytical work on kinship has been done along the line laid down for us by Morgan's preoccupation with the gens. We have now at any rate a body of propositions concerning unilineal kinship which make it comparatively easy for the student of a particular unilineal system to relate his findings to the general fund of ideas on the subject.[2]

[1] I may refer the non-anthropological reader to the following recent discussions by anthropologists on models: S. F. Nadel, *The Theory of Social Structure*, London, 1957, pp. 147–152; R. Firth, 'Social Organization and Social Change', *Journal of the Royal Anthropological Institute*, vol. 84, 1954, pp. 6ff.; E. R. Leach, *Political Systems of Highland Burma*, London, 1954, pp. 4f., 283ff.; C. Lévi-Strauss, 'Social Structure' in A. L. Kroeber, ed., *Anthropology Today*, Chicago, 1953, pp. 525ff.

[2] The most lucid and comprehensive exposition of these ideas is to be found in Fortes, 'The Structure of Unilineal Descent Groups'.

The most obvious characteristic of a thoroughgoing unilineal system of kinship is the continuity it ensures between the past and the present. A structure which perpetuates itself by recruitment through one line allows each new member to repeat, as it were, the role of his predecessors, and all living members to think of themselves as being part and parcel of a distinct group which includes their forebears back to its foundation. A lineage, as a corporate unit of society, may—as it in fact often does—work on a conceptually fixed time scale, or it may, like the Chinese lineage, incorporate biological generations in a constantly unfolding series of genealogical generations. In either case past and present participate together in a discrete and continuous unit. The ancestors worshipped by the Chinese in their halls were more than mere figures of history; they were the religious correlates of a social structure achieving permanence through time. If men remained in their lineage they continued to be associated with the sacred and secular objects which, however they may have been modified in fact by the passage of the years, still provided what seemed to be an unbroken link with the source from which the lineage flowed. Flesh and blood themselves entered into the perpetual corporation which was transmitted from generation to generation.

Maintaining itself by strict rules of patrilineal descent and patrilocal marriage—of which the married-in son-in-law system was not a breach but an adjustment—the lineage in Fukien and Kwangtung exchanged women with other lineages in such a fashion as to lose nearly all control over its sisters and daughters in order to gain nearly full control of its wives and daughters-in-law. Thus, to take up a matter recently discussed by Leach,[1] the Chinese lineage was one in which the strength of its patriliny was to be gauged by the relinquishment of its female agnates and its incorporation of the women married into it. Having few ritual and virtually no economic ties with her own agnates,[2] the married woman was forced to cast her interests fully within the group of which she was a member by marriage. One of the consequences of this identification, as I have earlier tried to show, was that the tensions inherent in the allocation of property rights among men was reflected in the standardized abuse of women as disrupters of the family peace. Family peace in reality depended fundamentally on the suppression of the potential conflict between a man and his father and brothers, but his wife, as a relatively new member of the group, could the most readily be accused of mischief-making, and doubtless she may often have merited some of the blame cast upon her because of her attempts to secure the interests of her husband and her

[1] E. R. Leach, 'Aspects of Bridewealth and Marriage Stability Among the Kachin and Lakher', *Man*, vol. LVII, April 1957, art. 59.

[2] Lin, *The Golden Wing*, pp. 130f., mentions two cases in which married women made inheritance claims on their original families. As the events occurred in the republican period the women presumably had in theory a legal right. I know of no evidence to suggest that by custom married women had claims on their parental estates.

own children against those of other members of the family. The total configuration of stress in a patrilineal complex and the burden borne in it by women are exemplified by the Chinese case.[1]

The integration of married women into their husbands' groups is evidenced by their fate on widowhood. Although, as I have shown, the data are not absolutely uniform, the widow appears generally to have been treated so much as a member of the group that if she chose to remarry she was disposed of to another lineage, her own agnates having comparatively little voice in the matter. There was officially no question of widow inheritance within the group, because the legal rules regulating the sexual conduct between kinsfolk provided strong sanctions against congress with the women married into the group, even when they had become widows. In theory at any rate, the women brought into the group were assimilated to the status of female members; as sexual objects they were available to their husbands only, so that while their fertility was a contribution to the group into which they had married it could not be continued after the lifetime of their spouses. Indeed, chaste widowhood was so much an ideal that memorial arches were put up to mark the distinction of women who had lived up to it. Further, the rules of the secret societies show us that the prohibition of sexual relations with the widows of agnates was carried over to stress the bond between ritual brothers. We are used to thinking of levirate and widow inheritance as accompaniments of agnatic systems, but the Chinese material suggests that the very intensity of the incorporation of a married woman may lead to her sexuality being confined so exclusively to one man in the group that after his death she must pass into yet another group before her sexual life may be continued. It might be argued that the prohibition of widow inheritance was an aspect of the individuation of simple families within the wider kinship group, but this view is countered by the fact that it was precisely among the poorest people, who formed an area of society where one would have assumed such an individuation to have been carried furthest, that the prohibition was most often ignored.

The conflict over property was given its specific form by the system of equal inheritance among brothers, an equality which was modified only by what seems to have been an optional rule that the oldest of them might get an extra share in recognition of his duty to maintain the domestic ancestral cult. The systems of inheritance and succession were egalitarian, genealogical headship passing by age and generation and not by seniority in line of descent. Since there was no effective primogeniture, as there has been in other Far Eastern agnatic systems,[2] the ascription of high status and authority to men on a non-kinship basis did not conflict with any

[1] Cf. Gluckman, op. cit., pp. 56–60, and Fortes, op. cit., pp. 37f.

[2] See, e.g., Eisuke Zensho, 'The Family System in Korea', and Kizaemon Ariga, 'Introduction to the Family System in Japan, China and Korea', in *Transactions of the Third World Congress of Sociology*, vol. IV, London, 1956.

privilege vested in a particular segment. In this sense the Chinese lineage was well able to accommodate a class structure cutting across the genealogical system. But the question is sometimes raised of the degree to which a lineage can tolerate social differentiation and remain an effective group; so that we should look more closely at the cohabitation of kinship and class principles of social division in the lineages of Fukien and Kwangtung.

In his exposition of the character and correlates of unilineal descent groups, Fortes points out that 'it seems that corporate descent groups can exist only in more or less homogeneous societies'. And he goes on, having commented on the unsatisfactory state of our understanding of the vague concept 'homogeneous society', to suggest that what we might mean by it is a society in which any person can be replaced by any other person of the same category without the substitution leading to change in the social structure.[1] By a person, of course, he means an individual considered only in respect of his social position or role, so that the interchangeable persons in a homogeneous society are, for example, fathers, brothers, headmen, priests and so on, as such. Fortes tentatively suggests that 'any two persons of the same category have the same body of customary usages and beliefs' and that 'with respect to their achievable life histories, in a homogeneous society all men are brothers and all women sisters'.[2]

It seems to me that this definition catches only one aspect of the concept of homogeneity as we apply it to society. When we speak of a heterogeneous society we normally have in mind not only that like persons entertain unlike ideas and behave in unlike ways, but also that there is a scatter of persons wide enough to exclude many individuals from being many of these persons. Fortes seems to imply that homogeneity is measured by the degree of variance in the performance of roles which are universal or near-universal for all members of one sex. But a heterogeneous society is one in which there are important roles (such as those of business man, bureaucrat, sailor, actor, and so on) which are open to only a few individuals. In other words, we must treat heterogeneity in terms of social differentiation.

Yet however we define the category 'homogeneous societies' we can scarcely say that China falls within its scope. Since the heterogeneity of Chinese society can be shown to have operated within many localized lineages, and since these lineages survived as corporate groups over long periods of time, we must ask what conditions made this survival possible.

One of the factors at work seems to have been the absence of seniority in line of descent to which I referred earlier. When, as we have seen, a small group of agnates had attained in wealth and status a position which they wished to assert against their more remotely related agnates, they

[1] Fortes, op. cit., p. 36.

[2] Loc. cit.

could differentiate themselves ritually by setting up a new ancestor-worshipping unit endowed with its fund of property. The system thus allowed small segments of high status to be scattered through the lineage. There was no entrenched segment whose superiority could be challenged by ritual expressions of high status on the part of inferior co-ordinate segments. Class differences could thus be accommodated, at least ritually, by the system of genealogical segmentation. It would be interesting to know how matters went in Korean society, for example, where a main line of descent was marked out within the lineage; class differences there could not have found so ready a genealogical expression.

In a sense the south-eastern Chinese lineage worked better the more it was internally differentiated in social status, as model Z suggests. That is to say, so far from weakening the system, heterogeneity actually strengthened it. When power was concentrated in the hands of an elite and genealogical authority and status were kept firmly in the background, the lineage could more effectively hold its members together and fortify them against their neighbours and the state. Fortes says that in centralized societies with corporate lineages, such as Ashanti and Yoruba, the central political structure was unstable, and he goes on to generalize that 'the more centralized the political system the greater the tendency seems to be for the corporate strength of descent groups to be reduced or for such corporate groups to be nonexistent'.[1] The Chinese political system was centralized and yet allowed a great measure of autonomy to local communities. Of course, if the state relinquished its control of individuals as citizens and treated them politically and legally as members of corporate lineages even while maintaining the fiction of a centralized polity, then Fortes's contention is supported. When the lineage was strong the state was weak. Perhaps, indeed, the state often effectively counted for little in the countryside of the south-eastern provinces, and the lineages were powerful in harmony with this weakness. But even so, lineage and state were by no means out of touch with each other. The state made its presence felt strongly enough for people to want to oppose it, while some of the lineages and the bureaucracy had common members in the scholar-officials produced in differentiated communities. We might say that, just because they were partly independent of the central authority and at the same time closely tied to it through their elites, differentiated lineages developed their corporate functions to a high pitch.

It could be argued that in proportion as the lineage increased its corporate character, it diminished its character as an agnatic system. To stand against the state the lineage needed strong men; to promote these men to positions of power in the lineage, genealogical principles of recruitment had to be pushed aside. The result was, we might say, that the internal affairs of the lineage ceased to be regulated, at least in part, by the genealogical structure of the community. However highly developed

[1] Fortes, op. cit., p. 26.

in response to prosperity, its segmentation became less relevant to the maintenance of internal order.

Undoubtedly one of the keys to the viability of the south-eastern Chinese lineage lies in the interlocking of lineage elites and the national bureaucracy. Since the effective leaders of the differentiated lineage were neither appointed by nor under the orders of the magistrate, and since if they were themselves scholars they could confront the magistrate on an equal footing, the will of the state could be resisted without a breach of administrative duty. Unless he was prepared to bring in the militia, the magistrate could only deal and treat with a recalcitrant lineage; he could not command it. By preventing a bureaucrat from serving in his own province the system attempted to avoid nepotism and corruption; but by allowing lineage leadership to take on a strong bureaucratic colouring without imposing any bureaucratic checks upon it, the state weakened its control of the lineage, however much it may have suffused its leadership with the correct ideology. With the gentry as buffer, the differentiated lineage could oppose itself to the state and yet maintain its standing in official eyes. We may well wonder what changes took place when the bureaucracy ceased to recruit itself in the traditional manner, and the relationship between the magistrate and lineage leadership was in consequence modified.

The purest form of unilineal descent group is to be found in a society which is a segmentary system in its totality, for where there is no specialized institution of government the whole of political life can be expressed in terms of the relations between segments of varying span. As soon as political centralism appears, lineages are engaged in relations which are supported by values and sanctions from outside. When individuals within lineages are called upon to be agents or officers of external political institutions they become subject to the constraints of more than one system.[1] In the Chinese case men were not officers of the state in their own communities, but if they were bureaucrats living at home or were otherwise closely identified with the bureaucratic profession and its ideology, they enjoyed a status which rested on principles other than those given in the lineage organization as such. Weber seems to have supposed that the lineage ('the strictly patriarchal sib') faced the bureaucracy without conceding the force of the educated official's position. 'The strongest counterweight to officials educated in literature was a-literate old age *per se*. No matter how many examinations the official had passed, he had to obey unconditionally the completely uneducated elder in the traditionally fixed affairs of the sib.'[2] In fact, of course, if the official

[1] Cf. L. A. Fallers, *Bantu Bureaucracy, A Study of Integration and Conflict in the Political Institutions of an East African People*, Cambridge, n.d., pp. 16f., 227.

[2] Weber, op. cit., pp. 95f. Since I have for the second time cited Weber only to dispute what he says I should refer to a recent sinological appraisal of his work on China: O. B. van der Sprenkel, 'Chinese Religion', *British Journal of Sociology*, vol. V, no. 3, Se t. 1954.

deferred to lineage leaders, then these men were likely to be gentlemen rather than country bumpkins making a stand for their customary rights. The gentleman and the 'completely uneducated sib elder' might be members of one lineage, and any suggestion that 'a-literate old age *per se*' could prevail over gentrydom seems very wide of the mark.[1] Once we begin to think of the way in which the class structure of China could penetrate the local community, we see how strikingly the differentiated lineage adjusted its internal arrangements to take account of the positions of power and status based on the wider political system.

Fallers discusses in an African setting the difficulties experienced by men who are at once members of lineages and of a state apparatus. He propounds the general hypothesis: 'The co-existence in a society of corporate lineages with political institutions of the state type makes for strain and instability'.[2] By strain he means the conflict within and between individuals, and by instability he means a failure in the working of the institutions.[3] Now, to some extent there must have been what Fallers calls strain in the minds and relations of men who, while being members of localized lineages in south-eastern China, were also called upon in their capacity as gentlemen to support the actions and values of the bureaucracy. Conflict of loyalties there must have been on occasion, as when the gentry shared the hostility of their lineage against the lineages with which it was in feud and yet found it difficult to countenance violence. But the strain to which they were subjected was not that imposed on a man by the performance in his own community of a clearly formulated political duty. In their own communities the literati were never in office, and in this single fact we can see the success with which the Chinese political system encouraged men to seek bureaucratic employment and yet left them to enjoy the full fruits of their high status at home. A literatus could use unhindered all his influence on behalf of his lineage; doing so he could meet the expectations of his agnates and reinforce his position among them.

The instability of which Fallers writes can be seen in the Chinese case when the state was unable to combat sedition and inter-lineage affrays. Large-scale lineage organization, anti-state activity, and feuding between lineages seem to have been three phenomena associated in the south-east as they were nowhere else in China. When lineages were localized and highly corporate, they appear to have developed a bellicosity towards the outside world which was a denial of the bureaucratic peace pursued by the centralized government. In this sense lineage organization and the state system were in conflict. Rebellion and feud were a constant challenge to a government which, by feeding influence back into at least some lineages

[1] Weber, op. cit., p. 135: 'Within the sib, however, the authority of old age was a strong counterweight. . . .' to the influence of the literati.

[2] Fallers, op. cit., p. 17.

[3] Ibid., p. 227.

by its method of recruiting officials, seems only to have succeeded in strengthening the corporate and resistant qualities of its obstreperous charges.

Even though China was not 'a more or less homogeneous society' it produced large-scale corporate lineages. But up to what point of increasing social differentiation could they survive? In the People's Republic, we might assume, the radical reshaping of government together with legislated changes in land tenure will have put an end to a system which bent social inequality to the service of resisting central authority. In the Hong Kong New Territories, on the other hand, we still have the opportunity of observing how far lineage organization can stand up to the encroachments of an industrial economy and an administrative system which is both more intensive and less geared to the support of social differentiation along traditional lines. It is appropriate that I end by referring to the observations which have yet to be made, because in writing this essay I have allowed myself a high ratio of guesswork to facts, and I ought to leave the reader with the conviction that, if there is anything in what I say, it should be put to the test of thorough research. By a combination of historical research and sociological field work, sinologues and anthropologists should be able to bring the south-eastern Chinese lineage fully within the framework of modern political and kinship studies.

List of Works Cited

ADDISON, J. T., 1925. *Chinese Ancestor Worship, A Study of its Meaning and Relations with Christianity*, Shanghai.

Agrarian China, 1939. Institute of Pacific Relations, London.

ARIGA, KIZAEMON, 1956. 'Introduction to the Family System in Japan, China and Korea', *Transactions of the Third World Congress of Sociology*, vol.iv, London.

BALL, J. DYER, 1911. *The Chinese at Home or the Man of Tong and His Land*, London.

BALLER, F. W., 1892. *The Sacred Edict, With a Translation of the Colloquial Rendering Notes and Vocabulary*, Shanghai.

BIELENSTEIN, H., 1947. 'The Census of China During the Period 2–742 A.D.', *Bulletin No.* 19 *of the Museum of Far Eastern Antiquities*, Stockholm.

BOHANNAN, L., 1952. 'A Genealogical Charter', *Africa*, vol. xxii, no. 4, October.

BOÜINAIS and PAULUS, A., 1893. *Le culte des morts dans le Céleste Empire et l'Annam*, Paris.

BOULAIS, G., 1924. *Manuel du code chinois*, Variétés Sinologiques, no. 55, Shanghai.

BUCK, J. L., 1930. *Chinese Farm Economy*, Chicago.

1937. *Land Utilization in China*, Nanking.

1937. *Land Utilization in China: Statistics*, Nanking.

CHAN WING-TSIT, 1953. *Religious Trends in Modern China*, New York.

CHANG CHUNG-LI, 1955. *The Chinese Gentry, Studies on Their Role in Nineteenth-Century Chinese Society*, Seattle.

CHAO YUEN REN, 1943. 'Languages and Dialects in China', *The Geographical Journal*, vol. cii, no. 2, August.

CHEN HAN-SENG, 1933. *The Present Agrarian Problem in China*, China Institute of Pacific Relations, Shanghai.

1936. *Agrarian Problems in Southernmost China*, Shanghai. (Also published as *Landlord and Peasant in China*, New York, 1936.)

1937. 'The Present Prospect of Chinese Emigration', in *Limits of Land Settlement*, I. Bowman (ed.), New York.

CHEN TA, 1939. *Emigrant Communities in South China, A Study of Overseas Migration and Its Influence on Standards of Living and Social Change*, London and New York.

1946. *Population in Modern China*, Chicago.

CHIAO CHI-MING, 1933. 'A Study of the Chinese Population', *The Milbank Memorial Fund Quarterly Bulletin*, vol. xi, No. 4, October.

Chinese Law and Custom in Hong Kong, Report of a Committee Appointed by the Governor in October 1948, 1953, Hong Kong.

'Clanship Among the Chinese', 1836, *The Chinese Repository*, vol. iv, no. 9, January.

CONWELL, R. H., 1871. *Why and How. Why the Chinese Emigrate...*, Boston.

CORDIER, H. M., 1888. *Les Sociétés secrètes chinoises*, Paris.

COULING, S., 1917. *The Encyclopaedia Sinica*, Shanghai.

DOOLITTLE, J., edited and revised by HOOD, P., 1868, *Social Life of the Chinese, A Daguerreotype of Daily Life in China*, London.

DORÉ, H., 1912. *Recherches sur les superstitions en Chine. 1ère partie: Les pratiques superstitieuses*, vol. ii, Shanghai.

DOUGLAS, R. K., 1901. *Society in China*, London.

EBERHARD, W., 1952. *Conquerors and Rulers: Social Forces in Medieval China*, Leiden.

ELLIOTT, A. J. A., 1955. *Chinese Spirit-Medium Cults in Singapore*, London.

D'ENJOY, P., 1904. 'Associations, congrégations et sociétés secrètes chinoises', *Bulletins et Mémoires de la Société d'Anthropologie de Paris*, Series V, vol. v, Paris.

FALLERS, L. A., n.d. *Bantu Bureaucracy, A Study of Integration and Conflict in the Political Institutions of an East African People*, Cambridge.

FAVRE, B., 1933. *Les sociétés secrètes en Chine, Origine—rôle historique—situation actuelle*, Paris.

FEI HSIAO-TUNG, 1939. *Peasant Life in China, A Field Study of Country Life in the Yangtze Valley*, London.

1946. 'Peasantry and Gentry: An Interpretation of Chinese Social Structure and its Changes', *American Journal of Sociology*, vol. 52, no. 1.

revised and edited by REDFIELD, M. P., 1953. *China's Gentry, Essays in Rural-Urban Relations*, Chicago.

and CHANG CHIH-I, 1949. *Earthbound China, A Study of Rural Economy in Yunnan*, London.

FÊNG HAN-YI (FÊNG HAN-CHI), 1948. *The Chinese Kinship System*, Cambridge, Mass. (reprinted from *Harvard Journal of Asiatic Studies*, vol. ii, no. 2, July 1937).

FIRTH, R., 1954. 'Social Organization and Social Change', *Journal of the Royal Anthropological Institute*, vol. 84, Pt. 1.

1955. *The Fate of the Soul, An Interpretation of Some Primitive Concepts*, The Frazer Lecture, 1955, Cambridge.

FORREST, R. A. D., 1948. *The Chinese Language*, London.

FORTES, M., 1953. 'The Structure of Unilineal Descent Groups', *American Anthropologist*, vol. 55, no. 1, January–March.

and EVANS-PRITCHARD, E. E., eds., 1940. *African Political Systems*, London.

FREEDMAN, M., 1950. 'Colonial Law and Chinese Society', *Journal of the Royal Anthropological Institute*, vol. lxxx, pts. 1 and 2 (published 1952).

1956. Review of Chang Chung-li, *The Chinese Gentry*, in *Pacific Affairs*, vol. xxix, no. 1, March.

1957. *Chinese Family and Marriage in Singapore*, London.

FRIED, M. H., 1953. *Fabric of Chinese Society, A Study of Social Life in a Chinese County Seat*, New York.

GAMBLE, S. D., 1954. *Ting Hsien, A North China Rural Community*, New York.

GARDNER, C. T., 1897. 'Amoy Emigration to the Straits', *The China Review*, vol. xxii, no. 4.

GILES, H. A., 1880. *Freemasonry in China*, Amoy.

1912. *A Chinese-English Dictionary*, 2 vols., 2nd edition, Shanghai, &c.

GLICK C. and HONG SHENG-HWA, 1947. *Swords of Silence, Chinese Secret Societies—Past and Present*, New York.

GLUCKMAN, M., 1955. *Custom and Conflict in Africa*, Oxford.

GRANET, M., 1951. *La religion des Chinois*, 2nd edition, Paris.

1953. *Études sociologiques sur la Chine*, Paris.

GRAY, J. H., edited by GREGOR, W. G., 1878. *China, A History of the Laws, Manners and Customs of the People*, 2 vols., London.

GROOT, J. J. M. de, 1885. *Het Kongsiwezen van Borneo, eene Verhandeling over den Grondslag en den Aard der Chineesche Politieke Vereenigingen in de Koloniën, Met eene Chineesche Geschiedenis van de Kongsi Lanfong*, The Hague.

1885. *Buddhist Masses for the Dead at Amoy*, Leiden.

trans. CHAVANNES, C. G., 1886. *Les fêtes annuellement célébrées à Emoui (Amoy), Étude concernant la religion populaire des Chinois*, Annales du Musée Guimet, vols. 11 and 12, Paris.

1892. 'De Lijkbezorging der Emoy-Chineezen', *Bijdragen tot de Taal- Land- en Volkenkunde van Nederlandsch-Indië*, vol. xvi.

1892–1910. *The Religious System of China*, 6 vols., Leyden.

1903–04. *Sectarianism and Religious Persecution in China, A Page in the History of Religions*, Verhandeling der Koninglijke Akademie van Wetenschappen te Amsterdam, Afdeeling Letterkunde, New Series, Part IV, nos. 1 and 2, vol. i, vol. ii, Amsterdam.

GUTZLAFF, C., 1846. 'On the Secret Triad Society of China, Chiefly from Papers belonging to the Society found at Hong Kong', *Journal of the Royal Asiatic Society of Great Britain and Ireland*, vol. viii.

HILL, A. H., 1955. 'The Hikayat Abdullah, An Annotated Translation', *Journal of the Malayan Branch Royal Asiatic Society*, vol. xxviii, part 3.

HOANG, P., 1897. *Notions techniques sur la propriété en Chine avec un choix d'actes et de documents officiels*, Variétés Sinologiques, no. 11, Shanghai.

1898. *Le mariage chinois au point de vue légal*, Variétés Sinologiques, no. 14, Shanghai.

HOMANS, G. C., and SCHNEIDER, D. M., 1955. *Marriage, Authority and Final Causes, A Study of Unilateral Cross-Cousin Marriage*, Glencoe, Illinois.

HSIA CHING-LIN et al., trans., 1931. *The Civil Code of the Republic of China*, Shanghai.

HSIEH PAO CHAO, 1925. *The Government of China (1644–1911)*, Baltimore.

HSU, F. L. K., 1940. 'The Problem of Incest Tabu in a North China Village', *American Anthropologist*, vol. 42, no. 1, January–March.

1943. 'The Myth of Chinese Family Size', *American Journal of Sociology*, vol. xlviii, May.

1945. 'Observations on Cross-Cousin Marriage in China', *American Anthropologist*, vol. 47, no. 1, January–March.

1949. *Under the Ancestors' Shadow, Chinese Culture and Personality*, London.

1949. 'The Family in China', in *The Family, Its Functions and Destiny*, R. N. Anshen (ed.), New York.

1953. *Americans and Chinese, Two Ways of Life*, New York.

HU HSIEN-CHIN, 1948. *The Common Descent Group in China and its Functions*, New York.

HUGHES, G., 1872–3. 'The Small Knife Rebels (An Unpublished Chapter of Amoy History)', *The China Review*, vol. i, no. 4.

HUMMEL, A. W., ed., 1943. *Eminent Chinese of the Ch'ing Period (1644–1912)*, 2 vols., Washington.

HUNTINGTON, E., 1924. *The Character of Races*, New York.

HURLBUT, F., 1939. *The Fukienese, A Study in Human Geography*, n.p. [U.S.A.].

HUTSON, J., 1928. 'Chinese Secret Societies', *The China Journal*, vol. ix, nos. 4, 5 and 6, Shanghai.

The Indo-Chinese Gleaner, vol. i, no. 3, February 1818, and vol. ii, no. 18, October 1821, Malacca.

JERNIGAN, T. R., 1905. *China in Law and Commerce*, New York.

JOHNSTON, R. F., 1910. *Lion and Dragon in Northern China*, London.

KULP, D. H., 1925. *Country Life in South China, The Sociology of Familism, Volume I, Phenix Village, Kwangtung, China*, New York.

'Kwangtung Agricultural Statistics', 1928, *Chinese Economic Journal*, vol. ii, no. 4, April.

LANG, O., 1946. *Chinese Family and Society*, New Haven.

LE VAN DINH, 1934. *Le culte des morts en droit annamite (Essai historique et critique sur le Huong-Hoa)*, Paris.

LEACH, E. R., 1952. 'The Structural Implications of Matrilateral Cross-Cousin Marriage', *Journal of the Royal Anthropological Institute*, vol. lxxxi.

1954. *Political Systems of Highland Burma*, London.

1957. 'Aspects of Bridewealth and Marriage Stability Among the Kachin and Lakher', *Man*, vol. lvii, article 59, April.

LEONG, Y. K. and TAO, L. K., 1915. *Village and Town Life in China*, London.

LÉVI-STRAUSS, C., 1949. *Les structures élémentaires de la parenté*, Paris.

1953. 'Social Structure' in *Anthropology Today*, A. L. Kroeber (ed.), Chicago.

LEVY, M. J. and SHIH KUO-HENG, 1949. *The Rise of the Modern Chinese Business Class* (mimeographed), New York.

LI CHI, 1928. *The Formation of the Chinese People, An Anthropological Inquiry*, Cambridge, Mass.

LIN-LE [LINDLEY, A. F.], 1866. *Ti-Ping Tien-Kwoh, The History of the Ti-Ping Revolution*, 2 vols., London.

LIN YUEH-HWA, 1936. 'An Enquiry into the Chinese Village-Lineage from the Viewpoint of Anthropology' (in Chinese), *She Hui Hsüeh Chieh*, no. 9.

1946. 'The Kinship System of the Lolo', *Harvard Journal of Asiatic Studies*, vol. 9, no. 2, June.

1948. *The Golden Wing, A Sociological Study of Chinese Familism*, London.

LIU HSING-T'ANG, 1936. 'The Structure of Kinship Groups in Fukien' (in Chinese), *Shih Huo*, vol. 4, No. 8.

MCALEAVY, H., 1955. 'Certain Aspects of Chinese Law in the Light of Japanese Scholarship', *Bulletin of the School of Oriental and African Studies*, vol. xvii, no. 3.

MAO TSE-TUNG, 1954. *Selected Works of Mao Tse-tung, Volume One*, London.

The Marriage Law of the People's Republic of China, 1950, Peking.

MASON, M. G., 1939. *Western Concepts of China and the Chinese, 1840–76*, New York.

MASPERO, H., 1950. *Mélanges posthumes sur les religions et l'histoire de la Chine, I, Les religions chinoises*, Paris.

MEADOWS, T. T., 1847. *Desultory Notes on the Government and People of China and on the Chinese Language; Illustrated with a Sketch of the Province of Kwangtung. . .*, London.

1856. *The Chinese and their Rebellions*, London.

MEDHURST, W. H., 1832. *A Dictionary of the Hok-Këèn Dialect of the Chinese Language. . .*, Macao.

1840. *China: Its State and Prospects. . .*, London.

MORSE, H.B., 1932. *The Gilds of China*, Shanghai.

NADEL, S. F., 1957. *The Theory of Social Structure*, London.

NEWBOLD, T. J. and MAJOR-GENERAL WILSON, 1841. 'The Chinese Triad Society of the Tien-ti-huih', *Journal of the Royal Asiatic Society of Great Britain and Ireland*, vol. vi.

'Notices of Modern China. . . .', 1836, *The Chinese Repository*, vol. iv, no. 12, April.

'Oath Taken by Members of the Triad Society and Notices of its Origin', 1849, *The Chinese Repository*, vol. xviii, no. 6.

Papers Laid Before the Legislative Council of Hong Kong, 1899, 1900, Hong Kong.

Papers Laid Before the Legislative Council of Hong Kong 1900, 1901, Hong Kong.

PELLIOT, P., 1928. 'The Hung Society' (compte-rendu of Ward and Stirling, *The Hung Society*), *T'oung Pao*, vol. xxv, Leiden.

PICKERING, W. A., 1878–79. 'Chinese Secret Societies', *Journal of the Royal Asiatic Society, Straits Branch*, no. 1 and no. 3.

PLOPPER, C. H., 1926. *Chinese Religion Seen Through the Proverb*, Shanghai.

PURCELL, V., 1951. *The Chinese in Southeast Asia*, London.

RADCLIFFE-BROWN, A. R., 1952. *Structure and Function in Primitive Society*, London.

REICHELT, K. W., trans. TETLIE, J., 1951. *Religion in Chinese Garment*, London.

Report on the New Territory at Hong Kong, 1900, Cmd. 403, H.M.S.O., London.

SCARBOROUGH, W., revised by ALLAN, C. W., 1926. *A Collection of Chinese Proverbs*, Shanghai.

SCARTH, J., 1860. *Twelve Years in China*, Edinburgh.

SCHLEGEL, G., 1866. *Thian Ti Hwui, The Hung League or Heaven-Earth-League*, Batavia.

SCHURMANN, H. F., 1956. 'Traditional Property Concepts in China', *The Far Eastern Quarterly*, vol. xv, no. 4, August.

SHEN, T. H., 1951. *Agricultural Resources of China*, Ithaca, New York.

SHIH VINCENT YU-CHUNG, 1951. 'Interpretations of the Taiping Tien-Kuo by Noncommunist Chinese Writers', *The Far Eastern Quarterly*, vol. x, no. 3, May.

SIMON, G.-E., 1886. *La cité chinoise*, 3rd ed., Paris.

1887. *China: Its Social, Political, and Religious Life*, London.

SMITH, A. H., 1899. *Village Life in China, A Study in Sociology*, New York.

SPRENKEL, O. B. VAN DER, 1954. 'Chinese Religion', *British Journal of Sociology*, vol. v, no. 3, September.

SPRENKEL, S. VAN DER, 1956. *A Sociological Analysis of Chinese Legal Institutions with Special Reference to the Ch'ing Period, 1644–1911*, unpublished M.Sc. (Econ.) thesis, University of London.

STANTON, W., 1900. *The Triad Society or Heaven and Earth Association*, Hong Kong.

STAUNTON, G. T., 1810. *Ta Tsing Leu Lee; Being the Fundamental Laws, and a Selection from the Supplementary Statutes of the Penal Code of China; . . .*, London.

TAN POW TECK, 1924. *The Pek Kah Seng*, Kuala Lumpur.

TAWNEY, R. H., 1932. *Land and Labour in China*, London.

TAYLOR, G. E., 1933. 'The Taiping Rebellion: Its Economic Background and Social Theory', *The Chinese Social and Political Science Review*, vol. xvi, no. 6, January.

TENG SSU-YÜ, 1950. *New Light on the History of the Taiping Rebellion* (mimeographed), Cambridge, Mass.

THÉRY, F., 1948. 'Les coutumes chinoises relatives au mariage', *Bulletin de l'Université l'Aurore*, Series III, vol. 9, no. 36, Shanghai.

THOMSON, J., 1875. *The Straits of Malacca, Indo-China and China*, London.

T'IEN JU-K'ANG, [1953]. *The Chinese of Sarawak: A Study of Social Structure*, London.

'Tomb of Ancestors', 1833, *The Chinese Repository*, vol. i, no. 12, April.

VALK, M. H. VAN DER, 1956. *Conservatism in Modern Chinese Law*, Studia et Documenta Ad Iura Orientis Antiqui Pertinentia, vol. iv, Leiden.

VLEMING, J. L., 1926. *Het Chineesche Zakenleven in Nederlandsch-Indië*, Weltevreden.

WARD, J. S. M., 1926. *The Hung Society or The Society of Heaven and Earth*, vols. ii and iii, London.

and STIRLING, W. G., 1925. *The Hung Society or The Society of Heaven and Earth*, vol. i, London.

WEBER, M., trans. and ed. GERTH, H. H., 1951. *The Religion of China, Confucianism and Taoism*, Glencoe, Illinois.

WERNER, E. T. C., edited by TEDDER, H. R., 1910. *Descriptive Sociology . . . Chinese. Compiled and Abstracted Upon the Plan Organized by Herbert Spencer. . . .*, London.

WIEGER, L., 1909. *Folk-lore chinois moderne*, Sienhsien.

WIENS, H. J., 1954. *China's March Toward the Tropics*, Hamden, Conn.

WILLIAMS, S. W., 1883. *The Middle Kingdom*, 2 vols., London.

WITTFOGEL, K. A., 1938. *New Light on Chinese Society, An Investigation of China's Socio-Economic Structure*, New York.

and Fêng Chia-shêng, 1949. *History of Chinese Society, Liao (907–1125)*, Transactions of the American Philosophical Society, New Series, vol. 36, Philadelphia.

'The Worship of Ancestors among the Chinese: A Notice of the Kiá-lĭ Tieh-shih Tsih-ching . . . or Collection of Forms and Cards used in Family Ceremonies', 1849. *The Chinese Repository*, Vol. xviii, No. 7.

Wu, Leonard T. K., 1936. 'Merchant Capital and Usury Capital in Rural China', *Far Eastern Survey*, vol. v, no. 7, March 25.

[Wylie, A.], 1853. 'Secret Societies in China', *Shanghae Almanac for* 1854 *and Miscellany*, Shanghai.

Yang, M. C., 1948. *A Chinese Village, Taitou, Shantung Province*, London.

Yuan I-chin, 1931. 'Life Tables of a Southern Chinese Family from 1365 to 1849, *Human Biology*, vol. iii, no. 2, May, Baltimore.

Zensho, Eisuke, 1956. 'The Family System in Korea', *Transactions of the Third World Congress of Sociology*, vol. iv, London.

Zi (Siu), Etienne, 1894. *Pratique des examens littéraires en Chine*, Variétés Sinologiques, no. 5, Shanghai.

Index

LONDON SCHOOL OF ECONOMICS
MONOGRAPHS ON SOCIAL ANTHROPOLOGY

A complete list of the Monographs is given below. Those marked with an asterisk are now out of print.

*1, 2. Raymond Firth, *The Work of the Gods in Tikopia*, 2 vols., 1940.
*3. E. R. Leach, *Social and Economic Organization of the Rowanduz Kurds*, 1940.
*4. E. E. Evans-Pritchard, *The Political System of the Anuak of the Anglo-Egyptian Sudan*, 1940.
5. Daryll Forde, *Marriage and the Family among the Yakö in South-Eastern Nigeria*, 1941.
*6. M. M. Green, *Land Tenure of an Ibo Village in South-Eastern Nigeria*, 1941.
*7. Rosemary Firth, *Housekeeping among Malay Peasants*, 1943.
*8. A. M. Ammar, *A Demographic Study of an Egyptian Province (Sharqiya)*, 1943.
*9. I. Schapera, *Tribal Legislation among the Tswana of the Bechuanaland Protectorate*, 1943.
*10. W. H. Beckett, *Akokoaso: A Survey of a Gold Coast Village*, 1944.
11. I. Schapera, *The Ethnic Composition of the Tswana Tribes*, 1952.
12. Ju-K'ang T'ien, *The Chinese of Sarawak: A Study of Social Structure*, 1953.
13. Gutorm Gjessing, *Changing Lapps*, 1954.
14. Alan J. A. Elliott, *Chinese Spirit-Medium Cults in Singapore*, 1955.
15. Raymond Firth, *Two Studies of Kinship in London*, 1956.
16. Lucy Mair, *Studies in Applied Anthropology*, 1957.
17. J. M. Gullick, *Indigenous Political Systems of Western Malaya*, 1958.
18. Maurice Freedman, *Lineage Organization in South eastern China*, 1958.

For Product Safety Concerns and Information please contact our EU representative GPSR@taylorandfrancis.com
Taylor & Francis Verlag GmbH, Kaufingerstraße 24, 80331 München, Germany

www.ingramcontent.com/pod-product-compliance
Ingram Content Group UK Ltd.
Pitfield, Milton Keynes, MK11 3LW, UK
UKHW021956180926
475701UK00003B/56

* 9 7 8 0 3 6 7 7 1 6 9 7 4 *